মজৰূঢ়
THE MAGICAL SOULS

TRANSLATED, ADAPTED AND COMPILED BY
SHARAD KAMAL BEZBORUAH

INDIA · SINGAPORE · MALAYSIA

Copyright © Sharad Kamal Bezboruah 2022
All Rights Reserved.

ISBN 979-8-88704-369-2

This book has been published with all efforts taken to make the material error-free after the consent of the author. However, the author and the publisher do not assume and hereby disclaim any liability to any party for any loss, damage, or disruption caused by errors or omissions, whether such errors or omissions result from negligence, accident, or any other cause.

While every effort has been made to avoid any mistake or omission, this publication is being sold on the condition and understanding that neither the author nor the publishers or printers would be liable in any manner to any person by reason of any mistake or omission in this publication or for any action taken or omitted to be taken or advice rendered or accepted on the basis of this work. For any defect in printing or binding the publishers will be liable only to replace the defective copy by another copy of this work then available.

Dedicaton

A Tribute to my Grandparents, grand-aunts, grand-uncles, Uncles and Aunts; and to 'Aaji'.

Remembering fondly; Late Anandamoyee Bezboruah, Late Damodar and Sewali Baruah and Late Mukul Chandra Chaliha; Granduncle Lt. Jimmy Varma and Grandaunt Lt.Malthi Varma; and Uncle Lt. Dr. Rajen Barua; to the 'miracle bachcha'; to her everlasting 'Naaz'. And, to, many more such untimely losses...

Dedicated to my land, to its people; to my school(s), to the town of 'Digboi', a place called 'home'; to friends, family and relatives who have stood by me through thick and thin; to poets and lyricists across the subcontinent, alive and immortal, and to the 'past'; to the 'future'; and to 'everything in between'.

Contents

Acknowledgements

Among my greatest ideals have been; Shri. Dhirendra Nath Bezboruah; Mrs. Dipika Phukan; Shri. Bhaben Baruah, and Late Mr. Syed Ahmed Shah; to name a few.

Team 'The North-Eastern Chronicle'.

Team 'Baartalaap'; the greater 'Baartalaap' family, Madhu Raghavendra da, Namrata Pathak ba and others.

Team 'Irshaad', Poetry Social and other circles; Virsaaa, and more.

YourQuote, Airplane Poetry Movement (Shantanu and Nandini) & Kommune; among others.

MINIMI, A.Void, Basshole, Tanuj Nath, team 'Tumaloi', and many more.

Proofreading, Foreword and Misc: Syeda Jebeen Sabira Shah 'Jethai', Namrata Sarma, Shaheen Akhtar.

Cover Art: Shreya Chetia/dona illustrations.

'Drenched: Projects & Productions'; 'ART-ALAAP', Nephews and Nieces; and their respective kins; and to all those who have inspired me to sail this through.

Foreword / Opening Words by Syeda Jebeen Sabira Shah

"Maj-Rooh: The Magical Souls"!

What an apt name for a book containing hundreds of poems and lyrics translated, sometimes adapted; and compiled by Sharad Kamal Bezboruah of Assam. Few months ago, he had shown me a translation of the State Song of Assam, "O Mor Aponar Dex", by Lakshminath Bezbaroa. While discussing the translation, he happened to mention that he would include that in a book he has been working on for seven years. When he sent me the initial draft of the book, I was amazed by the amount of work he has put into it. It has poems and lyrics from different languages of the Indian Subcontinent. It is undoubtedly a very ambitious literary project that he took up. Translation is not an easy task, at all. First, one has to know and understand both the languages well, the original and the language one is translating to. Secondly, often there are no equivalent of the exact words or phrases, or the words or phrases in the original language could mean something totally different to the native speakers and literal meaning may mean nothing to the speakers of the language one is translating to. Getting to the soul, the spirit of the original poem is very important. And I think, Sharad still being a student, has strived to do his best in conveying the meanings of the originals to the readers in English, and in doing so, he wisely decided to adapt some of those. Sharad has written in detail all the literary greats that he is trying to pay his tribute to through this book.

Readers who love listening to Indian songs, especially the old ones, will find almost every song in this collection, only, in English. I am very impressed by his choice of poems and songs. From the beautiful "Aogey Jab Tum" of Faaiz Anwar to the most romantic, "Abhi Na Jaao Chod

Kar", of Sahir Ludhiyanvi Sahab. Then, there are Gulzar Sahab's "Ae Ajnabi" and "Dil Se Re".Kafeel Aazer Sahab's lyrics made famous by Jagjit Singh Ji's soulful rendition, the "Baat Niklegi To Phir Door Talak Jaayegi", which has very special significance in my own life.Another famous one which everyone who knew me in Aligarh Muslim University, might remember me by, Majrooh Sultanpuri Sahab's, "Jalte Hai Jiske Liye", finds its place in this beautiful book.

One of my favorite Urdu poets, who I have met at Mushairas in New York,

Nida Fazli Sahab's "Kabhi Kisiko Muqammal Jahan Nahin Milta" is nicely done by Sharad.Javed Akhtar Sahab's, "Panchi Nadiyaan Pawan Ke Jhonke", for- "the birds, the rivers, and the gusts of wind, Their movement no fences ever bind,

Only for human these fences are meant".

Sharad believes in not having these artificial barriers, and that is why he picked this for translation.And Akhtar Sahab's "Woh Jahan", where the conclusion is that the beautiful, happy world exists right here on this earth, if only love rules in life.This shows the translator's own belief.

I am elated to see translation of Faiz Ahmad Faiz Sahab's, famous "Mujhse Pehli Si Muhabbat".I was fortunate enough to be part of the Centennial Celebration of Faiz Sahab in New York, as President of AMU Alumni Association,New York Tristate, during World Urdu Conference in 2011, where his daughter Muneeza Hashmi had also, come from Lahore. From the hauntingly beautiful poems and lyrics, like, Makhdoom Mohiuddin Sahab's, "Aapki Yaad Aati Rahi", he goes on to includepatriotic ones.Prem Dhawan's famous, "Aye Mere Pyare Watan/Oh My Country, so Close to My Heart"; Atal Bihari Vajpayee Ji's, "Kadam Milakar Chalna Hoga"."Hum Laaye Hai Toofan Se Kashti Nikaalke".

It is great to see Sharad select some of our very own from Assam.He has translated many contemporary Assamese poems, including his own, "An Ode to Cotton College", written on its 115th Year.

My English Teacher at Cotton College, Sahitya Akademi Awardee Nabakanta Barua Sir's "Kune Aji Aabeli", takes me back to my childhood and brings so many thoughts on how years later the singer of that song Dwipen Barua would marry a cousin, and the main child actress would become my classmate from class Six to Pre-university. Sahitya AkademiAwardee Hiren Bhattacharyya's, "O Jibon"..."I am awake counting, the musical stars of the night" how beautiful is that!

There is Dr.Nirmal Prabha Bordoloi's, "Akou Notun Probhat Hobo", "There Shall Be A New Dawn".Indeed, everyone everywhere in this world should remember that the "Dark Night shall not last, there shall be a new dawn." Glad that Sharad picked this one of hope. Sharad has included Bharat Ratna Dr. Bhupen Hazarika's, "Xagor Xongomot", and "Oye Oye", among others.It warms my heart to see my late elder brother Syed Ahmed Shah being kindly acknowledged by Sharad, while translating Dr. Bhupen Hazarika.My brother's "Winged Horse" has the English Translation of 76 songs of Bhupen Hazarika, and I happened to be Contributing Editor of the book. My late brother was very fond of Sharad, and his literary enthusiasm, and that is how I got to know Sharad through Facebook, we have yet to meet. I feel so honoured that Sharad has asked me to write something for both myself and my brother, who he lovingly addresses as Bordeuta.In Assamese, it means father's elder brother, and I am Jethai, father or mother's elder sister. That is how we Assamese are, regardless of backgrounds for centuries, and that is how it shall remain.The rainbow of a State, which is like no other, and that, is why it is called 'Oxom', meaning peerless.

Congratulations to Sharad, and all the best for all his future literary efforts.

With Warm Regards,
Syeda Jebeen Sabira Shah (Jebeen Jethai)
President, Sahitya Sabha of North America.
Ex-President, Life Member, AMU Alumni Association, New York Tristate;
Ex-Councilor, Federation of AMU Alumni Associations, North America;

Former Head of Compliance, QA and Production for 3 Groups of American Multinationals,(1994-2019);- New York City. 28 March 2022.

Pic 1   Pic 2

pic-1; Exclusive Translator of songs of Bharat Ratna Dr. Bhupen Hazarika; Lt. Syed Ahmed Shah 'Bordeuta' (seated right) with Sharad and his distant relative Monava.

pic-2; The Brother-sister duo, Lt. Syed Ahmed Shah and Syeda Jebeen Sabira Shah 'Jethai', launching 26 poetry books of others, on birth anniversary of Lt. Shri Hiren Bhattacharyya.

"Raah Dekha Karega Sadiyon Tak,

Chod Jaayenge Yeh Jahaan Tanha"

– MEENA KUMARI 'NAAZ'
(Chaand Tanha, Aasmaan Tanha, Translation no. 160).

I wish to illuminate my eternal motherland,
into the warmth of my first love.)2
Gentle and tender like song you would listen to more than once,
moist like the clouds near the sun.....
Such is my motherland.....)3
In this place, my every song shall come and end.
In my motherland.....

(With my life and my death,
I wish to groom my motherland....
into the warmth of my first love.)2....

-Translated on 14th April,2013 by Sharad Kamal Bezboruah.

👍 Like   💬 Comment   ↪ Share

Archita Krishnatriya Sarma and 10 others

Syed Ahmed Shah
Bravo.. !

9y   Like   Reply   1

Sharad Bezboruah
Syed Ahmed Shah Sir,where have u been?
U don't seem to b posting very often.
M keen to hear more of u...
Do post whenever free...
U'r posts r eagerly awaited by me for around 1 - 1.5 months

9y   Like   Reply

Syed Ahmed Shah
... I am gladly handing over the baton to you Sharad..!

9y   Like   Reply

Lt. Syed Ahmed Shah bordeuta's take on my translation of Lt. Shri. Hiren Bhattacharyya's"Mur Jiwonore, Mur Moronere"; (Translation no. 97); back in 2013. The weight of the baton continues to overwhelm all-the-same.

Preface

Before I begin to compile my translations of selected works of noted poets and lyricists from across the subcontinent; I would like to express my deep and sincere reverence to Sahityarathi Lakshminath Bezbarua; for his invaluable contribution to Modern Assamese Literature. A translation of his piece 'Ami Asomiya', which was later composed into a song, follows:

Aami Asomiya...
-Lakshminath Bezbarua.

We, the people of Assam,
never shall we be poor.
We have it all;
the beauty, the charm;
but never did we learn to adore...

The saint Sankaradeva,
he taught us flawless religion...
and the martyr 'Lachit' gave us his strength;
and the blood that Lady Jaymati shed;
Mother Assam is now empowered, by its every droplet...

Play the Congo, blow the sacred conch,
beat the holy drum...
Assam again is on the path of development,
(come on,) say- "Glory to Mother Assam"!

Beat the Congo, blow the sacred conch,
beat the holy drum...
Assam again is on the path of development,
say- "Glory to Mother Assam".

"If they work hard", said 'Tamuli', an uncle of ours;
"miracles can be done even by tiny insects".
And, 'Rudra Singha' has shown,
us, that, even if you're the King,
you can always be one among your subjects.
The people of this land have thus shown
that impossible is nothing...!

Sankaradeva, forever the guru of the Assamese...
Kanaklata, the girl of seventeen;
shall always be remembered for her courage.
So many people of this land, we've seen,
have brought now to this land so much change....
And so, beat the Congo, blow the sacred conch,
beat the holy drum...
Assam again is on the path of development,
come on, say- "Glory to Mother Assam"!
Say- "Glory to Mother Assam"!

– Trans-created on 19th March, 2014
by Sharad Kamal Bezboruah.

The people of Assam shall be forever indebted to him, and all those who followed and raised Assamese Literature to where it today stands, and translations of whose works shall follow hereinafter. As much as I connect to my language and my people, I express my sincere apologies back home for having been able to cover only so much, owing to constraints, as regards my academics and formal education in the language. I am hopeful that this would at least help my friends from the other side to get a glimpse, and hear of the literary or cultural giants of the Assamese language.

Nevertheless, this compilation consists of translations of works of noted poets and lyrics, both from Assam, and other parts of the subcontinent. These translations have been done largely over a period of 7 years, or more; and thus the reader may find them of a varied nature, in terms of structure, or language in its literal sense; more so, because yours truly, as a translator has tried to give more importance or emphasis in keeping the structure and the very essence of the original in tact or alive, rather than its literal meaning. And as so, he might have gone overboard and taken certain liberties at several instances.

As the title of this compilation goes, it is a tribute to the popular Indian poet and lyricist, Late Majrooh Sultanpuri; whose centenary year we celebrate now, in 2019, and thereafter. Also, the title aims to highlight the characteristic of this compilation, of breaking the barriers of language, and thus being inclusive of all the three languages (English, Hindi/Hindustani and Assamese), or more. Though 'Majrooh' in literal terms means 'the wounded one', the title has been spilt into two, both syllables belonging to two very different languages. 'Maj', here, stands for 'Magic' in English, while 'Rooh' in Urdu, primarily (also Hindustani), is the word for 'Soul'. Thus explained is the hyphen used therein.

It would only be just to mention that Javed (Akhtar) Sahab played a crucial role in introducing me to this Magical Soul, along with many more, through his show 'The Golden Years with Javed Akhtar' screened on the Epic Channel between May and August 2016. This compilation would not have come this far if it weren't for him...Of course; there has been a series of events, both before and after, that have added to the development of the same.

Most importantly, Sahir Ludhiyanvi Sahab; who rightly deserves to be accredited with the pioneering of the providing of credits to the lyricist of the song, alongside the singer and composer, in the All India Radio and thus, a trendsetter in the same. Without his initiative, many of the noted and well-acclaimed lyricists of the yesteryears of the industry would have probably remained unnamed to our own generation, and many more to come. It is evident, that without the recognition they have received over the years, thanks to Sahir Sahab; this compilation would probably have never gotten through.

As much as I would love to open with Hiru Da's "O' Jiwon", considering I started compiling this in the centenary year of both Amrita Pritam and Majrooh Sultanpuri, it would be only just to dedicate the very first translation to Sahir Sahab on account of this year, 2021, being his centenary year.

Much has of course changed in the last three years; or four rather, ever since I have begun with the work of compiling this. Owing to the pandemic and the lack of mobility during my college days, I do regret not making the most of the time I had, but here, I continue to struggle to redeem myself, midst the chaos. While there's a lot to curse 2020 for, boons are merely to count on the fingertips. But one such boon I would not want to miss out counting in is the 'Clubhouse' app and it's much anticipated launch and use in India. It is not only a platform that celebrates art in its most intrinsic form, but also a great source of cross-cultural interactions, at least, to those who understand its use. I have been fortunate to have come across some phenomenally dedicated and learned people from across the globe; who cherish and celebrate a wide range of culture and literature from all over the subcontinent. The clubs "Hazaron Khwaishein Aisi" and "HindUrdu Poetry" have astounded me the most. I thank the founders; Dr. Himanshu Trivedi, Astha Deo, Vineet Prakash and all other core members for constantly inspiring, and throwing light on my very specific areas of interest. Furthermore, nuggets of wisdom shared by Mr. Satlaj Rahat Indori, Mr. Rakesh Anand Bakshi, Mr. Parvez Malikzada and Mr. Chandrashekhar Verma; and their very candid experiences with their respective elders which they were kind enough to share among us; were highly inspiring and evocative all-the-more. My first room, also the very first of Rekhta's on Clubhouse, on the night of 26th June 2021, shall forever be cherished.

For that matter, what HindUrdu Poetry started off with, was covering most of Amrita Pritam's work. Amrita Pritam; much of whom I was oblivious to, except as a name amongst the literary giants of India. Of course, my love for Sahir had made me stumble upon their tales, but only till the fact that 'they' existed as 'them' and left a mark in the history of tales of love, as regards the new-age India. As ill-fated of us as a generation to have not lived in the times of Sahir, so it is fortunate of us, to have witnessed love; not theirs in particular, but as a legacy in itself, to have been carried forward by Amrita Pritam ji, and her better half; a living legend and someone I would render as an epitome of love; Imroz sir. Hence, I offer my deepest reverences to Sahir Sahab and Amrita Pritam ji, as they complete 100 years of existence; both, as institutions in themselves; and as they continue to rule hearts eternally. Needless to say; here's to love, compassion, sacrifice, and much more; and also, a salute to the everlasting strength, endurance, persistence, perseverance, and the sport and spirit of 'Imroz'.

Names, as many taken, would fall short. But, on an honest note, after having paid my tribute to his 'beloved Didi', as I have learnt from Ms. Sehgal, Reena ji and others on clubhouse, I couldn't possibly leave out the very eloquent, versatile and stirring writings of 'Shiv Kumar Batalvi'; whose life and presence I have admired so deeply, but could not do justice to, owing to linguistic constraints, yet again. I also largely praise the spirit of Dr. Kumar Vishwas, not merely because of his prolific skill and knowledge, through which he creates magic each time he delivers performances; but also for, or rather only much more, for his attempt to keep alive the spirit of the 'Magical Souls' of the yesteryears among us. Having said that; his contemporary, though much senior, 'Rahat Indori Sahab', shall continue to live in our hearts; or, for that matter, many more of his time and genre, despite the fact that I might not have been able to pay a specific tribute to each one of them in this compilation...

So, here it is, a tribute to 'The Magical Souls'; alive and immortal... Happy Reading!

'Your eyes, oh, so kohled....
I lost my heart to them, uncanny!
Unknowingly, these eyes;
have made promises so many....

The waves of the breath
flow intermediate....
And thus, to you they state....
"The monsoon shall shower,
dancing away, tapping its feet...
And, drenched thus,
two hearts shall meet."
Oh, beloved! Whenever you shall come;
along my doorway, flowers shall bloom...'

– Faaiz Anwar (Aaoge Jab Tum)

Blurbs

"Maj-rooh is a beautiful collection of English translations by Sharad Kamal Bezboruah from Assamese, Hindi and Urdu poems by some of the most pheneomenal poets and lyricists. It is exhilarating to learn that voices from such different times and geographies could be coolly put together. The collection serves as a medley cafe for Lakshminath Bezbarua, Kalaguru Bishnu Prasad Rabha, Hiren Bhattacharya , Faiz Ahmed Faiz, Harivansh Rai Bacchan, Jyoti Prasad Agarwalla and many other avant garde poets to naturally blossom in the same string of pages like never before."

– Madhu Raghavendra.

(Founder, Poetry Couture; emminent Indian Poet, currently based inthe US.)

"As if someone has said it before, as if someone has come to remind me of all the beautiful things, that for once I forgot. That deja vu, that "shayari-wallah" has come with his magical translations to take all of us to a ride of nostalgia, love, life and every human emotion inch by inch. Sharad's translations are not just literal ones but something that comes far from somewhere. Every line, every paragraph takes you to an odyssey and you delve deep into finding meanings, yet to be understood, yet to be written. Sharad, you are one of your kind in making."Love;

– कलमकारी aka Himanshu Trivedi.

(Founder, HindUrdu Poetry; Alumni- Aligarh Muslim University; Hathras, UP.)

"Maj-rooh is a translation and compilation of multiple voices, ranging from Assamese poets to Urdu and Hindi---- the translator's renditions are smooth and delectable, delicious and enticing! Without losing the essence of the original verse, the translator has successfully straddled worlds and realms."

– Namrata Pathak.

(Assistant Professor, English, North Eastern Hill University, Shillong.)

"Music propagates to the hearts of millions, irrespective of the language. Breathing through the verses, adhering to the meaning , connects the audience to the world of music. Sharad Bezboruah commendably executed his translations of songs from different languages , giving the reader an insight to the meaning of the songs. Songs become more melodious, when we immerse ourselves to it with a greater sense of understanding. A book which stands out in the world of literature being one of its kind."

– Sreekala P Vijayan

(Best Selling Author; Poetess, Academician, Newscarter, Host of Literary Events; Bangaluru.)

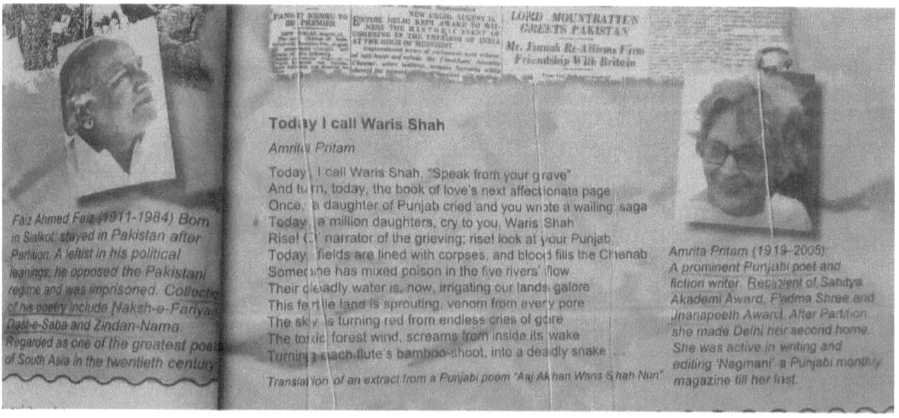

A SNIPPET FROM A DEAR FRIEND'S TEXTBOOK, A TRIBUTE TO FAIZ AHMAD FAIZ and AMRITA PRITAM JI, (CIRCA, 2016)

1. Abhi Na Jaao Chodd Kar...

Lyricist:- Sahir Ludhiyanvi.

Male:
Don't leave now;
for the heart still isn't content…
You've just arrived,
and dispersed like the spring fragrant.
Let the fragrance at least fill the air,
Let the eyes get a chance to wander…
Let the evening set in and chase away the sun's glare,
Let the heart revive from the shock of the splendour….
Let me live for a little while at least,
Let me at least drink sips of intoxication…
We haven't even talked of anything yet,
Nothing has been heard,
nor anything said…
Don't leave now;
for the heart still isn't content…

Female:
The stars have begun to glitter…
The lamps have begun to burn; flicker…
Enough now me, to pause,
you ask not, better…
Do not come forth to obstruct my path; because…

If I don't leave now… I shall not be able to go ever…
And, that "the heart still isn't content",
the same words you shall continue to utter…
One that at some point or the other comes to an end,
this isn't at all such a tale…

Male:
Not now, Not now…

Female:
No! No! No! No!

Male:
Don't leave now;
for the heart still isn't content…

Male:
With a thirst,
only half quenched…
In a partially unfulfilled desire,
with a heart that's drenched…
If you leave, then how shall we continue!!?
For, in the love of the young hearts,
of life, along the path wretched;
many such places, we shall come across,
by which we shall be tested.
Do not mind, for, these words gross,
I speak in love, not in reproach…

Female:
That "the heart still isn't content",
the same words you shall continue to utter…

Male:
Yes…!!
The heart still isn't content…

Female:
No! No! No! No!

Female:
The lanes of sorrow and joys…
are meant for all…
Defeated by sorrows,
like this if you fall…
If you leave, then how shall we continue!!?
Be it joy, be it sorrow…
Together we both, shall share…
Come, try and test me, and let me show!
Look into my eyes, with of your eyes the pair…
Perhaps the bodies are two but,
between the hearts there isn't a distance…
They're at the same place…
Who has ever such been born on earth,
sorrow who has never had to embrace!!??
In the name of your love, I swear…
Your pain is my pain…
What's in your heart, share…
Do not stay extinguished like this…
From me too if you begin to hide,
to whom shall you say then!?
You, how shall I convince,
that I am no stranger…!
How shall convince you,

that from you I am not separated…
And that, from me you aren't separated…
From you I am not separated…
And that, from me you aren't separated…

– Translated on 27th June, 2014 by Sharad Kamal Bezboruah.

2. *Ajj Din Chadheya...*

*(SHIV KUMAR BATALVI)**

Today it dawns, in shades of you.

Today it dawns, in shades of you.
Your kiss from the past,
I carry along.
With the rays too does come,
the same stupor,
as in the 'kisses' of a snake's venom.

Today it dawns, in shades of you.

I wish time hands me over
this day entire.
And thus me it immortalizes,
this day; just like the colours you shower.
I confess the sin of death,
thus accept the debts, that to repay I offer.
Scribble two alphabets of the
sunrays, onto this pale paper.

Today it dawns, in shades of you.

Each day, overhead another debt;
each day, something I ought to borrow,
each day, something you ought to lend.

The books open, the credit shall rise;
never shall the accounts be equal set.
For of my body, a ray sleek,
your sun would have to be, for a bid laid.

Your stove void of ember,
your pitcher void of water;
this day, in shades of you which dawns;
turn away, and all of it shall shatter.

Today it dawns, in shades of you.

I wish not dies an untimely death,
such a day, so fair.
The nights bleak,
I wish to see this day's light scare.
Whatever comes my way,
to fight it all, I dare.

Whatever my debts with time,
all I shall clear, without an arrear.
I wish time hands me over
this day entire.

Scribble two alphabets of the
sunrays, onto this pale paper.

Today it dawns, in shades of you.

– Trans-created on 2nd October, 2017 by Sharad Kamal Bezboruah.

---

*Here's celebrating the spirit and legacy of the youngest recipient of the Sahitya Akademi Award, 'ever'.

3. Ae Ajnabi...

Lyrics: Gulzar.

Oh Beloved Foreigner....!!
Oh Beloved Foreigner....!!

Listen oh stranger!
From somewhere, a call even you must utter...
I live on here in bits,
and you live elsewhere and deep within shatter.
Listen oh stranger!
From somewhere, a call even you must utter...

'Everyday,
the silk-like breeze...
Does come and say,
"Tell me please..."
The breeze
as smooth as silk...
says – "Tell me please...
As pure as bathed in milk,
that tender blossom,
which everyone's heart did seize....
Where is she?
Where is she?
Where is that light...?
The one beloved to all....

Why do I not get her sight?"
I am incomplete,
so are you...
Let us meet...

Call out from somewhere....
Listen oh stranger!
From somewhere, a call even you must utter...
I live on here in bits,
and you live elsewhere and deep within shatter.
Listen oh stranger!
From somewhere, a call even you must utter...

Oh Beloved Foreigner....!!
Oh Beloved Foreigner....!!'
Oh Beloved Foreigner....!!
Oh Beloved Foreigner....!!

You though are not around,
your smiles are here.
The sight of your face is nowhere found,
but your footsteps are heard loud and clear.
Where are you?
Where are your traces?
Where is my world?
I am incomplete,
and incomplete you too live on...

Listen oh stranger!
From somewhere, a call even you must utter...
I live on here in bits,
and you live elsewhere and deep within shatter.

Listen oh stranger!

From somewhere, a call even you must utter...

Listen oh stranger!

From somewhere, a call even you must utter...

– Trans-created on 23rd February, 2014 by SharadKamal Bezboruah.

4. Dil Se Re...

A sun had arisen
Something it did melt
Melted, it was found
A storm, was felt;
when by them,
from the hearts, a sigh was given out
From the hearts…
From the hearts…

The heart after all,
is a heart, indeed…
Such is the difficulty,
a difficulty so sweet…
Oh beloved…! Oh beloved…!
Have I drunk or the goblet I have only held?
My life…! My life…!
In its true sense, a life, have I led?

Two leaves of autumn
From the trees,
down they did come;
From those branches,
they did descend…
Then, so many seasons,

they came and went…
The two leaves, the poor leaves;
in desire of growing again,
they passed through the heaps of sand…
Oh, what pain!!!
The two leaves were, in fact hearts;
Oh!!
They were… They were hearts…

If there is a heart,
there shall be pain…
If there is pain,
there's a heart, there again…

The heart after all,
is a heart, indeed…
Such a difficulty,
a difficulty so sweet…
Oh beloved…! Oh beloved…!
Have I drunk or the goblet I have only held?
My life…! My life…!
In its true sense, a life, have I led?

There are restrictions
in relations…
Fences of barbed wire…
The walls of stones, of stones the doors…
Still, the flowers and blossoms one does desire
to see; bloom and each grows;
and, the fictitious tales and fables…
They go on!
Even the characters match;

those relations were, in fact hearts…
Oh!!
They were; they were hearts…

Sorrows are the anxious feet of the heart
that tremble;
of water,
these sorrows are bubbles…
They burst and come up again,
in the hearts, from the hearts of people…
From the hearts…
From the hearts!

– Trans-created and Adapted on 21st September, 2014
by Sharad Kamal Bezboruah.

5. *Hum Laaye Hai Toofan Se, Kashti Nikaal Ke...*

– Kavi Pradeep. *(Ramchandra Baryanji Dwivedi)*

"Door Hato aye Duniya Waalon, Hindustan Humaara Hai!"

The dice have all flipped;
at the enemy's throw;
The letters of India's fate,
have too changed at one go;
The nation's has come to the gate,
as all hurdles it did forego;
After centuries, colours of joy have showered,
pink, blue and yellow!

With great effort, out of the storms,
this boat we have managed to row;
now, no matter what disaster comes,
you are to save it; I let you know;
into the future of this very nation,
dear children you are to grow…
Now, no matter what disaster comes,
you are to save it; I let you know!

Watch out, this garden,
it must not be wiped out;
Watch out, this garden,

it must not be wiped out!
With blood from his vein,
Baapu has nurtured it through…
This lamp, they did brighten,
the martyrs of this land…
So, no matter what disaster comes,
you are to save it; dear children…

With great effort, out of the storms,
this boat we have managed to row…
Now, no matter what disaster comes,
you are to save it; I let you know…

Do not link yourself to the happenings,
of the world… For you have a long way to go…
Let no one leave you lost,
the wrong way let no one show…
Now, no matter what disaster comes,
you are to save it; I let you know…

At the might of atom bombs,
the world is based…
On of gunpowder, a tomb,
the world is now placed…
Take every step a little carefully,
for this nation's honour;
by you it is to be raised…
With great effort, out of the storms,
this boat we have managed to row…
Now, no matter what disaster comes,
you are to save it; I let you know…

In the maze of shelter and safety,
do not be lost…
In the swing of dreams,
do not fly or be tossed…
Dear smiling flowers;
the time has come…
Jump… And touch the skies,
with all your powers…
Place the flag of this nation,
at that very point…
Turn it into a sensation,
us, do not disappoint…

With great effort, out of the storms,
this boat we have managed to row…
Now, no matter what disaster comes,
you are to save it; I let you know…

– Trans-created on 20th December, 2014 by Sharad Kamal Bezboruah.

6. Kal Ho Na Ho.

– Javed Akhtar

'Every moment, life is transforming,
somewhere there's light, somewhere there's shade.
Live life to your fullest,
enjoy these wonderful moments god has made.
Who knows, tomorrow these may not exist,
who knows, if this time, away shall fade.

One who loves with all the heart,
such a guy is difficult to find.
If you ever find anywhere anyone so,
he's the one most delightful, keep that in mind.
Take that hand today, for you never know…
tomorrow where that generous one may go.
Along with the shadows below the eyelids,
when someone it meets...
You try and hold back a zillion times;
yet this heart, so fast it beats.
But, think for once, whether for sure, you know,
that this story shall last beyond tomorrow.

You have your sorrows hidden;
I sit with a head, down bent.
Silence alone does speak,
what's within, who would vent?

If such is the distances,
whether or not, we meet tomorrow!

True that hurts the heart,
but I have given a thought;
that why does the heart ache,
why the eyes wet;
when what happens, is only what ought.

Whatever it is, let go;
for we know not if it's traces
we shall even find, tomorrow.'

– Translated on 18th April, 2013 by Sharad Kamal Bezboruah.

Extended: 10th July, 2018.

7. Panchi, Nadiyaan, Pawan Ke Jhonke....

– Javed Akhtar.

Both: The birds, the rivers and the gusts of wind...
their movement, no fences ever bind.
Only for humans, these fences are meant.
So, think for once, being born as humans,
what did we ever get!

Male: If you and I were birds...
we would float about in the skies with each other,
flapping our wings with feathers.
Female: Ours would be the entire world;
ours would be all the different sceneries and terrains.
Male: We would fly in the air open,
with all the love in our hearts.

Both: The birds, the rivers and the gusts of wind...
their movement, no fences ever bind.
Only for humans, these fences are meant.
So, think for once, being born as humans,
what did we ever get!

Female: Just think if I were to be a river,
and you the winds that blow on earth forever...
what would happen.
Male: When the winds touch the river's surface,

innumerable waves are raised.

When a meeting of ours would have been,

something similar would be seen.

Female: All say that all these waves,

even if one loses one's life, none say anything,

no matter how they behave.

Both: The birds, the rivers and the gusts of wind…

their movement, no fences ever bind.

Only for humans, these fences are meant.

So, think for once, being born as humans,

what did we ever get!

– Translated on 30th November, 2013 by Sharad Kamal Bezboruah.

**NOTE: The above piece by Javed Sahab for which he had been awarded the 48th 'Silver Lotus' Award in the year 2000; 'for his inimitable style'; 'speaks of transcending borders and countries, with beautifully written words for love and compassion'.

8. Woh Jahaan!!

– Javed Akhtar.

Female:
In the blue skies,
which is a vast ocean;
is there somewhere a star;
where lies another world,
where life awakens?

But, different from us,
from us opposed.
Of pain where lies no traces;
to live on,
where difficulty none faces.

Where no one cries,
no one is anxious.
Where everyone believes,
they aren't alone.
Where never do hearts break or heave!

The world where,
there be no pain, no sorrow;
the world where,
tears don't flow;
where between hearts,

there be no distances, nor walls;
the world where,
come true dreams all.

Everyone ought to know,
every heart has a deep river
of love flowing through.
In the blue skies, shining silver,
is there such a star?

Male:
This, an ocean of the blue skies,
the moon, across it I row.
If you look for such world;
it's right here, it's here somewhere,
and, to you I show-

Look; on its face,
of hatred, of tyranny,
of their dirt, this layer.
Look; it is tied, held back,
by shackles of greed, so many.
Thus, that world, almost here,
stopped at a distance, there!!

If this dirt is removed,
and are cut open the shackles.
On this very earth, you shall find;
the very world that sparkles.

The world where,
there be no pain, no sorrow;

the world where,
tears don't flow;
where between hearts,
there be no distances, nor walls;
the world where,
come true dreams all.

Let a light smile on these faces,
Let life be one of love;
and with love let live the masses.

– Translated on 24th June, 2017 by Sharad Kamal Bezboruah.

9. Rehna Tu...

Lyricist: Prasoon Joshi.

Stay as you are…

A little pain;
a bit of ease;
Stay as you are…
A pleasant breeze,
or a raging passion.

A little velvety
you are beloved, and a bit rough…
Sometimes, it runs,
sometimes get into a fight mighty…
Or full of fragrance…
Even a wee bit,
you I do not want to change.
Without decorations,
without any blending….
neither a bit nor more…

I need you;
to remain what you are…!
As your rains pour,
I wish to get wet…
fade away.

I need you
to remain what you are…!
I wish to burn,
in your flame…and, turn to ashes!

Though you give me many a scar,
many wounds… And then,
to put the heeling gel on them too, you do seem.
Every wound seems to be a star,
and I fall in love with those…
Stream! Oh, stream…
Let me drown in you, stream…

You know well,
if the two must walk holding hands…
then how do you expect both hands right
to be together… One would be right, one left.
You have to walk thus… So, hold the hand…
Hold the hand tight…
For you have to walk thus…

Stay as you are…

A little pain;
a bit of ease.
Stay as you are…
A pleasant breeze;
or a raging passion.

A little velvety
you are beloved, and a bit rough…
Sometimes, it runs,

sometimes get into a fight mighty…
Or full of fragrance…
Even a wee bit,
you I do not want to change.
Without decorations,
without any blending….
neither a bit nor more…

I need you;
to remain what you are…!
As your rains pour,
I wish to get wet…
fade away.

I need you
to remain what you are…!
I wish to burn,
in your flame…and, turn to ashes!

    – Trans-created on 16th June, 2014 by Sharad Kamal Bezboruah.

10. Baat Niklegi Toh Phir... Door Talak Jaayegi...

(Late Jagjit Singh.)
LYRICS BY: KAFEEL AAZER...

When the talk is out,

in no time, things shall have gone far…

People shall unnecessarily ask

what the sorrow is all about;

and that, why you look so troubled….

They shall point out to your dry hair,

and ask why it is so;

to olden days, they shall glance,

and ask "where is that flair?"…

At the slightest of chance,

they shall comment on your wrinkles, freckles…

Over your shivering hands,

they shall express concern from all angles….

People are cruel,

at every point, they shall taunt…

As their talks go on,

my mention too shall be brought…

Their words, dear mate,

at all, note not…

Otherwise, by the expression on your face,

all your feelings shall be caught…

No matter what happens,
do not ask what they mean….
About me,
don't have any word with them…
Or…. By them, all of it shall be seen…

When the talk is out,
in no time, things shall have gone far…

    – Trans-created on 5th May, 2014 by Sharad Kamal Bezboruah.

"রাত্রিপ্রভাতিল, উদলিরবচ্ছিছবপির্ব-উদয়গরিভিালে –
গাহবেহিঙ্গম, পূণ্যসমীরণনবজীবনরসঢালে।"

       – রবীন্দ্রনাথঠাকুর ॥

("Raatri Prabhatil, Udil Ravi-chavvi, Purv-udaya giri Bhaale; Gaahe Vihangam; Poonya Samiran, Nav-Jivan Ras Dhaale…)
       – Gurudev Rabindranath Tagore.

11. O Jibon.../O' Jivon...

– Lyrics By: Hiren Bhattacharyya.

Oh life...
Strum your fingers of lightning,
across the strings...
Of the incredible lyre
of my land so full of greens....

In the silent night, across the lyre strings,
who strummed one's fingers so skillfully?
The night's jasmine at my doorway,
wipes its teardrops silently, alone, lonely...
Far away in the skies,
bloom the flowers of jasmine.
Gathering and collecting
the stars of the night, so charming.
I am awake, counting,
the musical stars of the night...
One...two...three...!!
One...two...three...!!

– Trans-created on 6th March, 2014 by Sharad Kamal Bezboruah.

Credits: Kasturi, Anuraag, Bhaskar Sarma; YouTube, the album Dhemaali; Namrata Sarma.

12. *Kune Aaji Aabeli.*

(Dwipen Barua)
Lyrics: Nabakanta Barua.

Adult:
Look, oh children doting;
who takes away
the affection,
this evening, floating...
floating into the skies,
who does send?

Children:
This balloon,
this balloon deep red.
And thus, they soar;
into the clouds...
of the skies, into the core.

Adult:
Then, come along,
on this balloon;
let's all head
for the moon.
On its back,
go play a beat.

Children:
Blow the balloon large,
so that we all fit.
To go there,
and have a fete…
We are already
all set.

Adult:
But, if you miss home,
how will you descend.

Children:
This very land
will pull us back
with its mystic thread.

Adult:
If those skies scatter,
those twinkling petals
of the stars in descent?

Children:
Of the flowers wild,
the familiar fragrant
gusts, towards the skies
up we would send.

Adult:
Then tell me where
the bee buzzes and goes?

Children: We don't know.
Adult: Neither do I know!

No one knows,
no one ever knows.

– Translated on 28th June, 2017 by Sharad Kamal Bezboruah.

13. Akash'e Botaahe...

Dr. Birendranath Datta.
Lyrics: Nabakanta Barua.

All around,

so much music;

about does float!

But to my songs;

comes not

even one note.

So much they know!

The woods of the spruce pines;

to the winds, they speak.

Listen, oh listen!

Read between the lines,

for not one word comes

into ears mine.

All around,

so much music;

about does float!

But to my songs;

comes not

even one note.

The seeds of trees unfamiliar,
play their anklets
do you hear?
But, my soul, never it gets,
of the dancing waves
the rises, the sets.

All around,
so much music;
about does float!
But to my songs;
comes not
even one note.

– Trans-created on 15th July, 2017 by Sharad Kamal Bezboruah.

14. Heruwa Dinor Xunaali Xopun...

*– Artist: Jyotish Bhattacharyya.
(13th September 1937 – 23rd September 1991)*

The golden dreams of lost days,
floated away in the river of time...
On the bank, lay there, only,
the pearls of memories sublime...

The garlands of poetry,
woven with hope...have now withered...
The stanzas of songs half sung,
now lay, all over, scattered...

The golden dreams of lost days,
floated away in the river of time...
On the bank, lay there, only,
the pearls of memories sublime...

The skies vast, moonlit...
In the heart, such a chaos!
The skies within, bleak,
and, every moment...a loss...

The golden dreams of lost days,
floated away in the river of time...
On the bank, lay there, only,
the pearls of memories sublime...

– Trans-created on 13th September, 2016 by Sharad Kamal Bezboruah.

15. Akou Notun Probhat Hobo...

Lyrics- Dr. Nirmalprabha Bordoloi.

There shall be a new dawn;
this dark night shall not last.
The hoot of the owls,
of wolves the howls,
shall become a thing of the past.

There shall be a new dawn;
this dark night shall not last.
The hoot of the owls,
of wolves the howls,
shall become a thing of the past.

There shall be a new dawn,
you shall not see this dark night.
The hearts of the devils of darkness
shall be smashed by that new light.

There shall be a new dawn,
this dark night shall disappear.
The flame of courage and bravery
shall chase away the haunted night's terror.

There shall be a new dawn;
this dark night shall not last.
The hoot of owls,
of wolves the howls,
shall become a thing of the past.

There shall be a new dawn;
the bright sun shall bring a smile to every face.
To this generation that has come to a pause
the light of the dawn shall give a new pace.

– Translated on 5th May, 2013 by Sharad Kamal Bezboruah

16. Sokuye Jodi Kotha Koi....

– MAYUKH HAZARIKA...

If eyes too can speak,
then words, why do you seek!??

If only unknowingly, there is an error,
where's the need for forgiveness!?
Why all the terror??

If the heart too does cry,
then to express in language,
why does someone try??

If eyes too can speak,
then words, why do you seek!??

Of far, a chilled breeze…
why does it come and touch??
A beautiful melody, with so much ease,
why does it bring stupefaction such!!!??

I question…everyday, every season….repeatedly…

If in streams, away they flow,
why hold memories tight…!??
If the stars adorn,
the skies at night!

Then why be flying up there,
this kite??
If burns enough…
If to burn is enough,
alone, this fire bright…!
Then why be there this life
to add to the plight!!??

If eyes too can speak,
then words, why do you seek!??

This night, solitary…
Why does it never end!!??
Why me it loves to worry!??
Yet again, the dawn!
Why does it give life the hope of glory….!!??

I question…everyday, every season,
repeatedly…
I look for an answer, a reason…
repeatedly…

– Trans-created 20th February, 2015 by Sharad Kamal Bezboruah.

17. Saagor Songomot

– Dr. Bhupen Hazarika.

At the junction of many a sea,
for so long I have swum…
Even then, I seeketh not for rest…
Yet, among the waves
in the Pacific in me come,
many a wild tempest…

In the heart of the Pacific,
of my heart...
The endless waves showcase,
a brilliant spirit, epic...
In the Pacific in me come,
many a wild tempest…

In the lives of the noble,
the peace is breached;
along the Pacific shore...
Thereafter, new creations stumble,
at the harsh blow,
made by the demons... "Roar"!!
the demonic forces, oh so evil...
And therefore, restive they flow,
the waves in the Pacific in me...

With the blows of destruction, rash,
innumerable soldiers of creations,
come into many a clash...
The clash brings forth,
into the Pacific in me...
Horizons of new progress afresh...

The power of the deep Pacific in me baffles,
the forces of destruction...
And the endless march of peace loving men,
generates new ripples...
in the waters of creation...
And so, the storm among the restive waves
in the Pacific in me, forever rages, never settles.

At the junction of many a sea,
for so long I have swum…
Even then, I I seeketh not for rest…
Yet, among the waves
in the Pacific in me come,
many a wild tempest…

– Transcreated and Adapted on 2nd November, 2014
by Sharad Kamal Bezboruah.

Inspired by Lt. Syed Ahmed Shah's version of the translation of "Saagor Songomot"!

18. Oye Oye Akaax Xubo...

– Dr. Bhupen Hazarika...

The skies shall fall asleep...
so shall this breeze!!
At the horizon,
a chaos shall unleash...

Like time comes to a pause,
and then...trembles, fears...
Shall turn into
stones, these tears...
And thus, time shall fall asleep!

If wrong are sins
why was given this thirst...
If wrong is attachment, then,
these tunes be here why must??
Why shall be there, this separation,
if feelings are the worst...?
With the answers to these secrets,
who did the lords entrust...
Who shall give,
give the answers to us!!
Who??
And, time shall fall asleep thus...

A night full of riddles,
'my' piece of the moon shall sleep!
The question of what is just,
and what is not shall arise!
Thus, at the horizon
a chaos shall arise....

– Trans-created and Adapted on 5th November, 2016
by Sharad Kamal Bezboruah.

19. Dure Dure Kune?!(JAGJIT SINGH)

– Tafajjul Ali.

Far away,
who plays a flute, as hours elapse?!
On every note,
he shook the earth's lap…

Which bronzed lady set out,
and turned repeatedly,
looking at us with lowered, eyes…
The skies, to touch, the lady does sought.

The wondrous flute, its call is heard,
at of life, each and every rhythm.
The wondrous flute, its call is heard,
at of life, each and every rhythm.
My two eyes it has blurred,
and now pours the essence of wonder.
With tender poetry,
the heart it makes to overflow…

Far away,
who plays a flute, as hours elapse?!
On every note,
he shook the earth's lap…

– Trans-created on 6th April, 2014 by Sharad Kamal Bezboruah.

20. Mur Bonere, Mur Monere…

– Hiren Bhattacharyya.
Credits: Prayash Majumdar.

Through my grasslands,
my heart
flies a honey-bee, buzzing on.
Oh my…!!
Deep within, the feeling makes me die.

Through the dew,
in the middle of the grass
the sunlight does pass
and then giggle.
It's arrives like a golden-winged angel.
Oh my…!!
Deep within, the feeling makes me die.

Through the heart,
the light lustrous
like a lotus…
Gently sets foot…
Oh my…!!
Deep within, the feeling makes me die.

Through my grasslands,
my heart
flies a honey-bee, buzzing on.
Oh my…!!
Deep within, the feeling makes me die.

– Translated on 14th November, 2013 by Sharad Kamal Bezboruah.

21. Baahi….(Hero'o Baahi)

— By Hiren Bhattacharyya.
Sung by: Zubeen Garg.

Listen, oh dear flute….
You're very dear to me.
My flute…..
You really are dear to me.

Holding on to your tunes tight,
I shall go off far really,
one fine, full-moon night.
Holding on to your tunes tight,
I shall go off far really,
on a fine full moon night.
You're very dear to me.
Do you hear, oh dear flute….!!

Amidst the trees of gooseberries,
the ways graze the deer and does.
The same way, even I shall go far very,
on my toes.
Holding on to your tunes tight,
I shall go off far really,
on a fine full moon night.
My flute…..
You're really dear to me.

However far I go,
whenever I fail to recall the tune.
I shall return, let me let you know,
to you at once, soon.
Holding on to your tunes tight,
I shall go off far really…
on a fine full moon night.
Listen, oh dear flute….
You're really dear to me.
My flute…..
You're really dear to me!!
Listen, oh dear flute….
You're really dear to me.

 – Translated on 6th December, 2013 by Sharad Kamal Bezboruah.

22. *Bohudin Xuna Nai Jiya Xile Kotha Kua*

Sung by: Manojyostna Mahanta.
(Lyrics: Keshab Mahanta)

It's been long since I've heard the live stones talk…
inscribed within the warmth of the heart;
Affection… Affection…
For long, haven't heard words from the rock…
Do you
recall too…
Ever!?
Beloved, with a pause,
the heart does shiver;
what's the cause!!
Perhaps a fact forgotten….
It's been long since I've heard the live stones talk…
For long, I haven't heard words from the live rock…

The currents raise waves, so many…
In the heart of the rock,
lay, of love, the sweet and pure honey…
The honey of love in the heart of the rock….
Affection… Affection…
Could the waves possibly wipe, washing them away…
The immortal, eternal lines of the rocks…
It's been long since I've heard the live stones talk…

For long, haven't heard words from the live rock…

Our hearts immortal,
their stories itself… the live stones do tell….
Bylive stones, the green tales of the hearts are said…
By the stones live…!!
Come… Your hand beloved,
in my two hands do keep….

It's been long since I've heard the live stones talk…
written with the warmth of the heart…
Affection… Affection…

  – Trans-created on 11th May, 2014 by Sharad Kamal Bezboruah.

23. Kor Ejaak Xopun….Jen Boruxun…

– Dr. Bhabendra Nath Saikia.
Sung by: Anindita Paul.
(Tabla: Zubeen Garg) Credits: Namrata Sarma

Oh! From where comes this rain,
as if, of dreams a bunch...
It comes floating midst clouds,
pushing aside the dust...
The soothing song of the earth is such!
Oh! From where comes this rain,
as if of dreams a bunch...!!

It comes and awakens the sleeping forests...
The green beauty too awakens.
Somewhere rings the unseen, unknown anklets;
Jingle, Jingle, Jingle...

Awaken, innumerable birds in their nests...
I do not see them... Where are they?
I have searched entire forests...
Only a faint song rings in my ears,
Hum, Hum, Hum...
Oh! From where comes this rain,
like of dreams a bunch...!!

Oh! From where comes this rain,
as if of dreams a bunch...
It comes floating midst clouds,
pushing aside the dust...
The soothing song of the earth is such!
Oh! From where comes this rain,
like of dreams a bunch...!!
Oh! From where comes this rain,
like of dreams a bunch...!!

– Trans-created on 5th March, 2014 by Sharad Kamal Bezboruah.

24. Tai Ketiyaba Mon Gole.

– Hiren Bhattacharyya.
Credits: Namrata Sarma

Artist: Khagen Mahanta.
Music: Jaminidhar Baruah.

Sometimes, when she wishes to,
she scatters in my yard,
plucking flowers from the garden
like she's only a little girl,
among the other young children.

Sometimes, when she wishes to,
she scatters in my yard,
plucking flowers from the garden
like she's only a little girl,
among the other young children.

Sometimes, right at dawn
she moves by my window,
humming a song.
If my face I happen to show,
she turns and just runs along…
As though she never did come this way…
like she's only a little girl,
among the other young children.

She had come this evening, silently.
And on the leaves of the tree at my gate,
with strange letters of dust: had written something.
And before I had even read,
she wiped those letters away with her two hands
like she's only a little girl,
among the other young children.

Sometimes, when she wishes to,
she scatters in my yard, plucking flowers from the garden
like she's only a little girl,
among the other young children.

– Translated on 14th November, 2013 by Sharad Kamal Bezboruah.

25. Mur Kobitaa'r Chondo Laagi...

– 'Kalaguru' Bishnu Prasad Rabha.

Touched by the prosody of my poetry,
does your heartbeat awaken?
By the aroma of flowers,
are your golden dreams broken?
Are they broken?
Are they broken?
Are your golden dreams broken?

The stars dance,
all around…
Filling the world,
with joy profound…
On the joy emerging all over…
does your heart not fill
with joy….?
Does it not will,
to dance?!
By the aroma of flowers,
are your golden dreams broken?
Are they broken?
Are they broken?
Are your golden dreams broken?

At the prosody of my poetry,
does your heartbeat awaken?

The flute of my heart plays,
in every bit of me, raising a tune…
Among those tunes too, tell me if,
if the heart shall fall cool…
At every rhythm, flowers bloom,
Spilling fragrance all over…
At that very rhythm, raising ecstasy,
Does your heart dance even once?!
By the aroma of flowers,
are your golden dreams broken?
Are they broken?
Are they broken?
Are your golden dreams broken?

At the prosody of my poetry,
does your heartbeat awaken?

– Trans-created on 7th April, 2014 by Sharad Kamal Bezboruah.

26. *AHIBA TUMI by Tarali Sarma.*

Lyricist: Dilip Bora.

You shall come at midnight,
when the world will sleep…
The river of our love in the heart,
shall reach for the brims,
for the seas, it shall leap.
For the seas, it shall leap.
Oh beloved!!
For the seas, it shall leap.

Flowers shall blossom…
in our hearts.
As the moon so awesome,
in our eyes, to gleam it starts.
His face hidden behind,
of Bermuda grass, the leaves;
he shall come…
My beloved!!
And finally a sigh the heart shall heave.

In the waters of river Luit,
shall rise a flood…
The waves shall rage much…
The vast skies, it,
your hopes and dreams shall touch.

The vast skies they shall touch!!
Oh beloved!!
The vast skies they shall touch!!

You shall come at midnight,
when the world will sleep…
The river of love in the heart,
shall reach for the brims,
for the seas, it shall leap.
For the seas, it shall leap.
Oh beloved!!
For the seas, it shall leap.

– Trans-created on 5th March, 2014 by Sharad Kamal Bezboruah.

27. Xile Xile Theka Khale....

– Keshab Mahanta.
Credits: Namrata Sarma, team 'Baartalaap'.

On the rocks along its path,

hit itself, repeatedly; the water of the stream.

A faint ray of sunlight descends,

and the water is adorned by that gleam.

The colourful flowers, growing in the wild,

dancing and swaying, expressing elation…

what words do they speak,so timid and mild?

The heart craves for a heart;

I wonder who would bring it in!

A faint ray of sunlight descends,

and the water is adorned by that gleam.

The heart's cold; you are a distant call.

I am the pain,

of the low plain….

You are the peak of a mountain so tall.

On every peak,

whose creak,

did generate such waves with power?

Each ear,

whose song did it softly hear,

this sweet honey, whose voice did shower?
The principal wife, of which king,
is this dancing stream?
A faint ray of sunlight descends,
and the water is adorned by that gleam.

On the rocks along its path,
hit itself repeated; the water of the stream.
A faint ray of sunlight descends,
and the water is adorned by that gleam.

– Translated on 25th December, 2013 by Sharad Kamal Bezboruah.

28. Ohaar Dore Ubhoti Aatori Gola...

Lyricist: Hiren Gohain
Artist: Manidra Lahiri Sarma.

In fond memory of Bidisha Bezbaruah; and beloved Aita.

You walked away,
the same way you had come.
Along your way, you did scatter
many a blossom.
In the heat of the sun ever,
even if those flowers happen to wither.
About you alone,
they continue to utter.

You walked away,
the same way you had come.
Along your way, you did scatter
many a blossom.
In the heat of the sun ever,
even if those flowers happen to wither.
About you alone,
they continue to utter.

Like the cloud of the heavy monsoon,
you had come to take a scroll.
And showering on, you did wet,
of the path of my life, the dust all.

I don't know why ever,
did you walk away this way,
with a heart full of pride.

You walked away,
the same way you had come.
Along your way, you did scatter
many a blossom.
In the heat of the sun ever,
even if those flowers happen to wither.
About you alone,
they continue to utter.

The celerity of the rains, again no more;
only lay now on the banks, the coarse sands.
Of the boat of my life, your love was the oar,
on it alone, now, everything depends.
Today oh my!
The flowing river,
of love is dry…
Now, I am, lonely forever.

You walked away,
the same way you had come.
Along your way, you did scatter
many a blossom.
In the heat of the sun ever,
even if those flowers happen to wither.
About you alone,
they continue to utter.
About you alone,
they continue to utter.

   – Trans-created on 27th December, 2013 by Sharad Kamal Bezboruah.

29. Pranor Madhuri Butoli Butoli,
(Zubeen Garg)

– Asom Keshari Ambikagiri Raichoudhury.

Come let's gather the essence of life,
and offer our love so innocent….
And, by such devotion,
may the world be illuminant.
Come let's gather the essence of life,
and offer our love so innocent….

You oh mother…! You have been
illuminating this land for so long since then…
Even today, come shower your benevolence,
bring back great days like those again…
Come let's gather the essence of life,
and offer our love so innocent….

Shower unto us, the dusts of benevolence,
play the flute the world that would enchant….
Shower unto us, the dusts of benevolence,
play the flute the world that would enchant….
Let it awaken the world so static,
tearing open, the lid of ignorance….

Come let's gather the essence of life,
and offer our love so innocent.

And, by such devotion,
may the world be illuminant.
Come let's gather the essence of life,
and offer our love so innocent...

– Trans-created on 3rd April, 2014 by Sharad Kamal Bezboruah.

30. Porojonomor Xubhologonot...

– Kalaguru Bishnu Prasad Rabha.

If in our next birth too,
our togetherness we cherish.
I ask you, oh beloved! Will you fulfill,
of this heart, the unfulfilled wish?

The garlands you would make,
you kept them safe, carefully always;
never could you tie around my neck.
My heart is now void, like space.
I ask you, oh beloved! Will you fulfill,
of this heart, the unfulfilled wish?
If in our next birth too,
our togetherness we cherish.

Of this life, all the new-moon nights,
I have passed wiping tears, forever!
Never does the moon of happiness,
shine to shower into the heart its light silver.

Of this birth, a dozen tales untold
lay in this heart only to give pain.
Never did you see the portrait of sorrow in this heart;
never in the desert of the heart, did it rain.
I ask you, oh beloved! Will you fulfill,
of this heart, the unfulfilled wish?

If in our next birth too,
our togetherness we cherish.
I ask you, oh beloved! Will you fulfill,
of this heart, the unfulfilled wish?

– Trans-created completely on 29th January, 2014
by Sharad Kamal Bezboruah.

Edited: 20th June, 2017.

31. Tumar Kotha Jetya Bhaabu...

– Jayanta Hazarika.

The two eyes fill with tears,
whenever I think of you.
The tips of the grasses
shed two drops of dew.
The two eyes fill with tears,
whenever I think of you.

You are like a faint tune of a flute,
playing at a distance.
In the silent night, with the tide,
floating, you approach closer.
My doorway overflows with fragrance
of the long lost flower.

The two eyes fill with tears,
whenever I think of you...

When your thoughts come to my mind,
the heart feels so cold, it really does hurt.
Oh! Those dry leaves are blown off by a gust of wind,
so helpless I feel, like I'm left in a desolate desert.

The two eyes fill with tears,
whenever I think of you...

– Translated on 21st September, 2013 by Sharad Kamal Bezboruah.

32. Osto Aakashore....

– Dr. Bhupen Hazarika…
Credits: Bagmita Baishnabi

With the dreams of the skies that extend beyond the horizon,
the red water of the tired river Brahmaputra flows on and on.

Oh, which artist scatters the colors of a peacock's wing,
so beautifully with a boat of lotuses?
On both banks of this river, stand a lot of people, and sing…
The many episodes of history lay there.
Of innumerable ages, a hundred sighs,
of hope, relief and despair.

I f you aim for the horizons, oh! Talented one,
Do bring your pinnace to the shore for once. Then, you shall see
the incredible horizons of life, the setting Sun.!

With the dreams of the skies that extend beyond the horizon,
the red water of the tired river Brahmaputra…..flows on.

– Translated on 4th May, 2013 by Sharad Kamal Bezboruah.

33. Kimaan Nao Je Ghaatot Lagil....

– Keshab Mahanta.(Sung by: Archana Mahanta.)

So many boats and ships touched the shore,
just before sunset.
Perhaps you shall never come. For after this long too,
you still haven't arrived as yet.

The dark clouds cover the skies,
raging with thunder and anger.
Pausing at intervals, the red lightning sparks…
For how long more will you linger?

All the loved ones walked away together,
and it is you I need and want.
Just before sunset……

So many boats and ships touched the shore,
just before sunset.
Perhaps you shall never come. For after this long too,
you still haven't arrived as yet.
So many boats touched the shore…

Second by second, the darkness of the night nears.
Pausing, again and again, the heart, oblivious, shivers.

Second by second, the darkness of the night nears.
Pausing, again and again, the heart, oblivious, shivers.

Who knows, what may happen to you today?
Even my dreams may shatter, and break!
Just before sunset......

So many boats and ships touched the shore,
just before sunset.
Perhaps you shall never come. For after this long too,
you still haven't arrived as yet.

– Translated on 27th December, 2013 by Sharad Kamal Bezboruah.

34. Phool Nuphulile Ba…Ki hol Taate?!

Lyrics By: Hiren Bhattacharyya.
Credits: Monjit Rajkonwar, YouTube.

The flowers didn't bloom,

what does it matter?!!

The cuckoo,

the soothing call that it did utter….

It shook the skies, so that,

your dreams of onset of spring don't shatter…

The flowers didn't bloom,

what does it matter?!!

February, with its wondrous hands,

into the skies too it sends….

The fragrance of the memories of the Gamble tree,

along your way you tread…

In the air, the red flame-like flowers,

the beginning of spring, their warm breaths usher…

The skies are heated up again,

by the tender leaves of the Gulmohar.

If the dry branches of Palash call out…

If the tender leaves of the Gulmohar sing aloud….

Otherwise, the fragrance of flowers,

in every hand too it can be found.

The flowers didn't bloom,
what does it matter?!!
The cuckoo,
the soothing call that it did utter….
It shook the skies, so that,
your dreams of onset of spring do not shatter….
The flowers didn't bloom,
what does it matter?!!

– Trans-created on 7th April, 2014 by Sharad Kamal Bezboruah.

35. Ekhon Nedekha Nodir Xipaare....

(Dwipen Barua)
Lyrics: Nabakanta Barua.

Beyond the bank of an unseen river
the blossoms of laughter bloom.
I look on from the bank to the other bank,
for to go and pluck them, there isn't room.

Along the strings of dreams,
garlands with the flowers of reality-
you cannot weave, adjust.
In the gardens of hope,
there are only games and play
of mistakes and dust.
My doorway is full of darkness;
far away I see light…beyond the waters vast.

Today, after coming across to this bank,
I saw that the lamps are now lit.
And, that with the dust from the familiar road,
the sparkling dirt on the flowers is now mixed.
Looking for familiar fragrances, in vain
I have searched the entire skies, far and abroad.

Beyond the bank of an unseen river
the blossoms of laughter bloom.

I look on from the bank to the other bank
for a chance to go and pluck them, there isn't room.
Beyond the bank of an unseen river!

– Translated on 24th November, 2013 by Sharad Kamal Bezboruah.

36. Bilot Tirebirai Podumor Paahi..

Lyrics: Kamalananda Bhattarcharje.

(Music: Vivekananda Bhattarcharje.
Music Arrangement: Ramen Choudhury.
Sung By:Zubben Garg/Anindita Paul.)Credits: Namrata Sarma

Petals of lotuses shine in the lakes,
and on the leaves sparkles water after it showers.
In the sunlight, the wings of a dragonfly;
in the garden shines the queen of flowers.

Petals of lotuses shine in the lakes,
and on the leaves sparkles water after it showers.
In the sunlight, the wings of a dragonfly;
in the garden shines the queen of flowers.

In the dark shine fireflies,
'Midst black clouds flickers the lightning.
Up there, the moon shines in the skies,
Wonder who shines in this heart within!

Petals of lotuses shine in the lakes,
and on the leaves sparkles water after it showers.
In the sunlight, the wings of a dragonfly;
in the garden shines the queen of flowers.

The live flame that burns in me,
even there pure gold shines...
The live flame that burns in me,
even there pure gold shines...
Shall I ever see such a day,
when this broken flute would play...
and the full moon would glow in this heart of mine?

Petals of lotuses shine in the lakes,
and on the leaves shines water after it showers.
In the sunlight, the wings of a dragonfly;
in the garden shines the queen of flowers.

– Translated on 11th April, 2013 by Sharad Kamal Bezboruah.

37. Korobire Mala Negaathiba...

Lyrics: Idris Ali

Do not weave garlands with the flowers of oleander,
for their petals shall dry out and their fragrance shall fade.
Therefore, do not weave garlands with flowers of oleander.

If your heart sings to forgotten tunes without a reason;
and you are called back by the long lost days.
While you are thinking,
if you shed tears on something,
with both your hands, you must wipe away.
Do not weave garlands with the flowers of oleander.

Why do you build a transient sand castle,
with the sand of dreams, in this desert of life!
If the flower of memories loses, many, or, a petal,
don't keep those memories safe!
Do not weave garlands with the flowers of oleander...

Do not weave garlands with the flowers of oleander,
for their petals shall dry out and their fragrance shall fade.
Therefore, do not weave garlands with flowers of oleander.
Do not weave garlands with the flowers of oleander...

– Translated on 3rd May, 2013 by Sharad Kamal Bezboruah.

38. *Xou Sirish Daalot Bohi Ejoni Sorai...*

Lyrics By: Hiren Bhattacharyya.
Credits: Himjyoti Talukdar, YouTube.

On the branch of that tree,
is a bird
and she sits hiding there.
The light of its feathers fine,
fall on the reddish leaves...
And Shine....
after the morning sun rays they receive.

On the bank of the stream, a fawn,
like in the sun, it roams about...!
In the same way, the bird plays on,
hide and seek on that branch.
Whistling a tune...

On the branch of that tree
is a bird
and she sits hiding there.
The light of its feathers fine,
fall on the reddish leaves...
And Shine....
after the morning sun rays they receive.

Of my fatigue in my heart, the island;
by its side raising a splash
as the river flows and bends...
Similarly, this morning,
the bird did come to see me.
New tunes it was humming,
new songs it was singing.
And then it dashed away...

On the branch of that tree,
is a bird
and she sits hiding there.
The light of its feathers fine,
fall on the reddish leaves...
And Shine....
after the morning sun rays they receive.

    – Trans-created on 6th March, 2014 by Sharad Kamal Bezboruah.

39. Phool Phulok Rowdor'e Phool...

– *Zubeen Garg.*
Original: Baikuntha Gogoi...

Let flowers of the sunlight bloom,

on the soils green of the heart...

Let there be blooming sunflowers,

in the hair bun on your head...

On the leaves of the ironwood tree,

let us see dancing, of clouds the shade...

Let the flowers of the clouds free,

of the skies of the heart bloom today...

Oh butterfly! Open thy wings....

in the mesmerized heart...

Let there be blooming sunflowers,

in the hair bun on your head...

Let flowers of the sunlight bloom...

Keep the path behind concealed,

dear dry, withered leaf shade...

Fly with your wings open,

the path of pilgrimage of love ahead...

Let the stars of the night dance,

to the tune of the flute...

In the two eyes, be glowing,

the moon sweet and beaut.

Oh sunflower…! Open up your petals,
full of dreams…
In my humble heart…

Let there be blooming sunflowers,
in the hair bun on your head…

Let flowers of the sunlight bloom,
on the soils green of the heart…
Let there be blooming sunflowers,
in the hair bun on your head…

– Translated on 28th June, 2014 by Sharad Kamal Bezboruah.

40. Xuoroni Kuwoli...

Lyrics: Achurjya Borpatra & Amritjyoti

Through the clouds now the mist of memories;
descends the blood red of pain and anxiety.
The clouds of dreams hid the moon of desire,
for its sight, I remained thirsty.

And now, burns the flame of sorrow,
the mirror in my heart you have broken.
... I didn't ever know to love. I got it all, but lost it all.
So, to me, now, you bring this token?!
This heart, in pain does call out a sigh,
o mate, it wets the eye!

Through the clouds now the mist of memories;
descends the blood red of pain and anxiety.

'Midst the silence all around, across a bridge, as you paced forth,
of dew, the frozen drops, did come, turn my love moist,
and my entire life distort.

And now, burns the flame of sorrow,
the mirror in my heart you have broken.
... I didn't ever know to love. I got it all but lost it all.
So, to me, this is your token!

This heart in pain does call out a sigh,
o mate, it wets the eye!

Through the clouds now the mist of memories;
descends the blood red of pain and anxiety.

– Translated on 8th June, 2013 by Sharad Kamal Bezboruah.

41. *Aji Mur Endharote Tuponi Bhaagil…*

– Lyrics By: Hiren Bhattacharyya.

Today, I have awakened in the dark.
The petals of a fanciful vision, one by one,
they fell off.
It was like by the rays of the sun,
made the flowers dreary;
in the coiffure of a fleeting, nimble fairy.

And now in the thorns of my body, I have within;
of earth, this land, the chaotic din.

And like a transient shadow, the curiosity
of the vision, so subtle;
retreating away….little by little.

– Trans-created on 29th January, 2014 by Sharad Kamal Bezboruah,

inspired by a translation by Syed Ahmed Shah.

42. MUGDHO HIYA...(In fond memory of Lt. Jonki Borthakur)

– Zubeen Garg.
(Acknowledging: Blissed Integration, 'Drenched' and Sampriti Goswami)

Before me lies
the new moon bleak;
teardrops wet
on both my cheeks;
these nights of silence,
when shall they pass;
reach out to the dawn
and with the sunlight, dance.
When shall you arrive,
and my eyes, tint;
and with love
make this heart brim?

This humble heart;
wonder who kisses and does stir.
Pauses by within,
and makes a flame unfurl.
All the love
of flesh and blood does fade,
and all that is left is only ashes.
And flows through the heart
a blazing cascade...

Of flesh and blood,
this world does fade;
losing all traces
and all that is left is only ashes.

Everyday;
I only paint a rainbow
along my heart and soul;
each and every moment,
today, I do recall,
the laughter, sorrow and play,
of those February days...
Turned to dust,
slip through the fingers;
of joy, the pearls...
And thus, in the heart
a flame unfurls...

Flows through the heart
a blazing cascade...
Of flesh and blood,
this world does fade;
losing all traces
and all that is left is only ashes.

The February winds,
this heart they elate...
For you are to arrive,
and put an end to my wait...

A voice distant,
I hear...

I tremble as I listen on!
The skies insane,
the earth stagnant;
by teardrops; these days,
graceful are made.
And thus, flows through the heart
a blazing cascade...
Of flesh and blood,
this world does fade;
losing all traces
and all that is left is only ashes.
All the love
of flesh and blood does fade,
and all that is left is only ashes.

At your sight, your touch...
The dusky dreams, flip over, such;
and these eyes,
all along; for you they search.

    – Trans-created 18th November, 2017 by Sharad Kamal Bezboruah.

43. Manuhor Dehaate...

– *Pārbati Prasad Barua.*

Within the body of man, the soul remains oppressed,
for to eat there is no grain.
Yet there's chaos, when in the granaries,
the same stock doesn't remain.

Within the body of man, the soul remains oppressed,
for to eat there is no grain.
Yet there's chaos, when in the granaries,
the same stock doesn't remain.

Hey listen, o' keeper of the granary,
why do you get engrossed in greed?
Listen to the call of the oppressed,
the cry of the souls in need,
the cry of the souls in need!!

By the flame in the tummy everyone shall be bitten,
for there's no one big or small.
If the ones who ought to listen to the screeches don't,
the victims shall soon make them crawl.

Within the body of man, the soul remains oppressed,
for to eat there is no grain.
Yet there's chaos, when in the granaries,
the same stock doesn't remain.

– Translated on 10th May, 2013 by Sharad Kamal Bezboruah

44. Okolxoria Batoruwa

– Parboti Prasad Barua Deu.

You are a lonely journeyman,
a lonely journeyman.
Along your way, play your flute and sing,
all through the journey span.
Oh, lonely journeyman!
You are a lonely journeyman,
a lonely journeyman.
If behind you a flame ignites,
your entire household and creates a dreadful sight.
What would you get,
if you turn around and lament?
Would you get it back?
You don't have any companion,
who give you the willpower?
You don't have wealth, who would write songs for you to sing?
If those the dark clouds shower,
raindrops in the middle of your road.
You mustn't stop
behind trees,
just because shelters too many they have endowed.
On the wet, slippery path of yours,
on foot carefully, you must move along.
For you are lonely journeyman throughout,
the one whom one would seldom think about…

– Translated on 14th June, 2013 by Sharad Kamal Bezboruah.

45. Kino Kopaal Xadhi...

Dr. Bhupen Hazarika.

With what ill fate did you come, fellow mate,
the home has turned to a graveyard.
With your own hands, you planted an entire garden,
in a second everything withered.
With what ill fatedid you come, fellow mate,
the home has turned to a graveyard.

With passion of the sky, you embraced the moon;
little did you know the depth of its ruse.
The moon too hid, the moonlight too fled,
now in deluge, by the two eyes tears are shed.
With what ill fatedid you come, fellow mate,
the home has turned to a graveyard.

The cattle are now orphans, the pigeon too are orphans,
and solitary now is the ever-restive handloom.
Now, memories are only that remain;
now the sight at the ancestral pond too is a doom.
Of the mirror in the heart, the lady of the heart too,
why ever so soon, so far she dashed!
Of this illusive world, the altar of hope,
in a second it is now smashed.

With what ill fatedid you come, fellow mate,
the home has turned to a graveyard.

"As a fish and a tortoise,
an avatar, half human-half lion;
you've taken these forms all by choice,
and also journeyed from the Dwarf, to Dowson.
As brother of Lord Krishna, Haliraam,
and also as a wild boar;
you were also born as Lord Ram;
you came down to earth and did roar.
Lord Buddha and also Kalki, your tenth form,
by all these names, you are complete.
As over the years, it has been the norm,
with due salutations, oh Almighty! I fall at your feet..."

{*An Assamese prayer, literally meaning-
"A fish, a giant turtle, an avatar half human-half lion,
and a Brahmin named Parashurama (equivalent to Dowson in the bible).
Haliraam (Balraam, brother of Lord Krishna), a boar and Sri. Ram…
Lord Buddha and Kalki. [10 forms of Vishnu]
By these names, you've taken form, oh Krishna.
At your feet, I offer salutations."}

Of my empty, solitary home, someone opens the gate,
the home-maker returns and sweeps….
With hands her own, my gateway left in such a shabby state,
oh! The withered petals bloom again. Finally; she reaps
the fruit of her efforts. In the dark skies, I seem to again see,
the long lost ray of the beautiful moonlight.
The lost home-maker, now that has come back to me,
the home is now full of delight……!!!

 – Trans-created on 2nd January, 2014 by Sharad Kamal Bezboruah.

46. *Jonti Ulaale Tora ti Ulaabo.*

Keshab Mahanta.

If the moon appears,
so shall the star,
to the moon, does it ask?
The heart calls out a screech,
and then, on realization;
it does shatter and sunk.

When the petals unfurl,
the air turns fragrant...
Do they blossom or not,
the innocent buds of love?
Whether or not are by winds bent?

If the moon appears,
so shall the star,
to the moon, does it ask?
The heart calls out a screech,
and then, on realization;
it does shatter and sunk.

The winds, oh, the raging cyclone,
takes away, shredding the petals, yes.
The innocent bud weeps and mourns,
who shall come and console with a caress?

If the moon appears,
so shall the star,
to the moon, does it ask?
The heart calls out a screech,
and then, on realization;
it does shatter and sunk.

    – Trans-created on 18th August, 2017 by Sharad Kamal Bezboruah.

47. Akash Amaak Okoni Akash Diya...

Dr. Birendranath Datta.
Lyrics: Nabakanta Barua.

Oh mighty sky,
a bit of your skies do lend...

Oh mighty sky,
a bit of your skies do lend...
Our hearts, thirsty for the skies,
have lifelong wept on this land.
Oh mighty sky,
a bit of your skies do lend...

The pain is ours; however blue is your heart...
Midst all your clouds, plays our sun.
Even then, you are never ours;
a part of you is got by among us, none...
With many harsh blows,
cruel become the hours
of our lives...
Hence, our own is only the land,
immortal, evergreen...
Oh mighty sky,
a bit of your skies do lend...

Oh mighty sky,
a bit of your skies do lend...
Our hearts, thirsty for the skies,
have lifelong wept on this land.
Oh mighty sky,
a bit of your skies do lend...

– Trans-created on 7th March, 2014 by Sharad Kamal Bezboruah.

48. Jonak Gola Jaaror Nixa.

Lyrics By: Hiren Bhattacharyya.
Sung by: Zubeen Garg; Acknowledging:
Sampriti Goswami.

On a wintry night,

when the moonlight melts;

I lay my head,

on the pillow cold...

Counting the droplets

at my finger tips;

oh how many more

such teardrops wet?

How many more

such pretty little pearls?

Am I tired? No... Not as yet!

I haven't lost life,

no, not as yet!

On a wintry night,

when the moonlight melts;

I lay my head,

on the pillow cold...

Every day,

every single day,

I watch life melt.
Every second,
every single moment!
Where, a hand of compassion
would you sought to be lent?
Every day, looking for it,
on I would went.
Every day!

Am I tired? No... Not as yet!
I haven't lost life,
no, not as yet!

Love, affection;
never is ample!
In your eyes,
those bits of sapphire twinkle.
Like the star up there,
tell me if by my window,
glitter you will?

Am I tired? No... Not as yet!
I haven't lost life,
no, not as yet!

On a wintry night,
when the moonlight melts;
I lay my head,
on the pillow cold...
Counting the droplets
at my finger tips;
oh how many more

such teardrops wet?
How many more
such pretty little pearls?

Am I tired? No... Not as yet!
I haven't lost life,
no, not as yet!

– Translated on 28th July, 2017 by Sharad Kamal Bezboruah.

49. *"Protidine Tumi Diya Aahi...."... (Rodor Chithi)...*

(Zubeen Garg and Angaraag Papon Mahanta)
Lyrics: Diganta Bharati.

Everyday, you bring me a bud of a flower.
Oh, life! You are the colourful strokes of colour.
A blossom of laughter and
a bud of sorrow that makes one mourn…
with the two alone, this face I adorn!
Everyday, you bring me a bud of a flower.
Oh, life! You are the colourful strokes of colour.

I wish to wear the skies around me.
I wish to sleep at the bottom of the sea….
Of the heart, the kite…
to it, life today gives flight.
Let our times together always stay golden,
sweet in your heart and mine, let them forever remain.

A song that does make…
this heart of mine, shake….
Amidst a tune of what has been got,
and what yet has not…
There itself, I miss a heartbeat perhaps.
In my dreams;

in the reality of my dreams, but yet;
I honour and felicitate you, on the path scarlet.

Everyday, you bring me a bud of a flower.
Oh, life! You are the colourful strokes of colour.
A blossom of laughter and
a bud of sorrow that makes one mourn…
with the two alone, this face of mine, I adorn!

– Translated on 28th January, 2014 by Sharad Kamal Bezboruah.

50. Gaane Ki Aane...

Zubeen Garg.

What do the songs bring,
at every step of music?
What do the songs ring,
in the ears of the clouds?
In the corners of the rainbow…!
At every step of music…!

The floods of moonlight,
the raise waves in the skies and flow…
The current that raises music in the fields…
Do they at all know,
what the songs bring, and ring,
at every step of music…!
In the corners of the rainbow…!
At every step of music…!

The songs cry,
like the monsoon sky…
With the flash of the silver lightning,
to laugh, the songs do try…
What the songs bring, and ring,
at every step of music…!
In the corners of the rainbow…!
At every step of music…!

What do the songs bring,
at every step of music?
What do the songs ring,
in the ears of the clouds?
In the corners of the rainbow…!
At every step of music…!

– Trans-created on 27th April, 2014 by SharadKamal Bezboruah.

51. Moi Eti Dinor Junaaki...

– Artist: Jyotish Bhattacharyya.
Lyrics: Nabakanta Barua.

I am a firefly in the daylight...
I lay seated on the withered grass,
dreaming of the night!
I am a firefly in the daylight...

I am a firefly in the daylight...

I familiar to, the skies,
the stars vibrant...
And to the earth, that is,
with the night's essence, fragrant...
But, alien to this daylight!

I am a firefly in the daylight...

I've heard there's a sun,
in a far away land...
Spreading his blazing wings
he shadows, the poetry of the night...
I really do not understand,
what is the need of so much light...
when beneath the basil plant,
alone does stand...

Illuminated,
a tiny earthen lamp!

I am a firefly in the daylight...

I am a firefly in the daylight...
I lay seated on the withered grass,
dreaming of the night!
I am a firefly in the daylight...

I am a firefly in the daylight...

– Trans-created on 13th September, 2016 by Sharad Kamal Bezboruah.

52. Rumaal...

Zubeen Garg.
Credits: Namrata Sarma.

Of the twenty-first century,
this is a love story.
And in the creases of this handkerchief,
lies the light of memories.
This story
from the twenty-first century
by me, often read.
And, in the creases of this handkerchief;
lay the memories of a beloved.
In every fold of the handkerchief, the calls of agony.
In the handkerchief is a story…
In the handkerchief is history…
In the handkerchief is a sigh…and whines so many.

A handkerchief….
A handkerchief that was red…
A handkerchief….
A handkerchief, whose colour did fade,

Long ago, the pair of black eyes I had seen.
When I recall, even today,
the pain chokes me within.
The afternoon after school,

when beneath the Gulmohar we would roam.
At the corners of different classrooms;
our talks; so sweet, so warm!
As I turn the pages,
I see only images….
Images of the handkerchief!

A handkerchief….
A handkerchief that was red…
A handkerchief….
A handkerchief, whose colour did fade.

A cold wintry evening I do remember…
All of a sudden,
when I had to let go of someone forever.
The kohl around the two eyes wet….!
The soft and sweet pain on the lips that lament……!!
In my heart, I have filled….
the tender dreams I have for so long held.
An ocean of love,
from which once flowed…
it is that handkerchief
that I in my hands still hold….

A handkerchief….
A handkerchief that was red…
A handkerchief….
A handkerchief, whose colour did fade.

Of the twenty-first century,
this is a love story.
And in the creases of this handkerchief,

lies the light of memories.
By me this story,
of the twenty-first century is often read.
And in the creases of this handkerchief,
lies the memories of my beloved.
In every fold of the handkerchief, lay the calls of agony.
In the handkerchief is a story… In the handkerchief is history…
In the handkerchief is a sigh…and whines so many.

A handkerchief….
A handkerchief that was red…
A handkerchief….
A handkerchief, whose colour did fade.

   – Trans-created on 17th February, 2014 by SharadKamal Bezboruah.

53. Nibir Bon'e Je...

Lyrics- Dr. Nirmalprabha Bordoloi

Look! You are called
by the grass beyond that fence...
Go, go to that far away land,
for you are now called by
that lost fragrance!

The golden cage,
leave...and go...
The golden sun
that lights up the age
now call you, go!
Go...go far into the skies blue!
Go...
For the moonlight too awaits you!!
Go... Go far away...
Go, go to that far away land,
for you are now called by
that lost fragrance!

Black beauty shall bring colour,
Fatigue, the heart it enwraps...
The River of life shall kill
the ruthlessness that saps
your zeal...

And, the stream in the wilds,
momentum it will make you gain!
Of this magical, illusive life,
the soulful essence:
Go look for it; break this chain,
these shackles...strong!!

The mountains high shall give you assurance,
why do you let fear break
your confidence...?
Of this magical, illusive life,
the musical fragrance...
In that jungle, midst mahua trees,
go looking for it! Go look for it
in the atmosphere, the ambience...

Look! You are called
by the grass beyond that fence...
Go, go to that far away land,
for you are now called by
that lost fragrance!

– Trans-created on 20th September, 2016 by Sharad Kamal Bezboruah.

54. Moi'u Ketiyaba Gaan Gau...

– Tafajjul Ali.

Sometimes, songs I too sing…
Midst the notes and the tunes, many a times,
I go in search of myself, deep within.
Sometimes, I too sing…

Sometimes, I too sing…

Of losing something, the pain…!!
And the consolation I got,
by going in search; to regain,
only I know…as for it I have sought…

Sometimes, songs I too sing…
Midst the notes and the tunes, many a times,
I go in search of myself, deep within.
Sometimes, I too sing…

In of life, the struggle,
I fall tired…
Not even leisure a little,
to weave the dreams desired.
Thus, with the tunes,
weaving dreams, I go on…
Sometimes,

I too sing a song…

Sometimes, songs I too sing…
Midst the notes and the tunes, many a times,
I go in search of myself, deep within.
Sometimes, I too sing…

Sometimes, songs I too sing…
Midst the notes and the tunes, many a times,
I go in search of myself, deep within.
Sometimes, I too sing…

– Trans-created on 2nd April, 2014 by Sharad Kamal Bezboruah.

55. Akash'e Diya Rowdor'e Chithi....

– Zubeen Garg.

The letter of sunshine sent by the skies,
that letter, this earth has clasped.
The ink of the sunlight,
all around is splashed.
The letter of sunshine sent by the skies,
that letter, this earth has clasped.

Underneath a tree's shade,
for a moment or two
if life does wait.
In return, it doesn't know to offer,
you very well do know mate.
Today, everyone all over,
at every step they put on the ground;
even after roaming about anxious,
themselves they do look for, all around.

Yourself to another,
you now must hand over...
Flow along generating waves,
as if you were a river.

The letter of sunshine sent by the skies,
that letter, this earth has clasped.

The ink of the sunlight,
all around is splashed.
The letter of sunshine sent by the skies,
that letter, this earth has clasped.

– Trans-created on 20th February, 2014 by SharadKamal Bezboruah.

56. Dhumuha't Moi Thoi Jaam Mur Goti...

Lyrics- Dr.Nirmalprabha Bordoloi.

In the storms, I shall leave behind my momentum.
In the storms, I shall leave my momentum.
In the storms......
My momentum!

Of this earth, I blow away the dust...
Even the strongest trees, in front of my might,
not for long do they last.
On the old, I throw light;
I go announcing the creations' new acceptance.
So that the storms too move as fast;
I shall leave behind my momentum.
In the storms......!
In the storms......!

I go announcing the race's new acceptance.

I shall leave behind my momentum,
so that the storms too move as fast.
My distant, great love;
it goes on to touch the skies so vast,
goes high, high above...
Like a thousand monsoons,
bring the floods that rock the mast

of the ship of my life.
In those waves, all the small and large bits…
Let them all flow…
At lightning speed, forth I shall go;
of all the boundaries, breaking the limits.
Breaking all the limits!!
I shall leave behind my momentum,
so that the storms too move as fast.

I do not fear death…
thus without turning back, I manage.
I do make a lot of new preparations,
in search of creations of the new age.
I shall leave behind my momentum,
so that the storms too move as fast.

I shall leave behind my momentum,
so that the storms too move as fast.

– Trans-created on 2nd February, 2014 by Sharad Kamal Bezboruah.

57. Bishwar Chonde-Chonde...

– Kalaguru Bishnu Prasad Rabha.

In every corner of the world filling your heart with extreme joy,
Dance, oh destroyer of evil and darkness,
you must dance and the gloom you must destroy.

Salutations....!
From the troop of the devotees...
salutations at thy lotus-like feet.

In every corner of the world
filling your heart with extreme joy,
Dance, oh destroyer of evil and darkness,
you must dance and the gloom you must destroy.

Burn the flame of meditation!
Let darkness be smashed,
by thy victorious flame of fire...
In the temple of the world,
of the lamp of knowledge...
the flame of light must dance.
Thus, slaying the darkness of ignorance,
with ecstasy and joy....

Salutations....!
From the troop of the devotees...

salutations at thy lotus-like feet.

In every corner of the world filling your heart with extreme joy,
Dance, oh destroyer of evil and darkness,
you must dance and the gloom you must destroy.

At every rhythm of dance,
flowers bloom in the forest...
At every beat dance the gardens,
so illuminated, so vibrant.
By the fragrant, flowery scent,
the lovely land is made redolent....

Salutations....!
From the troop of the devotees...
salutations at thy lotus-like feet.

In every corner of the world filling your heart with extreme joy,
Dance, oh destroyer of evil and darkness,
you must dance and the gloom you must destroy.

    – Trans-created on 17th March, 2014 by Sharad Kamal Bezboruah.

58. O' Phagunore... Utola Baa.... (Savita Choudhury)

Music: Salil Choudhury.
Lyrics: Anuradha Das.

Oh! Warm breeze of February…
Go away… Go away… Go away….

Don't awaken the flower bud,
feathers your warm wings don't stud.
Like one who's crazy, don't sway…
Oh! Warm breeze of February…
Go away… Go away… Go away….

Of Palash, the red flowers,
of the Nahor tree, the tender leaf.
Wonder who they look for,
midst all the dreams, with such belief….
with colours filled in the heart…?!
Oh! Warm breeze,
it's time you depart…..
Oh! Warm breeze of February…

Other the side of this river,
holding up; of love, in his heart a word!
Stands waiting my lover…
a word of love, carrying in his heart,
his heart full of colour…

Oh! Warm breeze of February…
Go away… Go away… Go away….

Oh! Warm breeze of February…
Go away… Go away… Go away…

    – Trans-created on 6th January, 2014 by Sharad Kamal Bezboruah.

59. Xurore Deulore…

– Kalaguru Bishnu Prasad Rabha.

The chains of silver
at the temple of music;
all of them, you did splinter…
and break open its golden doors.
Oh, humble priest…!!
Wondrous! Wondrous, oh priest!
Wondrous oh, humble priest…!!

Hymns immortal, sweet and evergreen
and folk-songs full to melody…
oh Assamese patriot! Sing…
sing for it shall soothe the mind and body.
Oh, humble priest…!!
Wondrous! Wondrous, oh priest!
Wondrous oh, humble priest…!!

At your humble touch,
in the vessel of music…
Came overflowing
so many tunes such;
so much music…
Gaining freedom,
of music; the idol epic…
Flies and floats about!!

Oh, humble priest...!!
Wondrous! Wondrous, oh priest!
Wondrous oh, humble priest...!!

Blow your sacred conch;
play the cymbals...
Light the lamps so that they
slay the evils.
Arrange for the prayers,
with true devotion...
Oh, humble priest...!!
Wondrous! Wondrous, oh priest!
Wondrous oh, humble priest...!!

– Trans-created on 17th March, 2014 by Sharad Kamal Bezboruah.

60. Rimjhim Rimjhim Boroxun'e.....

– Dr. Bhupen Hazarika…

Narration:
My mother's teardrops and sweat from my father's forehead,
on which land do they fall?!

Lyrics:
Of the pitter-pattering raindrops,
where do the anklets jingle?
Where do the roaring clouds,
play aloud their drums?
It all happens, in this land of Assam.
The land of Assam….

Where is sweet water,
served in a royal metal plate?
The orchid scatters
its fragrance at whose gate?
It all happens, in this land of Assam.
The land of Assam….

Where does a little river turn into an ocean?
Where is that vast ocean not feared by anyone?
It all happens, in this land of Assam.
The land of Assam….

Where do pearl-like teardrops fall from my mother's eyes wet?
Wearing a garland of those pearls, where do I gather courage?
Where is my father's sweat,
shed from his forehead?
Watching all that, where do I feel,
that I would rather be dead?
It all happens, in this land of Assam.
Oh, in the land of Assam….!

Where is the music of my heart
understood and by whom?
For the sacrifices made by the youth for their land,
where is there always room?
Where is another's ridicule pushed aside?
In this land of Assam…!
It all happens, in this land of Assam.
Oh, in the land of Assam….!

  – Translated on 6th November, 2013 by Sharad Kamal Bezboruah.

61. Luitore Paani Jaabi O Boi...

– 'Rupkonwar' Jyoti Prasad Agarwalla.

Flow on, oh Lohit! Flow on...

Flow on, oh Lohit! Flow on...
In the evening, your waters turn golden,
the setting sun, when on them shone!
Through the city and through the town,
Flow on, oh Lohit! Flow on...
Go about, narrating the story
of Joymoti;
speaking of her glory,
flow across the nation, and beyond;
through the cities and towns,
and into the seas,
flow on, oh Lohit! Flow on...

The frame of earth,
leaving behind...
Into the light,
she goes to reside!
Thus, she is gone,
immortalizing her glory,
for the world, setting an example...
Flow on, oh Lohit! Flow on...

Drop by drop,
her blood three drops;
for her land, fall she let...
Oh maiden of Assam; oh bride newly wed;
in the name of Joymoti, her glory,
your eyelids too, do wet;
a teardrop, you too, shed!
Flow on, oh Lohit! Flow on...

Flow on, oh Lohit! Flow on...
In the evening, your waters turn golden,
the setting sun, when on them shone!
Through the city and through the town,
Flow on, oh Lohit! Flow on...
Go about, narrating the story
of Joymoti;
speaking of her glory,
flow across the nation, and beyond;
through the cities and towns,
and into the seas,
flow on, oh Lohit! Flow on...

– Translated on 17th June, 2017 by Sharad Kamal Bezboruah.

62. Enekoi Bhaagene Xopun!

Keshab Mahanta.
Sung by: Manojyostna Mahanta.

Are thus broken, many a wish?
Do bonds ever break like this?
Who will answer me today,
silently coming my way?
Who will say?
Who is my own?

It's in vain, building a house of golden desires and,
it's merely a transient house built with sand.

Are thus broken, many a wish?
Do bonds ever break like this?
Who will answer me today,
silently coming my way?
Who will say?
Who is my own?

Curved out by the heart's affection,
of life, all the aspirations….
Into mere jokes and pleasantry,
why turned is all the hope?
I wonder how,
with this fact I shall cope...

Are thus broken, many a wish?
Do bonds ever break like this?
Who will answer me today,
silently coming my way?
Who will say?
Who, from where will say?

– Trans-created on 7th January, 2014 by Sharad Kamal Bezboruah.

63. Diya Muk Diya...

Music - Zubeen Garg.
Credits: Namrata Sarma.

Give to me...
Give to me,
like the skies, a heart so large
that its boundaries meet....
That vast, blue sea...
I shall cause
the stars and the moon to fleet.
I shall embrace
the carnival of innumerable stars.
Give to me... Do bless
me like the skies, with a heart so large
that its boundaries meet....

The pain of the clouds...
and all the games of the lightning!
The colours of morning and evening...
Give to me,
a heart so large....
I shall embrace the fears of the forests.
Give to me...
Give to me,
like the skies....

I shall embrace the wild seas,
and the roars of the storm.
And the crazy desert, the breeze,
which are borne....
by the mountain peaks,
that touch the heart.....

Give to me...
Give to me,
like the skies, a heart so large
that its boundaries meet....
That vast, blue sea...
I shall cause
the stars and the moon to fleet.
I shall embrace
the carnival of innumerable stars...

– Trans-created on 11th February, 2014 by Sharad Kamal Bezboruah.

64. *Juwar Porot Xora Xewali Butoli...*

– Artist: Jyotish Bhattacharyya.

As you leave, picking flowers of jasmine,
what will you get? Do tell…
To look back now, there is no time,
now bid farewell….

The words sweet
of your lip…
All of it,
secretly you did keep…
The new dawn, again shall come,
the past it shall come and sweep.
For me, there isn't the fragrance
that would make life overflow.

As you leave, picking flowers of jasmine,
what will you get? Do tell…
To look back now, there is no time,
now bid farewell….

In the shade of the sun,
alone and silent…
I was an illusion of the dark!
As a flower on the roadway of memories,
for you to pass, I did wait…

Dear mate, hark;
in my skies, for a new morning,
even if you search, you wouldn't find.
As you leave, picking flowers of jasmine,
what will you get? Do tell…
Now, there isn't time to look behind…!

As you leave, picking flowers of jasmine,
what will you get? Do tell…
To look back now, there is no time,
now bid farewell….

– Trans-created on 7th April, 2014 by Sharad Kamal Bezboruah.

65. O' Mur Pranore Xosa Shilpi.

– Tafajjul Ali.
– Artist: Jyotish Bhattacharyya

Listen, oh true artist of my soul…!!
Forgive me!
Forgive me!
At the doubts of my impotence,
do not be upset and tensed.
Forgive me!
Forgive me!

What you want me to say,
I can't tell…
The songs you want me to sing,
to sing them, I fail…
I know, struggling with me day and night…
You fall tired…
Forgive me!
Forgive me!

Listen, oh true artist of my soul…!!
Forgive me!
Forgive me!
At the doubts of my impotence,
do not be upset and tensed.

Forgive me!
Listen, oh true artist of my soul…!

At the harsh blows of injustice,
you call out a roar…
Helpless out of fear; I can only make peace…
Where you wish to perform a disaster-dance,
I lay helpless, groaning in agony on the floor…
Looking at all my compassionate dramatics,
I know you are astonished…
Forgive me!
Forgive me!

Listen, oh true artist of my soul…!!
Forgive me!
Forgive me!

Listen, oh true artist of my soul…!!

– Trans-created on 5th April, 2014 by Sharad Kamal Bezboruah.

66. Gonga Mur Maa/Gonga Aamar Maa

– Dr. Bhupen Hazarika.

The Ganges is my mother, and so is its tributary Padma,
and the Meghna and the Yamuna are two streams from my eyes.
Solve it if you can; the enigma.

The same sky, the same breeze,
everyone breathes in their lungs the same air.
The two birds, the cuckoo and the hornbill,
the same melody they do share.
And from my two eyes flow the two rivers,
the Meghna and the Yamuna.

On this bank or the other, I do not know,
I am all around.
Though I set my catamaran free in the Brahmaputra,
at Padma too, I give tune to the boatman's sound.
Like a swan, I open my wings and dance in both rivers.
To both rivers, I am bound.

The same affection, the same hope;
and the same language lay in both laughter and despair.
In the heart of all, midst happiness and sorrow,
the agony is still the same there.
And from my two eyes flow the rivers,
the Meghna and the Yamuna.

– Translated on 21st June, 2013 by Sharad Kamal Bezboruah.

67. Kuwoli Xona Botaah.

Lyrics: Biditpran Gogoi.(Artist: Jonak Priyam)

Of the blues,
a picture clear;
a bird tired,
a bird travelling, alien;
yet familiar.

At my doorway,
sits weeping, the moonlight.
Floats before the eyes;
the tiny lamp of the night.

Oh! The breeze carrying the mist,
Go back home, to your door...
oh kite,
In the February breeze,
take flight!
Into the skies, soar...

The play in dirt,
of childhood awesome.
The storms of romance;
go looking for autumn...
And of monsoon;
the rains,
Shower in my bosom.

Oh! The breeze carrying the mist,
Go back home, to your door,
oh kite,
In the February breeze,
Take flight!
Into the skies, soar...

On the floral paper,
the familiar patterns;
in the eyes glitters,
a love that never returns...
Along the carpet
of love,
Life, its feet set.

Oh! The breeze carrying the mist,
Go back home, to your door,
oh kite,
In the February breeze,
Take flight!
Into the skies, soar...

– Translated on 18th July, 2017 by Sharad Kamal Bezboruah.

68. Mur Raag/Mor Raag...

– 'Rupkonwar' Jyoti Prasad Agarwalla

My musical modes,
to you I offer...
Do accept my offerings,
I worship you with flowers of oleander.

With your musical note,
I have created...
So many songs
that are or are not interpreted.
Do accept my offerings!
My musical modes,
to you I offer...
Do accept my offerings,
I worship you with flowers of oleander.

All my incredible songs,
all my many a chorus...
They seem to be as sweet as
the fragrance of a blooming lotus.
In every heart dwells,
wondrous dreams golden.
The dreams of the dreams too,
your flashing lustre they do retain.

Of music, bloom flowers a hundred...
The teardrops in my eyes,
their warmth does evaporate.
Do accept the offerings of my soul...!
Do play the tune on the flute
that has never been played before...

My musical modes,
to you I offer...
Do accept my offerings,
I worship you with flowers of oleander.

– Trans-created on 18th March, 2014 by Sharad Kamal Bezboruah.

69. Junak Junak....XitolJunak..

– *Parboti Prasad Barua Deu.*

The moon-light….!
The cold, grave and lifeless moon-light,
looking on, my teardrops I begin to shed!
The heart of mine turns anxious and sad,
So much turbulence, within bred.

I recall, yet again, a long lost pain of a night of separation.
Amidst those jasmine plants, secret meetings and
those talks of admiration.

Somewhere in the heart, arises a memory of happy moments,
those lovely days from the past.
But, alas! I realize they're gone!
I stare on out there, oh, the cold moon-light,
seldom, for long, does all of it last.

The moon-light….!
The cold, grave and lifeless moon-light,
looking on, my teardrops I begin to shed!
The heart of mine turns anxious and sad,
So much turbulence, within bred.

The moon-light….!
The cold, grave and lifeless moon-light,
looking on, my teardrops I begin shed!

– Translated on 2nd August, 2013 by Sharad Kamal Bezboruah.

70. Bokul Phulor Dore....

– Hiren Bhattacharyya.

Like the flowers of olive,
the birds of the night fly.
In the dark,
in the dark…!
Like the flowers of olive…

Like the flowers of olive,
the birds of the night fly.
In the dark, in the dark…!
Like the flowers of olive…

Darkness sheds teardrops
that fall drop by drop,
onto the ground from the top.

Like the flowers of olive,
amidst the heart's silence.
It sits alone,
with no one else.
Like the flowers of olive…

Beyond the sky seen by your eyes,
awaits me my own limitless skies…
Silently!
Patiently!

Like the flowers of olive,
amidst the heart's silence.
It sits alone,
with no one else.
Like the flowers of olive…

Like the flowers of olive,
the birds of the night fly.
In the dark,
in the dark…!
Like the flowers of olive…

– Translated on 8th August, 2013 by Sharad Kamal Bezboruah.

71. Oh... Mayaa Bhoraa Ei Dhoraa...

Artist: Khagen Mahanta.

Oh! This world of illusions...
Worldly attachments
and darkness shadow...
Whichever way I head;
I stumble, whichever way I go...

Oh-ho...!
This heart broken...
Tired, devastated;
Songs of pain, I hum...
And, of pain,
the lyre I strum...

Oh! This world of illusions...

The lamp of devotion,
if in the wind extinguishes...
Oh lord! On me,
do not render any curses...
This boat with a dipping prow,
pull to the shore;
that's all the heart wishes...
Oh lord!!
The fragile boat of life,
facing the splashes...

Oh! This world of illusions...
Worldly attachment
and darkness, shadow...
Whichever way I head,
I stumble, wherever I go...

Oh-ho...!
This heart broken...
Tired, devastated;
Songs of pain, I hum...
And, of pain,
the lyre I strum...

Oh! This world of illusions...

– Trans-created on 22nd August, 2016 by Sharad Kamal Bezboruah.

72. *Mur Kontho Rudhile Kune... by*

– Bokulbonor Kobi Anandachandra Barua
(Sung by: Dr. Birendranath Dutta)

Thank you Himjyoti Talukdar…

"My voice within,
has stopped humming;
for someone has, into the orchard;
with this divine fragrance; come in…??
Who does bring in,
the divine fragrance to this orchard…
How? Shall sing now,
his songs, this bard!!?
Who does?? Oh, who??"…

You cannot hear my voice anymore,
for someone brings back fragrance into the orchard?
With the divine fragrance, he does come;
and hence, no longer, can sing, this bard?
Who?? Oh, who?

So beautiful, the ruler, O' Might…
so beautiful, this mine of silver bright…!!
Who cries alone, shedding tears,
and pours of numerous moons, the light?

On a new moon night,
very oft does darkness speak...!
Oh, almighty! Your solemn light, here,
is all that all of the world does seek…

You cannot hear my voice anymore,
yet today, who brings back fragrance to the orchard?
I cannot sing my songs anymore,
yet, who sings the songs of this bard?

– Translated on 29th January, 2014 by ©Sharad Kamal Bezboruah.

73. Moi Bisarisu Hejaar Sokut..

Lyrics- Dr.Nirmalprabha Bordoloi

I want to see a thousand eyes shine
With the light of the glowing sun;
And watch them wipe out the dreadful sight,
The dreadful sight created by the clashes between two generations.

I want to hear from a thousand mouths,
Words full of rage...
That would bring hope of a new sun,
And return the spring of the golden age.
I want to hear pledges of many saying,
That they will shine, like the rising sun at dawn...
In the midst of all the chaos in the crowd,
I wish to see a Hero born...
Yes..!!
To wipe out the dreadful sight,
The dreadful sight created by the clashes between two generations.

I wish to watch the trembling feet on the path of development,
Suddenly take up speed...
To awaken the sleeping public, so that they can heed
They can heed, to the chaos, this dreadful scene.
I want an individual, blessed by the Almighty
Who can take pledges of righteous leadership from within..
Yes!!

To wipe out the dreadful sight;
The dreadful sight created by the clashes between two generations.
I want to see a thousand eyes shine;
Shine with the light of the glowing sun...

     – Translated 11th January, 2013 by © Sharad Kamal Bezboruah.

74. Jodi Moi Prosno Koru. (Jayanta Hazarika)

Lyrics:

If ever, that music is no more;
wouldn't it be a dark day for humanity?
O' composer, if I question you,
what if the carnival of tunes turns empty!
What would you say?
What would you say?

If you ever lose all your words,
when you only begin to think!
O' poet, with what shall you create poetry,
if your boat of thoughts begins to sink?
If I question you, what would you say?

And if you have painted only half of your picture,
when you see all the colors vanish!
How would you complete the picture?
Won't you be filled with anguish!
If I question you, what would you say?

On the first morning of life
if hope too, turns into despair,
and the storm and rain come?
And they begin to completely tear,

the petals of the flower that hasn't even bloomed?
Can you stop the doings of who has decided our doom?
If I question you, what would you say?

– Translated on 17th June, 2013 by Sharad Kamal Bezboruah.

75. Oh Mur Apunar Desh....

— Lakshminath Bezbaruah.

Oh, my very own motherland!
Oh, your charm, the sorrow it pushes apart, motherland!
So mellifluous;
So much prosperous;
so close to the heart is my motherland.

Oh, my very own motherland!
Oh, your charm, the sorrow it pushes apart, motherland!
So mellifluous;
So much prosperous;
so close to the heart is my motherland.

Oh, the place of my birth,
Oh, my motherland Assam....
Let me look at your face for once,
only then shall settled down, this craving heart...
only then to this heart shall a bit of peace come.

Oh, my very own motherland!
Oh, your charm, the sorrow it pushes apart, motherland!
So mellifluous;
So much prosperous;
so close to the heart is my motherland.

Oh, my melodious voice!
Oh, the glorious voice of my Assam! You soothe the mind.

Looking all over the world,

even if one tries throughout life, none shall ever find.

Looking all over the world,

even if one scours through life, none shall ever find.

Oh, my very own motherland!

Oh, your charm, the sorrow it pushes apart, motherland!

So mellifluous;

So much prosperous;

so close to the heart is my motherland.

-Trans-created 17th November, 2013 by Sharad Kamal Bezboruah,
(on the occasion of 150th Birth Anniversary of Lakshminath Bezbaroa)

(with reference to the translation by Shri.Krishna Dulal Barua and the original track in the voice of Kalaguru Bishnu Prasad Rabha dated 1937.)

The words used Shri. K.D. Barua, I believe is suitable for representation in the global platform. For the present generation and the generations to come to feel and realize this piece of work from the heart, I felt the need for a simpler and more rhythmic version. Though, I agree that his version of translation is more accurate, I think the present generation desires a version which they can understand more easily.

And, hence, the above is a humble attempt to assemble something of the kind.

JOI AAI AXOM...!!

On an honest note, I feel like I can end this section that I had begun with my deep reverences to the Sahityarathi, on a similar streak of admiration and regard for him.

And now, I wish to present before you the section that I regard as the most tender, fragile and closest to the heart. This section contains translations of Assamese lyrics or works, done in the initial years of my pursuit; the ones; few of which I had an opportunity to share with

'Aita', only a year or two before she left us. I would always have this lingering sting within for losing her at the very onset of my modest yet zealous venture, but however, thank her for the courage and patience she bestows upon me from the skies to hold on to the same for this long, despite the odds and the hindrances along the way.

10 years have passed since the time our most loved state, Assam has lost its crown jewel, Lt. Dr. Bhupen Hazarika; my first translation being Dr. Amarjyoti Choudhury Sir's 'Eta Gaan Sesh Hol', which had been a tribute to the eternal 'Song'; Bhupen Koka, at his departure. We have come a long way since then, be it the 'Bharat Ratna' being conferred upon him; or the third Jnanpith ever, being brought home to Assam, by our respected 'Nilomani Phukan' sir; the award ceremony being held for the very first time, in our very own land, a moment to be written in golden letters in the pages of history in itself.The constant guide and mentor over the years as mentioned earlier in this compilation, 'Syed Ahmed Shah', is sorely missed every single day, as I sit down and compile a nearly decade's hard work, of course, upholding the constant guidance, inspiration and contributions of all others in the journey; and above all, his.

Having said that, amongst all the unprecedented developments in the global literary scenario, one that has stood out the most in my view is the fact that Bob Dylan sir had received the Nobel Prize for Literature in 2016, something that ought to be cherished and upheld for several decades to come. It is indeed prudent, and urgent, hence, for our generation to have a compilation like this one allthemore, after 'lyrics' having been accepted as a form of poetry; and of literature at large, worldwide.

In my later teens, I remember Aita mentioning that her younger sister, Lt. 'Malthi Varma' (Mahi Aita), a retired professor of L.S.R, Delhi; had translated few Sanskrit works of either Kalidas or Adi Shankaracharya into English, but could never delve further in, because we lost her soon after. This year, 2021; Mahi Aita left two weeks after she had lost her better half, Lt. Jimmy Varma; after having herself fought a prolonged battle with dementia over the years. Hence, there wasn't a way to find out, the only one time that I had visited them in Delhi in 2018. I was fortunate to have met my Uncle Rajen Barua, from Houston, US; a man who constantly strived to represent Assam in a global platform; and continued to inspire me and so many others till the very end. His spirit and endurance during his 17 year long battle with malignancy, is all-the-more commendable, but a different story altogether. Having translated Emily Dickenson during his later years, along with many other such endeavors; he asked me to keep at what I was up to; every time we met during his brief and few visits to Assam.

Also, my respect and all due admiration, to the 'Magic' enchanted by my close acquaintances and fellow artists who have been credited between Translations Sl. Nos 110 to 124; and of course, the next; that closes the Assamese sub-section of 'The Unsung'; (Jon Dhone Jonaalite); a tribute to Lt. Smt. Dipali Borthakur and Luitkonwar Lt. Shri. Rudra Barua Deu; shall forever be cherished and held onto for many, many years to come, if not beyond.

Moving on, the next section below also contains many of the songs from films and the non film genres; 'THE UNSUNG' as I would like to call them; or 'SUNG', but either lay forgotten, or have never seen as much light as they must have.

The latter, covers a number of pieces that largely uphold endurance and patience, and other across moods such as hope, vagrancy, ambiguity, along with the most common subjects of love, loss and melancholy.

The following section must also be considered as a tribute to artists who have largely served as role models to the younger generations, and have continued to inspire people like us to step forth. While, I have touched upon the works of the heartthrob of the Assamese youth, Zubeen Garg da in the section above, the remaining works of Angaraag da, and a few written by Lt. Keshab Mahanta koka, and dear and respected 'Sarat Barkakati' bordeuta, not highlighted there, follow. Alongside, I also wish tothrow light on works of artists like Shweta Pandit, Monali Thakur, Aayushmaan Khurrana, Ali Zafar, Lt. Sushant Singh Rajput, and severalothers who ought to be celebrated more often; anda good number of other underrated albums of bollywood, like 'Mausam' by 'Irshaad Kamil', 'Mohabbatein' by 'Anand Bakshi'; 'Ishk Vishk' and 'Saawariyaa' by Sameer Anjaan, 'Kabhie Kabhie' by Sahir Ludhianvi, 'Sujata' and 'Solva Saal' by Majrooh Sahab, 'Arth' by Kaifi Azmi Sahab and 'Woh Kaun Thi' by Raja Mehdi Ali Khan; to name a few.

Hence, I unfurl before you the translations of 'THE UN-SUNG', both Assamese and Hindustani.

'THE UN-SUNG'

"In the nights, at the moon I do stare,
in your hands, life now lies...
Come in the heavy rains,
for, the stars wait shimmering in the eyes.
The world of dreams shall again,
bloom and blossom....
Oh, beloved! When you shall come!
I'll see the monsoon
dance, tapping its feet...
And, drenched thus,
two shall hearts meet."

– Faaiz Anwar (Aaoge Jab Tum) continued....

"Apart from that one lane, the eyes seek no other;
Life, enough of passing by now, pass away altogether.

And, to speak of the losses therein, why even bother,
for, autumn has always been known to be a wretched weather!

For once, like I have, since forever;
darling, just shed yourself ...
'like October'."

– Sharad Kamal Bezboruah.

76. Moi Mur Santaanok…

– Shri. Sarat Barkakati. (Sung by Murchana Barkakati)

What…. shall I leave (behind) for my kids…?
I didn't teach them languages Mom taught!
Where our roots lie, I didn't explain…!
In tomorrow's world, full of chaos…
They shall give their identity, what!!??

What…. shall I leave (behind) for my kids…?

Without a circle,
like humans…- Can one live on??
Without a name, within the society,
Can one's head be held high, strong…??
The pride in history; one's own culture;
that's all that is one's true identity…

What…. shall I leave (behind) for my kids…?

Shrunken by networks,
in the world of this age…
Perhaps far away there's,
the nourishing soil of my village…
Even then, can the fragrance of the land…
Can ever be forgotten?
Can it be allowed/let to be lost...

The warmth gentle,
of mom's lap...
If I can give not,
the fragrance and loving expressions,
what shall fill the gap??

What shall fill the gap????

– Trans-created on 31st October, 2014 by Sharad Kamal Bezboruah.

77. Dhowe-Dhowe (Angaraag Mahanta)

– *Keshab Mahanta.*

As the river flows,
What words are spoken out...?
Sitting alone, of whom,
Does this heart think about..!!
As the river flows,
What words are spoken out...??
What does the river
speak of aloud??

A cluster of stars staring,
I go insane...
No one has seen,
Lays within (me) what pain;
So empty oh
why so empty today?
So many dreams of mine,
in those waves, they float away.

From the dawn golden,
Throughout life, all of it,
safe I had kept.
God knows unknowing…
All of it, who has swept!
The pain that makes, my heart shiver,

Do you know it, Dear River..?
The pain stinging since forever,
Do you know it, Dear River..?

Why my heart does weep,
Do u know dear one?
Are there memories u keep,
Oh dear one?
Do you long and yearn,
to hear my voice like you used to?
Does the flame of nostalgia burn
in your heart too, dear one?

As the river flows,
What words are spoken out...?
Sitting alone, of whom,
Does this heart think about..!!
As the river flows,
What words are spoken out...??
What does the river
speak of aloud??

    – Translated on 15th October, 2012 by Sharad Kamal Bezboruah.

78. Duporore Rodaali.....

– Angaraag Mahanta...

A ray from the afternoon sun
does descend onto your hair and shaken me,
do you know?
The sun this morning had come,
and on my forehead,
left a red spot beside the eyebrow.
Let the evening set in now,
and then the moon too shall shine…
Affectionately, somewhere there
let me drown.

With the hope of you becoming mine,
my dreams spread arms… awaiting your arrival.
I see your dark eyes shine,
as their beauty showers colours of revival.
The night is on its way,
and it's like you put back life into me.

Let the evening set in now,
and then the moon too shall shine…
Affectionately, somewhere there
let me drown.
A ray from the afternoon sun
does descend onto your hair and shaken me,

do you know?
The sun this morning had come,
and on my forehead it,
left a red spot.

The watery eyelids,
they today make those memories wet.
From the heart, this affectionate light,
does light up, this lonely night.
Come on with affection, let's weave a blanket.
And with that, let's build a tiny shelter of joy.
Let the evening set in now,
and then the moon too shall shine…
Affectionately, somewhere there
let me drown.

– Translated on 21ˢᵗ January, 2013 by Sharad Kamal Bezboruah.

79. Akash Akash Tumar Kotha....

Angaraag Mahanta.

Your words, they are like the skies,
this heart, like the clouds.
They're like riddles, your two eyes,
so light feels my warmth.
With your ample hope and aspirations,
lustrous shall be my way ahead.
Your words, they are like the skies,
my heart, like the clouds, unheard.

The more the night sets in,
the more the expectations shall increase.
No, I do not seek the moon and the stars,
asking for false illusions, I cease.
Wherever I go....
I seem to see you, you must know.

Your words, they are like the skies,
the heart, like the clouds.........

The two cheeks; this face;
shall be touched by the frozen breeze.
A bunch of desires too shall pause.
No, I do not seek withered petals along the gateway,
nor to walk along an unseen street....
I find you everywhere I go, wonder what'd be the cause.

Your words, they are like the skies,
the heart, like the clouds.
They're like riddles, your two eyes,
so light feels my warmth.
With your ample hope and aspirations,
lustrous shall be my way ahead.
Your words, they are like the skies,
my heart, like the clouds, unheard.

– Translated on 30th August, 2013 by Sharad Kamal Bezboruah.

80. *Kotoh Jouwanor Mrityu Hol!*

– Dr. Bhupen Hazarika.

Which soldier lost his life?
Whose heart was pierced with a knife?
If death itself can lead to immortality,
then why am I alive?) 2

Which mother couldn't stop crying?
Which father lost his heir!
Whose forehead that was once filled with vermillion,
now lies completely bare?
Whose child is that running,
with no one around to care?

Who left on earth but a puddle of blood?
Who left us all before, his youth could even bud?
It came to my knowledge only today, how one could,
be so merciless, so cruel, and at times so crude.

With eyes filled with tears,
I offer today my heart-filled prayers.
So, let those who fought, casting aside fear,
Rest in Peace... as the skies clear.

– Trans-created on 19th April, 2012 by Sharad Kamal Bezboruah.

81. Endhare-Endhare (Hiren Bhattacharyya)

Music: Dony Hazarika; Sung by: Shreya Ghoshal.

Who came to my heart and,
planted a rose on its flower bed?
In the gloom...!!
In the gloom,
Came flying a fire-fly,
And in the heart, it slept, laying down its head..!!
When I think of you,
Up there quietly in the sky…!
A star glows
Like a flower begins to bloom.
In the gloom..!!
Who came to my heart and,
planted a rose on its flower bed?
..In the gloom...!!

Pouring just a drop of perfume into my blood,
Who touched my heart?
Who came to my heart and,
planted a rose on its flower bed?

When I think of you alone,
The stars talk among themselves,
On the petals of the same rose!
In my blood,

On every bud of the rose plant,
A swarm of fire-flies glows.
In the gloom..!!
(In the gloom,
Came flying a fire-fly,
And in the heart,
It slept, laying down its head..!!
When I think of you,
Up there quietly in the sky...!
A star glows like a flower is blooming.)2...

– Translated on 29th January, 2013 by Sharad Kamal Bezboruah.

82. Kihor Raagit ....

Parboti Prasad Barua Deu.

By what so intoxicating are you being bothered?
Oh! Tell me by which loon has your behavior been lowered.

By what so intoxicating are you being bothered?
Oh! Tell me by which loon has your behavior been lowered.

Whose wonder has made you go astray?
You are now blind,
for you looked at that bright glare.
Whose wonder has made you go astray?
You are now blind,
for you looked at that bright glare.
Which loon has put such vexation into your mind?

Blinded, you can't find out your way.
Walking unsteadily, going left and right,
you move about here and there.
Blinded, you can't find out your way.
Walking unsteadily, going left and right,
you move about here and there.
The entire world seems wondrous today,
for you have lost your sight,

Oh! You lost your way.
Whose wonder has made you go astray?

By what so intoxicating are you being bothered?
Oh! Tell me by which loon has your behavior been lowered.

– Translated on 5th May, 2013 by Sharad Kamal Bezboruah.

83. Jonaake Bisaare Ki..!!

(Angaraag Mahanta)

What does the night want to find!
Of what does the breeze of February remind..!
You!! You!! You!! You!!
You!! You!! You!!

What does the night want to find!
In the dawn,
As the Cuckoo calls out its enlightening screams...
Sorrow and pain come and wet my eyes,
The clouds mist my dreams...
The wind blows them away…

What does the night want to find!
What does the breeze of February remind..!

In the full moon night,
It seems like every star...
Displays some illusion or the other
In my eyes;
My heart travels so far...
To the doorstep of my village,
Where lays that irreplaceable altar...

Of what does the breeze of February remind..!
What does the night want to find!) 2

– Translated 29th September, 2012 by Sharad Kamal Bezboruah.

84. *Endharere Jaute Jaute...(Baahir Maat)*

– by Hiren Bhattacharyya...

While I walked along my way, through darkness,
I heard light calling its conch,
all of a sudden.
While I walked along my way, through darkness,
I heard light calling its conch,
all of a sudden.
While I walked along my way, through darkness!

In the bones that I had kept safe for the lightning,
I felt the soothing sound of a flute somewhere within.
In my blood, among the bones that thing
had been hiding there, it always had been.

I had gathered dry leaves from the tree of time,
in the beach of my life, 'midst all the sand.
Who has come and swept away those leaves,
whose could be that soothing hand?

While I walked along my way, through darkness,
I heard light calling its conch,
all of a sudden.
While I walked along my way, through darkness,
I heard light calling its conch,
all of a sudden.
While I walked along my way, through darkness!

– Translated on 10th April, 2013 by Sharad Kamal Bezboruah.

85. Jonaaki Raati/Junaki Rati

– Angaraag Mahanta.

Where shall I go...?

Oh..! Fireflies of the night,
Why do you come?
On every note of mine,
Why do you,
Draw few pictures
And colour some?

Looking at your two eyes,
Every night, the loony heart cries.
Looking at that sweet smile,
My heart even today,
Sprints a mile!

Tonight, why do the fire-flies,
Ignite your picture in my memory.
My heart can't forget you,
It really tries...
But again it's the same old story.

Where are you today?
Whom do you await today?
Whose songs do you hum today?

Who comes; to your gate today?
Don't come now, as I dream..!!
You will scare me,
And the heart will scream..!!

Oh..! Fireflies of the night,
Why do you come?
On every note of mine;
Why do you,
Draw few pictures and colour some?

– Translated on 20th September, 2012 by Sharad Kamal Bezboruah.

86. Lorali...(Dikshu)

Lyrics:Bijiyeta..

The dust from the world of my childhood,
Today, comes to my heart..
The silly pranks I used to play then,
Still, float about in this heart.

Oh! Chasing those colorful kites,
When I run;
I even today meet,
the red evening sun..

The dust from the world of my childhood,
today, comes to my heart ..
The silly pranks I used to play then,
still float about in this heart.

When today, I see the fire-flies dance,
this heart too flies along..
I want back those days of laughter and cries,
for the days of my childhood, so much I long..
The whistles of those carefree days,
echo in this heart even today..

Oh.! Chasing those colorful kites,
when I run.

I even today meet,
the red evening sun..

Going in search of wild berries,
I remember us getting lost in the grove..
The olive-tree at our neighbors' gateway,
to steal from it, we're always on the move.
The picture of my childhood days,
though blurred, I see it all, even today..

– Translated on 23rd March, 2013 by Sharad Kamal Bezboruah.

87. Maaj Nixa Mor…

Parboti Prasad Barua Deu.

At midnight, who goes to and fro,
in my dark residence;
my sleep is interrupted,
again and again; in the silence.

Oh stealthy thief, who are you?
Will take away everything of mine?
I see you without seeing you…
and I recognize you without recognizing.
For, from your footsteps, a familiar rhythm is arising.
My sleep is interrupted, again and again.

Of my concealed home, the deep, dark loads.
What wealth lies within, I myself do not know.
Revealing everything yourself;
to yourself, all of it, show,
and take away everything.
Take the wealth of dark into light,
weighing it all, load by load.
My sleep is interrupted, again and again.

At midnight, who goes to and fro,
in my dark residence;
my sleep is interrupted,
again and again; in this silence.

– Translated on 22nd August, 2013 by Sharad Kamal Bezboruah.

88. Xaar Paam Moi...Puwoti Nixaate.

Lyrics- Dr.Nirmalprabha Bordoloi.
(Tribute to beloved Aita, Lt. Sharada Bezboruah.)

I shall wake up at dawn,

when the dew drops arrive on the grass;

the time which wets

the streets full with dry dust.

Awaken me then, oh! Mother...

Awaken me then, oh! Mother...

I wish to see how the red morning sun,

slays away darkness.

And how the ability, the resolution of blooming,

the flowers are taught to harness;

how the heart of the open air is filled with fragrance.

And, I ask you to awaken me, hence.

I shall wake up at dawn,

when the dew drops arrive on the grass;

the time which wets

the streets full with dry dust.

Awaken me then, oh! Mother...

Awaken me then, oh! Mother...

I want to know the secret spell,

hidden in this universe.

I want to know what song is sung,
to make emptiness move away.
I vow to bloom like the sunflower...
And hence, I shall wake up at that very hour.

I shall wake up at dawn,
when the dew drops arrive on the grass;
the time which wets
the streets full with dry dust.

– Trans-created on 7th December, 2013 by Sharad Kamal Bezboruah.

89. Tumar Kotha Jetya Bhaabu…

Jayanta Hazarika.

The two eyes fill with tears,
whenever I think of you.
The tips of the grass
shed two drops of dew.
The two eyes fill with tears,
whenever I think of you.

You are like a faint tune of a flute,
playing at a distance.
In the silent night, with the tide,
floating, you approach closer.
My doorway overflows with the fragrance
of a long lost flower.

The two eyes fill with tears,
whenever I think of you…

Whenever your thoughts come to my mind,
the heart feels so cold, it really does hurt.
Oh! Those dry leaves are blown off by a gust of wind,
so helpless I feel, like I'm left in a desolate desert.

The two eyes fill with tears,
whenever I think of you…

– Translated on 21ˢᵗ September, 2013 by Sharad Kamal Bezboruah.

90. *Xandhiya Jetiya Naame/Aailoi Monot Pore… (Angaraag Mahanta)*

Lyrics: Shri. Sarat Barkakati.

When Evening sets in,
And the crescent moon begins to shine.
I recall my land and mother.

When every bird returns to its nest,
When the noise, the racket lessens…
When almost everyone retreats to rest…
I recall my land and mother.
The inconsiderate emotions,
they sweep across to me to give pain…
From the two eyes;
it again begins to rain.

When Evening sets in
I recall my land and mother.

A gust of wind blows…
The rain from the skies
in strands, it flows…
The smell from my motherland comes,
Up there, in the sky,
a flash of lightning glows.
Looking at the roaring skies,

I once again recall, my home,
my land… My mother…

On a fine autumn morning;
On the streets, I wander.
I get the sweet fragrance
of many a shed jasmine flower…
My heart feels like
flying back to my childhood days…
To the time when I used to pick flowers;
Beneath the golden sun-rays!
As the sweet fragrance of jasmines,
I fail to trace;
All my hope is smashed,
And the heart is set ablaze…
The dew drops turn into tears,
They roll down my face…

When Evening sets in,
The moon starts shining.
I recall my land and mother… … …......……When Evening sets in…

– Translated on 14th September, 2012 by Sharad Kamal Bezboruah.

91. Sinaaki Sinaaki Mukh, Osinaaki Mon…
(Angaraag Mahanta)

Lyrics: Shri. Sarat Barkakati.

The faces so familiar, but the minds unknown!
All of them are so engrossed in themselves,
that none cares, even if a storm has blown.

Their masks hide everything, good or bad.

So, much chaos, I feel distressed…
With the blue sky, we were blessed;
but here, I don't seem to see the skies blue.
I hear the rhythm of the familiarflute,
every now and then, it gives me a clue.

So much honour…
In the voice of my mother,
There's the warmth of affection delighting.
The fragrant breeze blowing,
On the banks of the river…!
An inexplicable feeling; igniting!

On an autumn full moon night,
Dreams so sweet and tender, I sight.
Getting the aroma of familiar jasmine flowers,
My heart again and again takes to flight.

The faces so familiar, but the minds, unknown!

As I look back, I see how it feels,
That culture, so simple,
Yet filled with thrills…
Also, those days of joy and pleasure,
Not finding them now, my heart chills.
The story of my land,
The praise of the martyrs and
The days when grandma taught me the rhymes!
My heart is shaking,
That devotion awaking...
As I remember the church and its hymns.

The faces so familiar, but the minds unknown!
For people who are thirsty for the skies...
For the generation, that needs a mask to smile.
Bringing out a flute out of my chords,
I compose a new tune.
With true dedication and feelings,
I wish to offer to my people, this boon.

The faces so familiar, but the minds, unknown!

– Translated on 5th September, 2012 by Sharad Kamal Bezboruah.

92. *Ujaiye Jaa Noi... (Angaraag Mahanta)*

Lyrics: Ibson Lal Baruah.

Go upstream, oh! River,

go and let the sun know,

about the atmosphere, polluted so.

Then coming back,

downstream shall you flow,

and brush along, my pain and sorrow.

What colorful clothes laugh,

round me and tease my mind…

My heart, so cheerless, so rough,

that tears come rolling behind.

My rainbow comes to a pause…

awaiting the sun, for it has not arisen,

and there's not a drop of rain…

So, my rainbow has gone somewhere and has hidden…

That false glow of ornaments

remains on this side, oh! River…

Only the light of life that illuminates

crosses to your other side, oh! River…

What colours of madness and craze does time,

pour at the end of a cliff that has no mercy.

Passion makes me forget it all,

the blood splashed by the sun's redness, is all I see…

My rainbow comes to a pause…
awaiting the sun, for it has not arisen,
and there's not a drop of rain…
So, my rainbow has gone somewhere and has hidden…

Of what does this drama speak?
Today, what does reality seek?
Collapsing are all the four walls…
spotless the gateway, my heart recalls.
Can the skyscrapers ever reach out to
this humble heart's desires?
There are flames blazing in this heart…
Can the seven colours of the rainbow,
spread out, and put out those fires?

My rainbow comes to a pause…
awaiting the sun, for it has not arisen,
and there's not a drop of rain…
So, my rainbow has gone somewhere and has hidden…
Go upstream, oh! River,
go and let the sun know,
about the atmosphere, polluted so.
Then coming back,
downstream shall you flow,
and wipe out my pain and sorrow.
What colorful clothes laugh,
rounds me and tease my mind…
My heart, so cheerless n rough,
that my tears come rolling behind.

Time has things to say,
the storm only blows away.

There comes a smile on my face.
The sun rays again,
return and meet today,
the pearls of my musical notes.
Conscience shall block Dowson's path...
Remember, the seven colours are still there,
along that same path across the sky…
Calling out the Lord's name…

My life watches the sport shown by time,
the colours again bring alive, the rainbow…
My dreams wake up,
they try to revive, the rainbow.

– Trans-created on 16th October, 2012 bySharad Kamal Bezboruah.

93. *Mur Minoti...*

– Dr. Nirmalprabha Bordoloi.

If my solicitation becomes a star,
your skies it shall touch and adorn.
And if this set of lyrics somehow gains a tune,
it shall lay in your grassland, like a milestone.

If my solicitation becomes a star,
your skies it shall touch and adorn.
And if this set of lyrics somehow gains a tune,
it shall lay in your grassland, like a milestone.

If this song of mine gains a tune,
if that song, shines like the moon!
That moon shall with its moonlight, at the tiniest chance,
shall go stealthily and dwell on your lips soon.
Even if I leave the world, you shall see
that the evening star comes and talks of me.

If my solicitation becomes a star,
your skies it shall touch and adorn.
And if this set of lyrics somehow gains a tune,
it shall lay in your grassland, like a milestone.

If my solicitation becomes a star,
your skies it shall touch and adorn. ....

– Trans-created on 11th June, 2013 by Sharad Kamal Bezboruah.

94. Oh,Xiparor Bandhou..Xuna!

(Dr.Bhupen Hazarika and Manna Dey)
Lyrics- Dr.Bhupen Hazarika
Artists- Bhupen hazarika and Manna Dey.

Traveler: Oh...dear mate...
Oh...dear mate of the other bank...
Do you hear?
This bank is lonely and dark...
The black clouds cover the sky,
I see lightning sparks...
I beg of you,
please take me across in your ark.
Take me across in your ark.

Sailor:
Pushing aside, storm and tide,
I shall bring you across at any cost.
But, in search of what do you wander,
What have you lost?
Anyway,
Pushing aside storm and tide,
I shall bring you across at any cost,

Traveler:
My boat is delicate, made out of wood for a silk-cotton tree,
to cross this dilapidated bridge, I have to strive..

I don't know my destiny,
And, I want to know why I am alive...
So, please take me across...
Take me across...

Sailor:
Alright, supposing I bring you this side,
leaving the other bank behind.
But, if you want to return,
I can't take you back, let me remind.
I'm bringing you across...

Traveler:
No, I don't want the illusion of this side,
it is full of gloom.
I want to go to the other side,
to see petals of hope bloom.
So, please take me across...
Take me across...

Sailor:
If one gets to one bank, he wants the other,
one can never give up thirst.
Going from one bank to the other,
out of fatigue, each time, I burst..
If one gets to one bank, he wants the other,
one can never give up thirst.

– Translated on 13th January, 2013 ©Sharad Kamal Bezboruah.

95. *MoiJiBatere ....*

Lyrics: Hemanta Dutta; Singer: Jayanta Hazarika.

The path that I've set out on today;
I shall never again set foot on this way.
For, taking the new path that I find right;
I go in search of the Birds of Light.

The path I've left back,
is now shadowed by darkness.
The chariot I ride with faith
faces trouble no doubt. Nevertheless,
with brand new flame of courage in me,
I, even more courageous today,
shall not return along this way.

Why does fatigue come each time and trouble me?
The Birds of Light call me forth, I see!
As I, with new hope,growflowers,
Along my way,
as I move, I play..

The path I've set out on today,
I shall never again set foot on this way.
For taking the new path that I find right;
I go in search of the Birds of Light.

– Trans-created on 27th April 2013 by Sharad Kamal Bezboruah.

96. Moi Akou Ubhoti Ahisu...

Dr. Birendranath Datta.

I again return today to,
my familiar abode.
I come in search of rest and peace,
underneath the shade of the trees I had sowed.
I again return today to,
my familiar abode.

(Oh! How many times, when lost,
I sat on the river bank.
On an unfamiliar street, when tired,
I sat under the tree that I even today thank.)2
(Today, I again return on that familiar road where I raced,
for the sweet fragrances of memories wait to be embraced.)
I come in search of rest and peace,
underneath the shade of the trees I had sowed.
I again return today to,
my familiar abode.

(Where my childhood woke up;
and my life went through all kinds of seasons;
where my teenage, aloud laughed;
with or without reasons.)2

Yes,

(I return to the same place,

to sing a song or two, begin again from the forgotten note.)2

I come in search of rest and peace,

underneath the shade of the trees I had sowed.

I again return today to,

my familiar abode.

I come in search of rest and peace,

underneath the shade of the trees I had sowed.

I again return today to,

my familiar abode.

– Translated on 2nd May, 2013 by Sharad Kamal Bezboruah.

97. Mur Jiwonere Mur Moronere…(Moor Desh i.e. Mur Dekh)

Prem aru Rodali'r Kobi --Shri.Hiren Bhattacharyya

-"In the seams my shirt lies the salute of pain,
if you ever put your hand on my shoulder…
You shall find the poet named Hiren. "

With my life and my death,
I wish to groom my motherland…
into the warmth of my first love.

Now, you can't tell another about this pain!
Only a feeling in the heart, it shall remain.
Gentle and tender like the loved ones,
moist like the clouds near the sun…..
Such is my motherland…..)2
In this very place itself, my every song shall come and end.
In my motherland!

With my warm eyes and the flame of my body;
with my warm tears and the flame of my body!
I wish to illuminate my eternal motherland,
into the warmth of my first love.)2
Gentle and tender like a song you listen to more than once,
moist like the clouds near the sun…..
Such is my motherland…..)3

In this very place, my every song shall come and end.
In my motherland!

(With my life and my death,
I wish to groom my motherland…
into the warmth of my first love.)2….

– Translated on 14th April, 2013 by Sharad Kamal Bezboruah.

98. *More Bharotore More Soponore*

– Rupkuwor Jyoti Prasad Agarwala.

Of my land, my dreams,
so beautiful is the ever-green culture.
In my green heart,
on this green land of mine…
Shines, and shall shine on in future,
the light of new life,
the light so divine..

Today, any artist is no less than-
a humble heart's salutation.
Today, any artist is no less than-
eternal devotion.
Hail..!! The unbeatable, unmatched,
ever victorious culture, freedom and liberty of the people of India...
Salutations...!!!
Salutations...!!!
Salutations...!!!

– Translated by © Sharad Kamal Bezboruah on 26th January,2013.

99. Luitor Xutot Likha Robo…

Lyrics: Ratna Oja.

In the current of this river Luit,

all the stories of my life.

With sand, I shall write on,

on the sandy banks,

even after I have to embrace the pain of losses.

Of childhood, my childish laughter,

flow here, within these currents, so solemn.

Of my uncountable aspirations of my time,

the boat sailed off into them.

Read there, within the waves, of my life the rhyme.

After I depart…

In the current of this river Luit,

all the stories of my life.

With sand, I shall write on,

on the sandy banks,

even after I have to embrace the pain of losses.

Even **my** youth was overflowing with melodies,

dipped in the flames of the sun.

I shall not turn back and look at the sandcastles of agonies,

shall not allow these tears to be shed. Like these currents that run,

even in **my** life, the stories are vast.

Read there, within the waves, of my life the rhyme,
for these currents shall forever last.

In the current of this river Luit,
all the stories of my life.
With sand, I shall write on,
on the sandy banks,
even after I have to embrace the pain of losses.

    – Translated on 3rd September, 2013 by Sharad Kamal Bezboruah.

100. Loka-Motive (Eri thoi oha mur...
Xounigaon khoni)

Angaraag Mahanta.
Lyrics by: Manmath Baishya.

The golden memories of
that lovely village of mine on the river bank,
which I left behind long back.
Oh, how do I forget!
They still haven't stopped awaiting me yet.

How simple, oh! How adorable….oh!
The river, oh! What affection that it had!
In the mirror of love, highlighting the image of life,
it did ask me to move on ahead.
I did, oh! I've come so far,
so far I've treaded on the path of dreams and aspirations.
Oh! Shall I return to find them all where they are?

On mother's lap, I shall again romp and frolic;
I shall again going back to childhood.
From her mouth, again shall I hear those sweet lullabies;
chase away, all my tiredness and fatigue I would.
I've seen lot many streets, along many paths I have had chances to roam.
Somewhere among those streets, mother must be waiting at the gateway.
Oh god! I really feel like rushing back home…..

The golden memories of
that lovely village of mine…
Oh, how do I forget!
They still haven't stopped awaiting me yet.

The golden memories of
that lovely village of mine on the river bank,
which I left behind long back.
Oh, how do I forget!
They still haven't stopped awaiting me yet.

– Translated on 5th September, 2013 by Sharad Kamal Bezboruah.

101. Paribane..

– *Angaraag Mahanta*

Can you again add color,

to the black dress they wear to mourn;

the forehead now without the spot.

Can you put together again,

the heart that this storm has apart torn.

The lap that lays empty in vain…

Can you? Speak up!!

If you can wipe out the tears,

bring back the good from exile.

If you can return peace and joy,

come on make those victims smile.

Can you?

Who are you and what are you looking for?

Why must those innocent kids face the war?

Tell me now..!!

Watching everything happen,

why don't you make a sound?

Who will bring justice, then;

unshackle our hands bound?

Politics is only a game,

of the nation, no one does care.

Our leaders only want wealth and fame,

to call us their own, no one's there.

Can you again add color,
to the black dress they wear to mourn,
the forehead that's now without a spot.
Can you put together again,
the heart that this storm has torn.
The lap that lays empty in vain…
Can you? Speak up!!
If you can wipe out the tears,
bring back the good from exile.
If you can return peace and joy,
come on make those victims smile.
Can you?

– Translated on 11th December, 2012 by Sharad Kamal Bezboruah.

102. Pua'r Rodaali... (Angaraag Mahanta)

From my window, I see the morning sun-ray,
as it comes to me , comes to say.
That you will come this morning,
you will come , you will come today.

When you come, seems like flowers smile.
Like even reality turns, into a dream so sweet.
Like spring awakens in my garden,
I listen to the birds as they tweet.
The morning dew on the grass giggles.
This morning the autumn breeze wakes me up,
The first ray of the sun comes and tickles.
As they know that you will come today.

From my window, I see the morning sun-ray,
as it comes to me , comes to say.
That you will come this morning,
you will come , you will come today.

If you don't come, the wind comes to a standstill.
The fragrances of the flowers fade.
My finger wants to touch the dew drops.
It moves half way, and then stops.
Since you don't come, it too changes its will.
The flowers that fall
This autumn, dry out.

As the wait for your footsteps,
But you don't fulfill their call.
If you don't come,
Why does everything seem so helpless?
If it really has to be so,
Why o why don't you come always?

From my window, I see the morning sun-ray,
As it comes to me , comes to say.
That you will come this morning,
You will come , you will come today.

    – Translated on 19th September, 2012 by Sharad Kamal Bezboruah.

103. Nistobdha Nisha...

Angaraag Mahanta.

The cicadas of the motionless night,
gave me company of the morning.
Once again, I look back to sight,
so much loneliness.

So many truths of life turn to lies,
in front of me.
With the same lies, in front,
laughter in reality breaks free.
God knows when this night
shall turn to dawn;
I wait, a new morning that would bring light,
yet doesn't pass of this earth…this night so long.
They just can't be understood,
all the norms and regulations.
It is leisure, a calm mood;
I laugh and cry on this silent night.

God knows when,
the mist of the mind shall settle.
God knows when we shall see,
all the far away minds,
see all those minds break free.

– Translated on 4th September, 2013 by Sharad Kamal Bezboruah.

104. Mrityu Aahe Jibonole (Angaraag Mahanta)

Death comes and takes away someone close.
Seems like the heart is suddenly filled,
With pain and chaos, pain and chaos!
From the eyes, the river of tears flows.

I know you won't return;
to have with me a friendly word.
In my memory shall always burn;
the scene of your hand on my forehead.
On your lap, as I lay down...
Will you ever narrate, again
the story of the Merchants' Town?

In the evening, as I sit alone.
Alone, amidst my heart!
I recall your sheltering shadow,
your touch, so cold, as you depart.

And now, I see,
You are gone...
To dwell with the stars,
Leaving me alone!

Death comes and takes away someone close.

– Translated on 23rd September, 2012 by Sharad Kamal Bezboruah.

105. Biswa Xilpi.

– 'Rupkonwar' Jyoti Prasad Agarwalla

The poet- Jyoti Prasad!

An artist of the world,
I am an artist of all three times-
of the past, the present and the awaited future.

I journey through the beginning
and go off that which hasn't a beginning.
Midst chaos, destruction;
I take form through a change of form,
and hence I light
the wick of new creation to fulfill the norm.
In the hearts of the public lies my golden nation.
I wear the world class attire,
and stare on, unblinking;
at of creation, the fire.

Many languages; so many hopes
and many races now victorious;
over the colorful envelopes,
which separate them;
And vaguely, I do here from the same,
a brand new,
incredible song of the human race.

I raise the echo of that song too,
in my own creations of music.
To create on this land, a new world
where peace shall be at its peak.
With my imagination, understanding, intelligence and intellect,
I try and make myself, the incredible base of culture.
And I being the wick, burn the lamp of the world,
to offer devotion to the world; setting out on a venture.
Of that devotion, I being the principal medium,
award myself for its success,
broadcasting myself with my own voice.
Long live the human race! Long live the human race!
Long live the human race.

– Translated on 16th June, 2013 by Sharad Kamal Bezboruah.

106. Niyonr Xona Xandhiya...(Angaraag Mahanta)

Lyrics: Pankaj Mishra.

Seems like your affection,

adds colour to the dew-drops so grave.

Like the dew-drops, emotions too so stubborn...

how strangely these feelings begin to behave!

I do not know why it turns dark today,

why these dreams do shatter.

Only the hope of finding you dwells in my eyes,

I just can't figure out, with the heart; what is the matter...

Seems like your affection,

adds colour to the dew-drops so grave.

Like the dew-drops, emotions too, so stubborn...

how strangely these feelings begin to behave!

In both my eyes there is,

of getting you, only the thirst.

With true or false hope of getting you,

perhaps the heart would burst.

Shall I find you in the middle of the night?

Shall I find you in my heart?

Shall I find you when lamps glow to give out light,

in the wet evening, after the sun departs?

Seems like your affection,

adds colour to the dew-drops so grave.

Like the dew-drops, emotions too, so stubborn...

how strangely these feelings begin to behave!

When twilight sets in, like the dew-drops that roll forth...

will you too come close?

When evening sets in, like a wandering fire-fly,

god knows why so often this heart does pause!

Illuminating you, it burns today...

It flows down in the desire to get

you. In the dark clouds, why do the rains float away,

in this evening that the dew-drops did wet?

Seems like your affection,

adds colour to the dew-drops so grave.

Like the dew-drops, emotions too so stubborn...

how strangely these feelings begin to behave!

– Trans-created completely on 29th January, 2014
by Sharad Kamal Bezboruah.

107. Xora Phul Bokulor...

– Angaraag Mahanta.

The fallen petals of a flower,
thatlay at the other end of my gateway.
The wind does blow and sweep those petals away,
and they do fall quite near.
So, I think of picking up a few,
but they fly off again...
And this time they fall at a place quite far,
where they are wet by the morning dew.

The fallen petals of a flower,
thatlay at the other end of my gateway.
The wind does blow and sweep those petals away,
and they do fall quite near.
The fallen petals of a flower...

With many of those tiny expectations,
this heart begins to fly.
It dreams big and stretches for the moon,
and slowly moves away far into the sky.

I scream... "Don't go dear heart of mine, stay near.
I see that the skies up there aren't too clear.
.......You shall be lost in the middle of those dark clouds."

The fallen petals of an flower,
thatlay at the other end of my gateway.
The wind does blow and sweep those petals away,
and they do fall quite near.
The fallen petals of an flower…

From where does this crazy gust of wind come
and blow away this heart's pain?
From where does this crazy gust of wind come
and blow away this heart's pain?
Far away, it stands and looks on,
trying to speak again and again…
… "Don't go dear heart of mine, stay near.
I see that the vision up there isn't that clear.
…….You shall be lost in the middle of those dark clouds."!!

The fallen petals of a flower………

– Translated on 21st December, 2012 by Sharad Kamal Bezboruah.

108. Eta Gaan Xex Hol.

– Dr. Amarjyoti Choudhury.

A song has come to an end.

The song towards which the entire race used to bend,

That song has come to an end.

The song that carried along spring,

In a silver, decorated palanquin,

Now that it's gone,

What shall we sing) 2

In it, was a country's (blood) vein!

In it, was our winter grain!

In it, was our shining summer!

In it, was our monsoon rain!

Wherever it was,

On a mountain or plain;

It sounded loud in every terrain.

And now it's gone, leaving us in pain) 2

Dried is that clear brook!

Where will u now even have one look?

At the never ending seas

Of experience and of memories;

In the twilight of the November day,

The blazing flame that showed the way…

Blew out- as the raven flew!

And the storm that once blew,
Was now nowhere to be felt!
All seen now, was that colorless belt-
Claiming to be the rainbow!
But, who would even care,
It had no colors to show.

Now only a flame flickers...
as the song burns to become ash.
Gone shall be the song,
Leaving the space blank!
The song that built an entire tree-house,
With just one wooden plank!
Filled with joy and courage,
That was the over-flowing tank.
The flame now has extinguished;
the heart of all now sank…

Even time sits with its eyes closed.
Look-as the seed of a new song grows.
The new song is growing,
The change is now showing.
Watch the new flame burn,
As the race takes its turn,
to change the way of living…!
To show the way to learn!
But now, what shall replace this immortal song-,
That taught us to judge, what's right and what's wrong.
From its ashes rises another song.)3
All big and small...Come, come along.
Let's sing another song,

To praise this holy song
That sang till the end,
Sang all along...
Let's march ahead together…
To the place where we belong!
So, from the ashes of the holy song,
arises another powerful, new song.
So, from its ashes rises another Song,
from its ashes rises another Song.

– Translated on 2nd May, 2012 by Sharad Kamal Bezboruah.

109. Phoolor Ei Melaate...e

Lyrics- Dr.Nirmalprabha Bordoloi.

In this carnival of flowers,
the birds sing...
In this carnival of flowers,
the birds sing...
The bee buzzes,
and plays out a tune...
Looking at it, the Bulbul,
its Tabla, to play it begins...
And the Mynah, out of delight,
"Doe...Re...Me...." it sings...

Me...So, So, Sososososososo...
Me, so la, tea, la so, fa me, fa, fa...
re, so, fa , me...re fa me re...Doe me re do tea doe doe...
Doe, re me, fa, so la, tea, doe...
In this carnival of flowers,
the birds sing...
In this carnival of flowers,
the birds sing...
The bee buzzes,
and plays out a tune on its sitar...
Looking at it, the Bulbul,
its Tabla, to play it begins...

And the Mynah, out of delight,
"Doe...Re...Me...." it sings...

Me...So, So, So...
Me, so la, tea, la so, fa me, fa, fa...
re, so, fa , me...re fa me re...Doe me re do tea doe doe doe...
Doe, re me, fa, so la, tea, doe...

In this carnival of flowers...!

A little shy is the peacock
its wings, does open it...
And, it dances...
tapping o its feet...
In the carnival of spring,
in their voices, so sweet...
You hear the oriole and the cuckoo sing!!

And the Mynah, out of delight,
"Doe...Re...Me...." it sings...

Me...So, So, So...
Me, so la, tea, la so, fa me, fa, fa...
re, so, fa , me...re fa me re...Do me re do tea doe doe doe...
Doe, re me, fa, so la, tea, doe...

In this carnival of flowers...!

On that music, the bee does get anxious,
anxious, it roams around flowers...
Yes it does!!
The parrot....
only rhythms of music,

it now seems to rote
and sing on...

And the Mynah, out of delight,
"Doe...Re...Me...." it sings...

Me...So, So, So...
Me, so la, tea, la so, fa me, fa, fa...
re, so, fa , me...re fa me re...Doe me re do tea doe doe doe...
Doe, re me, fa, so la, tea, doe...

In this carnival of flowers...!

In this carnival of flowers,
the birds sing...
In this carnival of flowers,
the birds sing...
The bee buzzes,
and plays out a tune on its sitar...
Looking at it, the Bulbul,
its Tabla, to play it begins...
And the Mynah, out of delight,
"Doe...Re...Me...." it sings...

Me...So, So, So...
Me, so la, tea, la so, fa me, fa, fa...
re, so, fa, me...re fa me re...Doe me re do tea doe doe doe...
Doe, re me, fa, so la, tea, doe, la...
re, tea, so, doe....

– Trans-created on 18th March, 2014 by Sharad Kamal Bezboruah.

110. At the END of a TSUNAMI....

Trans-created and Adapted from and Inspired by....
TSUNAMIR SESHOT...
A poem by Prof. Punya Saikia...

Today, dear friend, do not try to console...
me.... for gone are the days....
of a golden age...
destroyed...devastated...is the civilization whole....
And, now... shall crumble... clod by clod...
The ancestral dome...
of His Highness, My Lord...
The Royal Palace, the home...
Like a ripe citron...shall shatter...
The floor of the dinning hall...
And, also shall collapse,
of the golden masonry...the walls...
So full of aspirations and hope,
the architecture that stood tall...!!
The bones and joints of the sun...
Shall unbuckle...
And the flame blazing for ages
too shall fickle...
And, shall cease to burn...
The Himalayan Ice....shall begin
to melt...with a noise!!
Hawks and Falcons shall rush about in the wind,

dust-storms...shall obstruct the pathway...
And, the garden of roses red...
Shall be devastated;
its each and every bed...
Destroyed!! And shall be stained badly,
the white pages of the epic.... oh!! What Dread!!
After all this too,
you come to console
me!???
Not a bit it shall work;
Not at all!!
For, to listen, I do not wish...
So, kindly, with words of consolation,
do not come and preach...
because, it shall fail to affect me,
only my deaf ears, it can reach...
I shall not be able to accept,
the consolation in your speech...
So, do not try, dear friend...
Leave me as I am, please!
For I wish to remain, restive
and restless...
Lost, confused...and without ease...
I wish to cry out loud, friend...
To remain silent, I now refuse...
I wish...to...rush along the banks
of Subansiri and Lohit...
So, your consolation, you yourself keep...
for I shall not accept it,
not a bit...
I shall cry out loud today,

with a voice true...
From places where battles were fought;
The battlefields and the land of martyrs...
From the birth place of the Legend,
to the gardens...to the banks of rivers,
Far and wide...within and abroad;
like the Mississippi, the Volga
and the Thames...
And, also a lot many others
with and without names...
I shall cry my heart out,
at the tomb, the grave of Mark Twain..
At the Dushanbe Minar of Ghalib too,
I shall cry out in pain...
I shall cry out from Paul Robeson's
Princeton and Philadelphia.
I shall cry out from the Dungeons;
the prisons of Pretoria...
Also, from the shrine of Azan Fakir...
and, I shall cry out from places another dozen...
The Palaces of Kings, their tombs,
and the hilly roads...the mountains frozen...
With the innumeral ladies beloved to him,
I shall sing out... "Come on! Come in the name
of the Lord...come to free this land!"....
And, also...songs of his...
On the banks of the Lohit...
On its sands...
And on the banks of Gadadhar,
I shall make the young lady of Gouripur,
dance...the Bihu, the Assamese folk dance...

I shall question Monalisa...
who hails from Shillong...
Quiz her...if her memories are still
as red as Chrysanthemum...
For, (from then, now)..it has been so long...
And to Liyeng-Makaw... I shall ask,
if even now, the whistles of the dew-drops
can be heard strong...!!
Facing the Brahmaputra,
I shall roar out...
"Why do you not raise innumerable Warriors
like Bhishma....of Mahabharata!!?
Why are they yet not born?"
The child, the infant who had high-fever....
And, who have fallen asleep, forever
in the arms of the mother...
I shall cry out loud...and,
that child I shall awaken!!
Do not ask me to remain calm,
friend, for this is the time....
The time to roar, the time to cry out
and dance in anxiety and alarm!
At which moment, did the Holy Discus,
fly out of the Lord's hands...
At which moment, did the armour unbuckle,
where did it go and land...
At which moment, did the earth shake
so wildly, that themselves none could defend!!??
Hastily,
Flew over our heads...
A foul of Ravens...

At which moment was the silver-lit city
of an autumn evening....shadowed
by the dark clouds...and even,
The Brahmaputra, that would seem like
a Zig-Zag kerchief from the Heavens...
hung so lifeless, so motionless...
The Jungles of Kaziranga, Doboka and Kohora,
In what pain have they turned so haunted!??
How has the map of this youthful earth been altered!!?
How is it that there is an untimely change,
in the blossoming season of spring?
Come friends, let us all together,
with letters bold...write an epitaph...
For, of music; the lord, the king...
Call the fireflies...and the butterflies...
Let them too write,
in the language of their flight...
An epitaph....
On the leaves of trees,
the petals of flowers....the laughter of waterfalls...
And, of the pleasing flute of "Kohua"...
the melodious calls...
Come... Let us ask the winds to...
Spread fragrance....
To spread fragrance, in directions all!

– Translated on 7th September, 2015, By Sharad Kamal Bezboruah....

111. Haariye Thikana, Khoje Ghor...

Lyrics: Srijato. Credits: Reliance Entertainment (Regional).

Your magnificence, how can I not praise…!?
How can I not fear you? In your hands are blessings and…
In case I miss a prayer, it is you who shall decide fate…
And, thus… Tell me, why I shall not place;
my prayers at your heavenly gate…
You are the keeper of my trembling prayers…
Oh my Lord!
My Almighty Lord!!

Where did I arrive?
Oh where have I come…?
The winds blow, the tears roll…
The soil, my soul it does revive…
How do I return from this land so awesome…??
If as it sails through the stream of the heart…
the boat of life is smashed…
By a wild, violent storm,
a storm whose rage, unmatched…
To this land's breaths below the chilled feet,
to these wet lands;
god knows how and when I am tied…
As I decide to turn away,
who is the kith who pulls me from behind.

At the river bend,
every speck of sand…
losing its dwellings, a home it wishes to find…

Where did I arrive?
Oh where have I come…?
The blows, the tears roll…
The soil, my soul it does revive…
To this land's breaths below the chilled feet,
to these wet lands;
god knows how and when I am tied…
As I decide to turn away,
who is the kith twho pulls me from behind.
At the river bend,
every speck of sand…
losing its dwellings, a home it wishes to find…

You are my Almighty…
My Lord…
My fate who keeps…
The words that were in the heart for so long,
now have come onto the lips…
Oh! Lord…
Oh my Lord! My Almighty Lord!!
Between us, whatever ties and beliefs,
only you can interpret…
How could another?

Your home, your fields… the storm did finish…
What did you ever get in your own land?
Back to the banks he did not reach…

Which way do you go forth, now?
To do what do you wish?
Vows that can't be broken;
Back never can be taken
the words once spoken;
not always can two hearts bind.
No!! They cannot return,
they can only look at the path they leave behind.
On a sunny afternoon,
somewhere in June;
Losing their dwellings, a home they wish to find…

Where did I arrive?
Oh where have I come…?
The blows, the tears roll…
The soil, my soul it does revive…
To this land's breaths below the chilled feet,
to these wet lands;
god knows how and when I am tied…
As I decide to turn away,
who is the kith who pulls me from behind.
At the river bend,
every speck of sand…
losing its dwellings, a home it wishes to find…

Come on…
Enough now, oh Lord!!
Now, you must do your job…
Enough now, oh Lord….
Show some mercy now…
or in this way, on I shall have to sob…

Your job…
Enough now…
Your job…
Enough now…
Or on I shall sob…
Come on now…
Do your job…

– Trans-created and Adapted on 20th September, 2014
by Sharad Kamal Bezboruah.

112. I am the girl...

Credits: Namrata Sarma,
Alumni, B.A (English Hons.)
Hindu College, Delhi University.

I am the girl....
Whom you meet often,
in busses, trains and trams...
Whose sari, earnings, and heels,
also the red spot that adds to her charms;
that you see everyday, and spy!!
And, your heart feels
like seeing a lot more...
In whichever way you think, imagine;
you find me the same, in your dreams...

I am the girl...

For whom, stepping on a shadow too,
is forbidden in the norms of the villages of Bihar!
And, whom...you send for, in the night bleak,
to be picked up from the slums...
And, for whom your royal, majestic lust
turns restless, on the bed well-prepared...
Waiting for the moment she comes!

I am the girl...

I am the girl, at midnight;
from the dingy labour quarters of Assam
whom you wish to invite...
and escort to the Sahib's bungalow...
And in front of the flashing fireplace,
you wish to drink her sight!!

I am the girl....

From her dreary front yard,
in Rajasthan...hot as hell!
Who has to go fetch
water from the public well...
10 miles away!!
And then, back she does head...
And, then again, when she arrives, devastated;
you make her sit and toast your bread
in front of a choking furnace!!
And she does, silently; in dread...

I am the girl...

I am the girl...
Whom you wish to melt away into...
On the banks of Ganges,
in the blue of the movie-theatre...
or in Victoria Memorial, among greeneries!!
Whose eyes you wish you paint,
with the kohl of dreams false...
And, whom you fling off;
like an empty cigarette pack!!

And then, rush off...attending to calls...
Not turning back; for you are already late...
To solemnly accomplish your wedding ceremony,
where for you everyone does wait!!
And, thus...you whoosh away in your car,
shattering my dreams so many....

That evening of the wedding,
the one whom on the street you leave!

I am the girl...
who stands alone, stranded...
Whom even the Lords fail to forgive...
And leave in her womb,
by force and power,
the sin of a maiden, her doom...
Who has to face the dark hour,
when she has to send that bit of herself, her own bloom;
floating way in the river!!

I am the girl...

When the home is in danger,
I am faith...
My mother's drugs come from,
the tuition fees that I get!
My brother's stationery and books,
from other incomes, like rent...
I am drenched in heavy rain!!
With the darkest skies above me...
I become an umbrella;
and thus, I maintain

peace over my home...

You!! You!!
You have,
you all have done a lot...
A lot for me!!
From you,
so much I have got.
I literature and poetry,
in scriptures and convention...
In history,
and where not,
me you did mention!!
Worshipped me as a mother,
I have been sketched, portrayed as nature...
And, also, made my statue stand at the square,
and, have placed my highly adorned images
in other nooks and corners
of your towns and villages...

Yes... I am the girl!

Perhaps,
perhaps someday
perhaps some other day
I shall throw away
all my false attire...
and become the incredible...
My wavy hair shall cover like a cloud,
my bare back!! My eyes shall set ablaze...
and, from the forehead shall beam out a light splendourous!!
My anklets shall call out loud,

and shall shine my bangles...
A dreadful laughter shall fill the skies,
and the Lords too shall call out, spellbound...

"Hail! The goddess of the south
brings with her the clouds of grave destruction...
With four hands, and hair let loose;
ornamented by human heads"
and to stop I refuse...

I shall move on ahead,
like a fanatic...
And, on along path shall tremble
innumerable headless corpses...
The corpse of civilisation,
the corpse of development...
the corpse of society!!

Perhaps, I am the girl...
Perhaps...
Perhaps....!!

-Trans-created and adapted from "Aami Shei Meye" by Shri. Subho Dasgupta; with reference to its Assamese translation "Moi'e Xei Suwali Joni" by Shri. Punya Saikia; on 3rd November; 2016 by Sharad Kamal Bezboruah.

113. Xeujiya

– Neelotpal Lahkar 'MINIMI'

I stand on this bank,
Look on in silence,
the tides fierce.
In the skies, of the clouds, the games;
The sun crimson,
hide and seek it plays...

In the heart,
the vermilion rays,
Hopes too,
stay ablaze.
Such is the thrill,
the sting;
So subtle, so sweet!

Underneath
the misty veil;
The green globe;
Turning pale...

I wish to touch,
Of joy, the droplets!
Comes floating in the winds,
A tune, so mellifluent...

The routes familiar,
Call out to me, call near;
The trees, they smile;
and spread smiles all over.

A distant dilemma,
(Slowly) closes in, encloses...
Don't know which way,
To take me it chooses.

In the fist, to hold
these moments of love, wishes...
To fly, wants the heart;
But don't know what,
its zeal diminishes.

Swimming across the river of anguish,
At the other end,
I find myself... at ease.

    – Translated on 24th August, 2018 by Sharad Kamal Bezboruah.

114. 'ROUD'.

– Diptanil Barua

The sunrays today,
to me, they preached,
these specks too sparkle,
when dusted off, sun-kissed.

To sunlight, call out,
even the leaves withered;
embracing the reminiscence,
into smoke, they scatter.

These songs, today,
turn moist.
The songs of the bosom
turn ice cold, freeze;
in the warmth of the sun;
little did I know, in my quest for your visage;
you were but to fade away into the breeze,
like those specks, alas.

By the river bank,
I stretched out for some sun,
tales, a zillion;
I let the waters wash away;
your poetry,

into the river, immersed;
I let the silver lining,
be shadowed by the dark clouds;
in the warmth of the sun,
little did I know in my quest for your visage;
you were but to fade away into the breeze,
like those specks, alas.

This love, safely kept aside for ages,
like a withered rose between the pages.

    – Translated on 6th July, 2020 by Sharad Kamal Bezboruah.

115. Tumaloi (Adapted into a song by Tanuj Nath)

– Jintu Kumar Kashyap.

From a far away land,
I hope you are fine.
From your window, do you still watch,
the tepid moonlight shine?

Dreams ambiguous,
Today, do they weep?
In the heart, the breath,
Beating, does it keep?

A fist full of stars,
For you,
i would pluck away from afar.

A heart full of '*kohua*' blades;
With those stars,
I could decorate.

A kiss of emotions,
Old and anew...
Floats across this heart,
as if it were you.

At a distance further,
than to reach,
with both arms open together;
awaiting in vain,
These eyes begin to pain.

In the bleakest of nights,
Will you speak, in the silence,
and utter those words polite.

Of the dark clouds, the arrogance;
these tears shall shatter,
and then, from the eyes
it shall rain; pitter-patter.

– Translated on 17th June, 2020 by Sharad Kamal Bezboruah.

116. Ratibur paar hobo.

– Narjee Mausum Sharma.

The nights shall dawn...
116 of them,
I await;
your shadow
and the moonlit paint...
To hum a tune,
And, for a smile faint.
Yes, I await!
I await that very smile,
and losing ourselves
Every once in a while...

Speak to these rays,
have a word polite.
And let them know,
that I prefer darkness over light.
Let us lose ourselves again,
Tonight... This very night!
All these desires, these wishes,
Of love; of embraces;
Let me fade away,
into your bosom...
Fade and lose all my traces...

Right there, where I have planted seeds
Of poetry, of those verses;
Where, we, our emotions,
our love, into one ocean it all immerses.

– Translated on 28th September, 2017 by Sharad Kamal Bezboruah.

117. *Kobitaa bur.*

– Narjee Mausum Sharma.

If only poems were poems;
how nice it would be.
But alas, sometimes, they're 'you';
and at other times, they're 'me';
and also, someone in between.
Sometimes; they are our playful hearts
that hide, among the seen-unseen.

If only poems, were poems alone,
busy poems;
and, not poems about 'us'.
It would have been far better,
for then, there wouldn't be all the fuss.

– Translated on 28th January, 2019 by Sharad Kamal Bezboruah.

118. Xendur

– Devashis Thakuria.

A live breath, in a silent bosom,
in the wild February breeze,
like a fluttering leaf, like your shadow;
walking by your side,
in the darkness too, never shall I cease.

Of my dreams, you are the breath and soul,
So much pain, within I burn,
and turn black, black as coal.

I painted; life's skies, in shades a million;
to create a colourful vision of life;
I draw all over, with vermillion.

– Translated in August 2017, by Sharad Kamal Bezboruah.

119. *Tumi Ekura Jui (You, a flame).*

(A poem by Junmoni Basumatary;
dedicated to Dr. Ananya Barua Choudhury.)

You are a flame ablaze
an epitome of strength
of merit,
Showing the way ahead,
like a torch lit.
To the nomads of the night,
you are a flame ablaze.
Who vexes at another woman's plight,
you, a flame ablaze;
a flame,
the fire of courage; a fire such;
that, lights up one's life, your touch!
So incredible, a flame,
as wondrous as your name;
Thus, move on ahead; forever,
salutations to your glory, the same.

– Translated on 30th September, 2018 by Sharad Kamal Bezboruah.

120. Ronga Sulir Suwalijoni (The Crimson Haired Gal)

– *MAITRAYEE PATAR.*

As the tender blossom,
she stealthily plucks;
and into her hair,
tucks...
We pass by,
the lanes along which
the rain had once embarked.

The day, it is,
like a prolonged tale
of innumerable tales.

Pouring out a cup each,
of bitter black tea;
where the whistles of Kongthong prevail...
We head in search of yet another tale,
along the trail.

In her silence lays the tale
of a war-wrecked land;
as she spake,
the tale of her grandfather's raincoat,
she; frozen and still... And, with her hand

her crimson tress;
she would
like a child caress.
I overlooked the blossom
hidden among those tresses.

And there, rises one,
delivering to us,
the secrets of Nirvana; wisdom;
"We could all be Gautama; it seems,
if we forget the innumerable times;
that the pain of life and death go and come"...
And, we, pacing through the rain,
listened on, spellbound.

With the blossom in her head,
she perhaps wondered,
about Nirvana...
And, I, silently walked away,
to the Khasi Hills of the East;
to that tiny little village.

Do the dead of Kongthong
plant in the hands of the little children;
another new seed of Nirvana...
that strives on songs,
and fades away, blends away in the soil;
each fastening to their bosoms;
a song of its own.

I strive for Nirvana,
sans suffering and despair...

I look at her, she who spoke of the wars;
and midst her crimson hair,
watch the white blossom glare.

– Trans-created on 8th May, 2018 by Sharad Kamal Bezboruah.

121. An Ode to 'Cotton College'.

– *Sharad Kamal Bezboruah.*

"What do I speak of how I feel, Cotton?
No matter how hard I try to control my emotions...
I just can't!!
You finally receive recognition,
of the nation...
After years hundred and fifteen!
Oh!! What tunes do you play
on the lyre of this heart within...

It's all a game of sets and subsets;
The fans of cricket will know,
You possibly can't win all the bets...
Slipping away are the sands of time,
Skip a heartbeat maybe;
and sing the holy hymn-
"From darkness to light;
from death to immortality"...

What not you have taught them,
Geography, Economics, History and Maths...
Those pilgrims, so many,
have come to you along different paths...
You have witnessed so much,
triangles, pentagons,

even many a hexagon,
Like those you find in chemistry...
So many articles, poems,
hundreds of debates
of an era bygone...
And, a hundred and sixteen year old history.
As I step forth to enter your gates,
I feel like those hundred and sixteen moonlit nights
are to now finally see the dawn!!

I shall speak no more,
only bow to you in honour...
Of this land,
may your light illuminate every corner...
Your glory shall sparkle,
through your age-old freckles,
like sapphire.
You shall live on thus,
for centuries to come,
grow new roots, lay new bricks...
Rise again, and again, and again;
from these ashes; like a Phoenix!!"

– Translated from an Original in 2017; by Sharad Kamal Bezboruah.

122. Lorali.

– SHANKURAJ KONWAR

Go on, free bird, fly away;
go and find the forgotten tunes.
Come, oh, winds of the south,
bring, on the wings of the past;
the sleepy hues.

My childhood, to relive
is what I today seek,
and ask;
tired; looking for sport and play...
and in mother's lap, to frolic;
on a rainy July dusk.
The little one, lays asleep;
Hush, oh jackal, hush!
Oh beloved childhood of mine,
just (for) this once...
Fluttering your wings,
return you must.

Up there, in the tiny heavens,
lay painted dreams,
of shades seven.
In the droplets of the rain,
dance the kin forgotten.

Playing all day in the mud;
we return home, all weary.
Sleepless were the nights,
counting smiles; of the stars, glary.

Solitary tears;
of memories,
are shed the pearls...
As you I remember, recall.
I have grown up now,
alas! To me, return;
my childhood,
oh, world cruel!
Oh Childhood,
My Childhood...

No, do not return,
to this earth, lifeless;
the skies, a jasmine, bloody;
in love,
no longer lays benevolence!
And thus, if you lay in mother's lap,
remain there, under her caress.
Oh Childhood,
My Childhood...

– Trans-created on 1st June, 2018 by Sharad Kamal Bezboruah.

123. Omaator Maat

Lyrics: Swaraj Priyo.

The palms, of the hands, gold,
that wish to hold;
those are blackened the most;
smeared in coal.
The stupor of the heart,
longing for sunshine,
but, only in the cold;
shall a triumph unfold.

Dreams a zillion,
unseen, undreamt, together shatter!
Deep within, lay in decay;
of words unspoken; a clutter...

The light of many a dawn,
walked away, by the door;
Songs that on the lips, born;
all of them were but uttered, mute; sore.

In a frame of flesh and bones,
the heart, in vain, clenched;
on the back, that every nibble worns;
not a patch of flesh, etched.

The tales, here, of eyes so stead,
no, not in hope;
only long dead.

Dreams a zillion,
unseen, undreamt, together shatter!
Deep within, lay in decay;
of words unspoken; a clutter...

The light of many a dawn,
walked away, by the door;
Songs that on the lips, born;
all of them were but uttered, mute; sore.

– Translated on 29th November, 2021 by Sharad Kamal Bezboruah.

124. Kasiyoli

– Himanshu Nath.

A reverb
that the early sunlight,
in the bosom utters;
and, the fatigue
of the heart in flight;
the butterfly of melodies; flutters
through, casting aside.
On the latch of the athirst heart,
come, and your sleek fingers glide;
lifting gently, the veil purple,
underneath which, modest, it hides.

On the lawn of dreams,
the pitter-patter of emotions; dense;
while every petal of desire,
with poetry; intense.
If you ever asked,
for a lifetime I could wait;
ask for once, come in search...
Within the warmth of my cloak;
that lay; the evergreen stead!

Over the words, shrouding a dress;
the nip shall hand over,

and, on your lap, place.
Once scaled, the heart's hill stiff;
I shall await you; at the doorway of the
cosy, loving home. Do embrace,
you can recollect, if.
I shall tuck myself in, into the warm affection;
gliding, shrinking, then sweep.

– Translated on 14th December, 2021 by Sharad Kamal Bezboruah.

125. Jon Dhone, Jonaalite...

Lyrics - Mukti Nath Bordoloi.

'A tribute to the Golden Voice, Dipali Borthakur and Luit Konwar Rudra Barua deu.'

The moon, my precious, away does glance,
at the stars; in moonlight, bathed.
The flashing Milky Way begins to then dance
all elated.

"Hey! Look here", to the star,
the moon thus spoke;
instead, she turned away,
pulling back her silver cloak.

And the star, oh!
Straight into the eyes,
and befall a trance...
Of the star, every twinkle, glance.
She found place, hence,
in the Moon's heart, this chance.
Thus, all elated;
the flashing Milky Way begins to dance.

The betel nut (star), into the heart,
the moon clutched.
Stained his mouth,

as, on he munched.
And, the light; flushes
of the betel nut; and the star;
the hind, that rushes,
to places far.
The night silent; the moon, forlorn; and so,
the flashing Milky Way begins to dance.

In the blues of the skies,
the moonlight plays.
Down here, on earth,
of their sparks, the carnival;
of light and shade, the magic,
of the moon, the spells.
And, again,
of lovers uniting, the tales,
hearing it all, oh, retreating bird,
a song does rehearse;
and, the flashing Milky Way, in dances, bursts.

The moon, my precious, away does glance,
at the stars; in moonlight, bathed.
The flashing Milky Way begins to then dance
all elated.

"Hey! Look here", to the star,
the moon thus spoke;
instead, she turned away,
pulling back her silver cloak.

And the star, oh!
Straight into the eyes,

and befall a trance...
Of the star, every twinkle, glance.
She found place, hence,
in the Moon's heart, this chance.
Thus, all elated;
the flashing Milky Way begins to dance!

– Translated on 24th October, 2021 by Sharad Kamal Bezboruah.

126. Aawaargi...

– Javed Akhtar.

For long have been
hither and thither;
changing towns
like the changing weather;
only we the two,
besides us no other;
me, and my; wanderlust.

Nor familiar every boulevard,
nor benevolent eyes
at every yard;
if we ought to
which way must we depart?
Me, and my; wanderlust...

I too was once at peace,
when was I ever this weary.
I was joyous,
I was merry.

Such, his steps he raised,
I smothered
while the heart blazed.
On fire we set,

our home; and then,
on we went.
Me, and my; wanderlust...

The heart alone
did go through;
the words harsh
that he threw...
To speak of now,
what remains due,
the rivers from both eyes
along did spew.
When he said,
for you, I almost died...
The entire night,
together, we cried.
Me, and my; wanderlust...

Signs of flaws
all around;
to be scarred today
I am bound.
All paths obstructed,
in vain the pawns hover.
There isn't a way out,
the game is now over.
The wheels of fate spin,
darkness all over;
yet indifferent always been,
me, and my; wanderlust...

Why feel the pain now,
what for?
Cry in vain now
what for?
This heart; let burn
what for?
Why bother, I ought to discern.
Whose isn't the passion;
to vex others
without a reason...
we shall find such a beloved,
somehow, somewhere...
me, and my; wanderlust...

For long wandering
hither and thither;
changing towns
like the changing weather;
only the two of us,
accompanying each other;
me, and my; wanderlust.

    – Trans-created on 17th October, 2017 by Sharad Kamal Bezboruah.

127. Aaj Jaane Ki Zidd Na Karo...

– FAYYAZ HASHMI.

Do not insist on leaving today.

Do not insist on leaving today,
seated as you are,
by my side, do stay.
Do not insist on leaving today,
alas! I'll be finished;
oh lord, I will be robbed,
come on now, such things don't say!

Do not insist on leaving today.....

Think for yourself,
why I wouldn't ask you stop;
for when you rise to leave...
To go along, this life too, out; does pop!
I swear to my life, oh beloved,
keep this little word of mine...

Do not insist on leaving today,
seated as you are,
by my side, do stay.
Alas! I'll be finished;
oh lord, I will be robbed...
come on now, such things don't say!

Do not insist on leaving today.

In the flacon of time,
life lays bottled...
These are the only few moments
for which we are to settle!
Losing these, oh beloved,
for eternity; your regrets don't battle...

Do not insist on leaving today.
Alas! I'll be finished;
oh lord, I will be robbed,
come on now, such things don't say!

Do not insist on leaving today...

This ambience, so innocent
so wondrous...
Of beauty and love,
today is the ascent!
Who knows oh beloved;
what bring tomorrow might...
Do not let the night pass;
oh, let be tonight!

Do not insist on leaving today,
seated as you are,
by my side, do stay.

Do not insist on leaving today.
Alas! I'll be finished;
oh lord, I will be robbed,
come on now, such things don't say!

   – Trans-created on 12th February 2017, by Sharad Kamal Bezboruah.

128. Ek Ladki Ko Dekha Toh Aisa Lagaa...

– Javed Akhtar.

When I saw her,
it was like...
Like how a rose,
Its petals unfurls…
Like the dream;
In a poet's verse;
Like a ray;
Full of zest;
Like a deer
In the forest;
Like moonlit is the night bleak,
Like a word spoken,
Soft and meek!
Like in the temple
of a lamp, the wick;
burns and brings
hope to the weak.

When I saw her,
it was like...
Like, of the morning, the elegance,
Like,
Like the winter sun's benevolence…

Like of sitar the call,
Like…of colours the soul…
Like of the vines,
The swirl; the crawl...
Like the games that the waves play,
Like they rise and they fall!!
Like the breeze fragrant,
Comes to please all…

When I saw her,
it was like...
Like there dance;
peacock a hundred;
like of smooth silk,
a thread...
Like the melody of angels,
like the fire of sandalwood;
like how beautifully adorn
the ornaments and bangles...
Like the showers,
like the intoxication
growing steady over the hours.

– Trans-created on 2nd February, 2017 by Sharad Kamal Bezboruah.

129. Ek Pyaar Ka Naghma Hai....

Lyricist-Santosh Anand.

There is a melody of love;
there are the currents of the waters...
Apart from a tale of you and me,
life seems to be nothing other…

Something is to be lost, after found,
Something to be found, after lost...
Coming and then being gone,
that's what life's all about....
From seconds few in hand,
an entire lifetime we are to gather...
Apart from a tale of you and me,
life seems to be nothing other…

There is a melody of love;
there are the currents of the waters...
Apart from a tale of you and me,
life seems to be nothing other…

You are the currents of the river,
I am the river bank…
You are my strength, my support,
and without me, your boat shall sank…
In the eyes, an entire ocean,

comprising of, of hope, the waters…
Apart from a tale of you and me,
life seems to be nothing other…

There is a melody of love;
there are the currents of the waters...
Apart from a tale of you and me,
life seems to be nothing other…

The one that soothes the heart,
raise such a tune...
Raise the voices,
before your peace is ruined...
Of joy, there are the waves,
and...the feelings, tears now utter...
Apart from a tale of you and me,
life seems to be nothing other…

There is a melody of love;
there are the currents of the waters...
Apart from a tale of you and me,
life seems to be nothing other…

– Trans-created on 14th February 2016, by Sharad Kamal Bezboruah.

130. 'Chand Roz'

– FAIZ AHMAD FAIZ.

Just a few more days;
oh beloved,
days, a few more!
In the shade of tyranny,
to breathe, compelled;
one last blow, let me endure;
for I have endured so many;
just a few more days, oh beloved;
days, a few more.

The body lies caged;
emotions, shackled.
Thoughts, confined;
speech restrained...
And yet, all of it, tackled;
such is my spirit,
that through life, I battle.
Is life the clothing of the penniless;
and stitched onto it, a patchwork of pain?

But, now, the days of tyranny;
are only a few more.
Days of pleading, not too many,
just a few more days, I must endure.

In the burnt ruins of this time,
I ought to live, but, thus, forever, nor;
the laden blows of alien arms,
only today; I ought to endure...
not forever.

This dirt of anguish layered
around your splendour;
the days of this transient youth...
the losses that outnumber;
of the pain of the moonlit nighs,
the blaze, worthless;
the senseless urge of the heart,
of the body, the anguished cries.
Just a few more days;
oh beloved,
days, a few more!

Just a few more days;
oh beloved,
days, a few more!

– Translated on 16th of June, 2018 by Sharad Kamal Bezboruah.

In fond memory of Lt. Abhijit Nath, Lt. Nilotpal Das, Lt. Raj Kishore Gogoi, dearest 'Aaji' and all the untimely losses.

131. Choti Choti Baatein Hai Jo...

– Angaraag Mahanta.

These small talks and small things that are there,
about them what do I say? Let them be…
You don't get a thing… So, with you those talks how do I share?
You don't get a thing, so what do I say!
When I touched you, a thought just came by,
the heart said, "Watch your heart!"
Oh! How do I tell you? How do I explain?
Put your ear on my chest for yourself and listen,
perhaps that would be a good start…

You are the only business of my every heartbeat,
may it be day or night, and you are the one employed.

These small talks and small things that are there,
about them what do I say? Let them be…
You don't get a thing… So, with you those talks how do I share?
You don't get a thing, so what do I say!
In the cold lonely nights,
may your hand be in mine.
And you stay right in front of my sight,
both awake till sunshine.
May neither you nor I be in between,
let silence itself be a silent voice.
Those tottering winters lie in the slow breaths within;

let's make those mistakes, by chance and yet by choice.
As we wander, let's travel far beyond the moon in the space vast.
Of tiny talks and tiny thoughts, is this world of ours...
Let it stay forever, forever may it last...

These small talks and small things that are there,
about them what do I say? Let them be...
You don't get a thing... So, with you those talks how do I share?
You don't get a thing, so what do I say!

    – Translated on 12th August, 2013 by Sharad Kamal Bezboruah.

132. Tu Chaahiye...

Lyrics- Amitabh Bhattacharya.

The heart is in a state,
where it needs a sooth.
A wish unfulfilled,
must now come true...
In a way which I've never sought anything,
why am I in this dearth need??
The heart seeks to feel your presence,
so....!!

It needs you... it's you...
Day and night,
you are sought...
Whatever it is,
at the top most height
to be seen, you are sought...

Each time I have a persistence,
every time so,
there must be your presence...

I seek not anyone,
apart from you... I know not why!
In every, every journey of mine;
be you my only guide...
To live on, now,

it is only your benevolence is sought…
I seek you by my side…

If in the chest, the heart,
you are the pain…
I seek not medicines to heal…
And, in every vein,
like blood, flowing, it is you I seek to feel…
Whatever the consequences, be;
thus must be the beginning…

It's you… it's you…
Day and night,
you are sought…
Whatever it is,
at the top most height
to be seen, you are sought…

Each time I have a persistence,
every time so,
there must be your presence…

My wounds,
they need your healing touch…
The flames of my torches,
they seek for your fires….
And, hence….for you, is the search…

You are sought,
in of my dreams, the nest…
And, on my awakening,
your are sought by the head rest…

 – Trans-created on 11th February 2016, by Sharad Kamal Bezboruah.

133. Chalo Ek Baar Phir Se Ajnabi Ban Jaaye...

Lyricist:- Sahir Ludhiyanvi

Come on, once again...
Let us be strangers...
Come on...
Let us be strangers...again...

Let neither me expect...
from you... Hospitality
of the heart...
Nor, you look at me,
with eyes of guilt and hurt...
Let neither,
the beats of the heart...
stumble or tremble in my speech...
nor, through your eyes,
the secret of your dilemma;
others must reach...

Come on, once again...
Let us be strangers...
Come on...
Let us be strangers...again...

You too are held back,
by some complicacies...

I too am accused of
having false conduct and identity...
My companions, my journey mates, too,
are the infamies I carry from the past...
You too carry with you,
the shadows of nights from the past...

Come on, once again...
Let us be strangers...
Come on...
Let us be strangers...again...

When acquaintances turn into illnesses,
they ought to be forgotten...
When ties turn into burdens,
they ought to be broken...
The tale that, to an appropriate end,
cannot be brought... we ought to abandon,
at some beautiful, graceful bend...

Come on, once again...
Let us be strangers...
Come on...
Let us be strangers...again...

Come on, once again...
Let us be strangers...
Come on...
Let us be strangers...again...

Come on, once again...

– Trans-created on 16th March, 2016 by Sharad Kamal Bezboruah.

134. EK GHADI…

Lyrics: Niranjan Iyengar.

For a second pause,
for I still breathe…

For a second pause,
for I still breathe…
And, a sign of my existence,
on your lips I can still read…

On the face of the night,
there maybe be the colours of sunlight…
But, in setting dreams, even now dwells,
my world, it holds on tight…

For a second pause,
for I still breathe…

Separating…so…
Separating from me so…
Yourself, do not punish…
For, their share of crimes and sins,
your hands are yet to finish…

For a second pause,
for I still breathe…

The tale of blooming blossoms…
Was just an excuse…
The story of extinguishing flames
are yet to come…

For a second pause,
for I still breathe…

Be it, my eyes bleak,
and my forehead bare…
So what!? On my palms, even now,
there are the lines sleek;
that add to my flare…

For a second pause,
for I still breathe…
And, a sign of my existence,
on your lips I still can read…

For a second pause,
for I still breathe…

– Trans-created on 1st February, 2016 by Sharad Kamal Bezboruah.

"While one roars out in pride,
and, oppressed…
the other is left shivering inside!
Who knows in what lies strength,
to solve this riddle who has tried!!?

One stands ashore,
one in the tide…
One has never heard of truth,

the other has never lied!
A flame burns out there,
while the heart burns inside...
Who knows which way of life,
to solve this riddle who has tried!!?"

– Inspired by 'Geet-Ageet' by Shri Ramdhari Singh 'Dinkar'.

135. Geet-Ageet...

– Shri Ramdhari Singh 'Dinkar'. (Credits: Namrata Sarma).

The river flows swift,
songs of separation it sings...
The banks, its waters rift,
and it goes on speaking its heart out!!
And, on of the bank, a side,
a rose wonders...within; if such
a blessing from the heaven did slide...
that I could spake,
of the songs of autumn...the world
aware I could make!!
Thus, flows on, the stream,
singing the songs of lament...
While on the bank, swallowing in
a lot, the rose stands, silent!
Who can tell, whether
the rose or the waters that glide!!?
Who knows which is more beautiful,
to solve this riddle who has tried!!?

Somewhere in the leaves,
on the branch dense...
the male parrot sits!
Below on the bough

the other, its eggs it heats...
When the male sings of spring,
when those notes sieve through...
The songs of the female arise within,
but, alas, she isn't able to sing!!
The voice of the male echoes in the jungle,
while swollen in excitement;
are the other's wings...open wide...
In which is there more delight!!?
To solve this riddle who has tried!!?

Two lovers here, when one sings out,
his songs in the time of sunset!
His very first word, from her home;
brings pulling, his Juliet...
There, behind...beneath the Neem,
in the shade...
Peeps she, listening, and thinking
"Why not a stanza, in my fate!!?"...
He sings, but, within is the
anxiety he can barely hide...
Who knows which is more beautiful,
to solve this riddle who has tried!!?

– Trans-created on 13th November, 2016 by Sharad Kamal Bezboruah.

136. Ghanan-Ghanan.....

– Javed Akhtar. *(Credits: Namrata Sarma)*

Male:
Roaring and pounding,
the clouds come surrounding...
Thick and dark grey clouds,
they cover the skies...
Look how they're sounding...
loud and clear...
Look out; the lightning flashes...

The clouds make the heart beat anxiously...

Both:
The clouds make the heart beat anxiously...

Female:
Listen oh grey clouds, Listen!
Do bring on the showers;

Male:
Listen oh grey clouds, Listen!
Do bring on the showers;
we are thirsty of water...
Do not use the sword of lightning...
Make with water-droplets,

of arrows, a quiver...
Then, use them on us...
The clouds spread,
they come roaring with a pound...
The rains they seem to bring,
finally here, perhaps now water shall be found.

Female:
They come closer and closer,
the entire village they seem to surround....

The heart rebellious does now tell...
Don't walk like this, watch it...

Male:
Oh! Times have changed now,
come out of the homes in which you dwell...

Both: the clouds shall shower thus, as if the divine ale.

Male:
Days of the troubles are now past,
come on...let's sing aloud, come fast....

Both:
Roaring and pounding,
the clouds come surrounding...
Thick and dark grey clouds,
they cover the skies...
Look how they're sounding...
loud and clear...
Look out; the lightning flashes!
The clouds make the heart beat anxiously...

Male:
When the liquid is showered,
who shall remain thirsty?!
The Cuckoo shall sing on the roofs.
As the birds shall sing with beauty,
new days shall arrive...
By the lights, darkness shall be smiled at...
By the rains of love, the soul and body is wet...
On this land, a mirror of waters
to see, we shall now get...
Go, wherever you go,
to you this time shall show
that the land here now does wear…
Both: a veil out of the seven colours of the rainbow....

Both:
Roaring and pounding,
the clouds come surrounding...
Thick and dark grey clouds,
they cover the skies...
Look how they're sounding...
loud and clear...
Look out; the lightning flashes!
The clouds make the heart beat anxiously...

Female:
On the trees, put the swings
and swing really high...
Both:
Listen oh grey clouds, come on now bring!
Bring on the showers;

we are thirsty of water...
Do not use the sword of lightning...
Make with water-droplets,
of arrows a quiver...
Then, use them on us...

Male:
The intoxicating times have come,
to spread greenery wide....
It has brought along the monsoons...
To adorn the land that is getting ready like a bride;
it has brought the lightning's anklets,
and the clouds as a shawl...

Female:
Now, every branch shall wear bangles of flowers...
Joy shall be brought to homes of all,
by these wonderful monsoon showers...

Male:
Now, every flower shall bloom,
every street shall laugh...
For of pain and gloom,
we have had enough...

Female:
The good times seem to have come,
for I felt the blowing breeze...

Male:
The sun-rays that burnt the body and heart,
the heat of those rays now decreased...

Both:
Listen oh grey clouds, Listen!
Do bring on the showers;
we are thirsty of water...
Do not use the sword of lightning...
Make with water-droplets,
of arrows a quiver...
Then, use them on us...

Roaring and pounding,
the clouds come surrounding...
Thick and dark grey clouds,
they cover the skies...
Look how they're sounding...
loud and clear...
Look out; the lightning flashes....
Roaring and pounding,
the clouds come surrounding...

– Trans-created on 22nd March, 2014 by Sharad Kamal Bezboruah.

137. Bhari Duniya Mein Aakhir Dil...

Lyrics: Shakeel Badayuni.

In this populated world,
to console the heart, where do I head...?
For those who are in love,
tell them, where is found a shed...
In this populated world,
to console the heart, where do I head...?

The torches are on guard;
with the eyes of the society...on it...
For to burn,
in the flames lit...
those who yearn;
where do those head...
Someone show them the way!
They ought to be led...
For those who are in love,
tell them, where is found a shed...
In this populated world,
to console the heart, where do I head...?

Those, that nor can be kept untold,
nor...can be said...!!
Oh heart, now you speak,
where those fables are to be kept, unread...

For those who are in love,
tell them, where is found a shed...
In this populated world,
to console the heart, where do I head...?

In the eyes, the sight...
there are complicacies, dilemmas...
In the heart, turmoil and anxiety...
Nothing can be made out as to where,
are to head...
For those who are in love,
tell them, where is found a shed...
In this populated world,
to console the heart, where do I head...?

– Trans-created on 26th March 2016, by Sharad Kamal Bezboruah.

138. Benaam Khwaayishyein... (Anweshaa)

Music By: Angaraag Papon Mahanta.
Lyrics: Pinky Poonawala

Anonymous desires, they don't utter a sound.
They aren't able to take flight,
by limitations…why are these dreams bound?
The heart though knows, it refuses to accept,
that for me you aren't meant.
Come back oh beloved of mine,
come, as for you my helplessness has sent.
Anonymous desires, they don't utter a sound.

Oh moon! Your light though is like the sun,
even after wanting to, the eyes of the two didn't meet.
Distances exist, day and night,
they just be covered by the feet.
Anonymous desires, they don't utter a sound.

Autumn passed, the monsoon approached,
flowers blossomed in spring, seasons continued to flip.
Even then, the frozen winds that dwell in the heart,
why do they just refuse to leave? Return oh, beloved!
The seasons of loneliness…they don't pass when we're apart.
Anonymous desires, they don't utter a sound.

– Trans-created on 10th November, 2013 by Sharad Kamal Bezboruah.

139. Khaamoshiyaan Awaaz Hai/Lafzo Mein Bas Inkaar Hai…

Lyrics: Sameer.

In the silence too, there is a noise…
Only denial seems to be uttered in words by that voice…

By words are chosen,
by words are woven;
whatever we have heard,
whatever we have spoken…

Neither I have an idea,
nor you do know…
When by the words,
there's a mistake made.
In words are vented,
somewhere something unsaid…
In the words one does lose,
somewhere something unheard…
God knows where in the heart, the bruise,
the wound felt so…that even words have tricked,
the sight of words, they have blurred…

In the silence too, there is a noise…
Only denial seems to be uttered in words by that voice…

There are secrets a hundred,
in the stacks of words…
Let the meanings disappear,
wherever words are exchanged, friend…
Words often bring you down,
to point where the road does bend,
and leaving you alone, everyone is gone…
With words, things often work out,
and with words itself, things come to an end…
Nothing did I think, I just flowed away in words…
I had to say something, and it was something else that I said.

In the silence too, there is a noise…
Only denial seems to be uttered in words by that voice…

By words are chosen,
by words are woven;
whatever we have heard,
whatever we have spoken…
So much they've given,
so much they've taken;
so much they've mended,
so much…. They've Broken…

In the silence too, there is a noise…
Only denial seems to be uttered in words by that voice…

Neither I have an idea,
nor you do know…
When by the words,
there's a mistake made.

In the silence too, there is a noise...
Only denial seems to be uttered in words by that voice...

In words....
Denial....

  – Trans-created on 25th June, 2014 by Sharad Kamal Bezboruah.

"Did u mean what u said,
did u say what u meant...?
Did the words that u meant,
were the words that u said....?
What u meant, was it less,
was it true what u said...?
Did the words that he said,
flip the words that u said...?
And when he changed what he said,
did that change what u meant...?
And did it hurt when he hurt,
by the words that u said...?"

140. Aapki Yaad Aati Rahi

– Makhdoom Mohiuddin.

You alone I did remember,
the night entire.
The watery eyes, smiled on with a shimmer,
the night entire.

Stayed ablaze, the torch of pain;
the flame of grief, on did flicker,
the night entire.

The wondrous, mellifluous call of the flute,
like a memory, did keep coming, here,
the night entire.

In the heart, the moon of memories did descend;
the moonlight; on did glitter,
the night entire.

The loon, in the lanes,
all along, he did pace;
all along, the noise I did hear,
the night entire.

You alone I did remember,
the night entire.

The watery eyes, smiled on with a shimmer,
the night entire.

You alone I did remember,
the night entire.

– Translated on 1ˢᵗ August, 2018 by Sharad Kamal Bezboruah.

(Edited: 10.12.2021)

(*fondly remembering 'Koka'; Lt. Dr. Nil Kamal Bezboruah, on the 9ᵗʰ year of his departure)

141. Seene Mein Jalan...

Suresh Wadkar. (Lyrics by Sharyar)

Why does there seem to a burning sensation in the chest,
and in the eyes seems to be a storm?
In this city, tell me why everyone seems in unrest,
anxious and troubled, why they all roam.

If there is a heart at all,
then for it to beat, look for an excuse.
If it lay as lifeless as a stone,
of having one, what use?

So filled with loneliness,
what kind of a place is this?
Tell me why friends!
To the extent seen,
why, a desert is all that one sees?

Within me lately,
did anything new arise?
Looking at me, I wonder why
the mirror seems so surprised.

Why does there seem to a burning sensation in the chest,
and in the eyes of all people seems to be a storm?
In this city, tell me why people all around me are in unrest,
anxious and troubled, why they all roam.

– Translated on 21st November, 2013 by Sharad Kamal Bezboruah.

142. Khaatir SE Ya Lihaaz SE...

– Dagh Dehlvi. *(Credits: Maitrayee Patar)*

By a plea or in due regard,
I'm convinced, consoled.
Your promises were but false;
your faith now but sold.

For free, I do hand over the heart,
she asks of what use!
With complaints alone she does revert,
long forgotten are the dues...

By a plea or in due regard,
I'm convinced, consoled.
Your promises were but false;
your faith now but sold.

I fear, yes, I do,
watching the heart turn so hopeless;
yes, the house of course, forlorn,
for, left has now the guest.

At the corner of the tomb;
does dawn upon me such ease.
That the fervours, the ardours, the desires;
all of it does cease.

By a plea or in due regard,
I'm convinced, consoled.
Your promises were but false;
your faith now but sold.

Ask not, oh Sheikh what the eyes
at the tavern, to me have shown;
of faith, you can speak so,
that faith is now but gone.

By a plea or in due regard,
I'm convinced, consoled.
Your promises were but false;
your faith now but sold.

The showers of the secrets of love,
thus they did humiliate;
but God's grace, she came to hear of it,
to her I could state.

With the postman before her eyes,
she was not pleased; nor glad;
but God's grace!
She could at least recognize,
when my name on it she read.

This heart turns a lover insane,
amidst all enemies callous;
At least I lose myself in you,
though I burn, turn jealous.

All the senses, the Consciousness,
the strength and the tolerance;

all of it is now but gone, damaged.
'Dagh' alone is left, he too shall leave soon,
already goes his baggage.

By a plea or in due regard,
I'm convinced, consoled.
Your promises were but false;
your faith now but sold.

       – Trans-created on 7th April, 2018 by Sharad Kamal Bezboruah.

143. Soona...Soona Man Ka Aangan...

Lyrics: Swanand Kirkire. (In memory of beloved 'Aita')

Forlorn…
The heart's courtyard is forlorn…
The jingles of the anklet,
it searches for, for it, it does yearn…
Forlorn…
The notes of the heart are forlorn…
Your beloved, he's in search,
of the songs that are now gone…
In the heart, be it evening,
be it morn…
Building their abode,
live there, your memories alone…
Why all the ties…have you broken?
It's better if you'd move away like this,
what thoughts made you reckon?
Tell me now… Tell me now… Tell me now…

To every blossom,
a bee does come…
And, In the heart, your memory…
In the garden, the cuckoo hums…
Asking where her beloved could be…

How do I pass…
solitary nights??
Tell me…
How do I forget…
the past,
the wondrous moments??
Tell me…
How can I claim,
that a place with you I held…?
How do I make again,
the courtyard of the heart fragrant…?
How can it be forgotten,
your love, oh beloved??
How do I mend again,
the ties that have been broken…

In the heart, let it be evening,
be it morn…
Building their abode,
live there, your memories alone…
Why all the ties…have you broken?
It's better if you'd move away like this,
what thoughts made you reckon?
Tell me… Tell me… Tell me…

To every blossom,
a bee does come…
And, In the heart, your memory…
In the garden, the cuckoo hums…
Asking where her beloved could be…

To every blossom,
a bee does come…
And, In the heart, your memory…
In the garden, the cuckoo hums…
Asking where her beloved could be…

– Trans-created on 14th September, 2014 by Sharad Kamal Bezboruah.

144. Gulon Mein Rang Bhare.

– FAIZ AHMAD FAIZ.

Blow, the winds of spring,
and colours, to the flowers, bring;
come now,
for the gardens too do their thing.

Let the breeze know, mates;
that my cage wails.
Somewhere today, for god's sake,
be mentioned my beloved's tales.
Come now,
for the gardens too do their thing.

Blow, the winds of spring,
and colours, to the flowers, bring!

Whatever I've been through;
I have; but on the night of separation;
my tears flow to adorn
your way ahead,
all along.
Come now,
for the gardens too do their thing.

Blow, the winds of spring,
and colours, to the flowers, bring!

For once, let it dawn
from of your words, the sweetness,
for once, let the night borrow,
the fragrance from your every tress.
Come now,
for the gardens too do their thing.

Blow, the winds of spring,
and colours, to the flowers, bring!

Faiz, now no place
along the way does suit;
from the lanes of my beloved,
to the gallows I head to be execute.
Come now,
for the gardens too do their thing.

Blow, the winds of spring,
and colours, to the flowers, bring!

Extended:
Much is my connection with pain;
and be, that the heart penniless rolls.
Yet, at the mention of your name;
every one of them comes to console.
Come now,
for the gardens too do their thing.

Come the winds of spring,
and colours to the flowers, bring!

If the arrows of the eye
lay in the half-pulled bow, what use?
It shall only be legit
when it goes through the heart,
to make flow blood profuse. (Mahendra Singh Bedi)

Come now,
for the gardens too do their thing.

Come the winds of spring,
and to the flowers, colours bring!

– Trans-created on 12th August, 2017 by Sharad Kamal Bezboruah.

(Edited: 28th August 2017).

145. 'Dono Jahaan Teri'...

– FAIZ AHMAD FAIZ.

Both worlds,
in your love, apart torn;
Passing the night of grief
there he goes forlorn.

Desolate the tavern;
the goblets alone do mourn.
With you, the days of spring
too, have turned away and gone.

A leisure, for sins,
but only days four;
I've seen the spirits,
of the one who sits above, on throne.

The world, it separates
me from your sore.
Yes, you have been beguiling,
but, duties have been more.

This day, though forgetfully,
when a smile she wore.
Ask not, what fervour,
the hapless heart had borne.

Both worlds,
in your love, apart torn;
Passing the night of grief
there he goes forlorn.

– Translated on 21st July, 2018 by Sharad Kamal Bezboruah.

(Edited: 10th December, 2021)

146. DHUAAN…

Lyrics: Niranjan Iyengar.

No longer there is,
of memories the caravan…
Wiped out is every sign of existence!
Why, has forgotten, this land,
why has forgotten them, these skies…??
Wonder where they have disappeared!

Those, by whose blood,
the dreams were coloured;
whose passion, determination;
paved new ways…
Why those, no one remembered!!?
Why, has forgotten, this land,
why, has forgotten them, these skies…??
Wonder where they have disappeared!

Those who could not
find room, in even the stars…
This, the story, the epoch-
of those forgotten by both Venus and Mars!!
Those…whom we
have blown away into smoke…

Not asking for; who always only gave;
for such was their language...
And thus, looting them, we have
woven this time, of our age....
If both on earth and in the skies,
them we fail to trace...
We shall be a shame,
a shame to the human race!!

Those who could not
find room in even the stars...
This, the story, the epoch-
of those forgotten by both Venus and Mars!!
Those...whom we
have blown away into smoke...

Those who could not
find room in even the stars...
This, the story, the epoch-
of those forgotten by both Venus and Mars!!
Those...whom we
have blown away into smoke...

Why did we,
blow them away...into smoke!!?

– Trans-created on 2nd October, 2016 by Sharad Kamal Bezboruah.

147. Tukrey Tukrey Din Beeta……

DHAJJI DHAJJI RAAT MILI
– MEENA KUMARI 'NAAZ'…

The day did pass in bits...
And, at night;
the same repeats!!
Each one got as much gifts,
as in their laps would fit...
Each one got as much gifts,
as in their laps would fit...

Whenever I wished,
the feelings of the heart
I've tried to read...
Also, I heard a laugh;
like someone spoke out,
'There you go; it's again defeat'...

What defeat??
What losses!!?
To move on are the two feet,
hours twenty-four...
A companion as the heart,
when I happened to meet....
Along with it, anxiety did pour!!

The day passed,
in bits...
And, at night...
the same repeats!!
Each one got as much gifts,
as in their laps would fit...
Each one got as much gifts,
as in their laps would fit...

– Translated on 20th June, 2016 by Sharad Kamal Bezboruah.

148. Ishq mein ghairat -e-jazbaat

– Sudarshan Faakir.

In love,
Of the dignity of emotions;
I did care.
Or what was it,
that didn't let shed a tear?

You had mentioned,
'crying shall not alter your fate';
Lifelong, your words thus,
to cry, didn't let.

Ask the weepers,
to weep their share;
for circumstances were such;
that didn't let shed the tears.

On seeing you this once,
a lot; I were to weep;
but alas;
for, the reunion, very brief.

I would have cried 'Faakir', if the trauma,
for a day or two were;
but an anguish of a lifetime,
didn't let shed the tears.

– Trans-created on 12th July, 2018 by Sharad Kamal Bezboruah.

(At the 'Bhuyan's'; Itavata, Digboi).

149. Iss Mod Se Jaate Hai...

Lyrics: Gulzar.

By this bend they all pass...
A few steps, steady
along the street!
And, a few along the highway,
run faster than the heartbeat...

From the palaces of stone,
to fragile homes of glass...
to the nests made of twigs;
all of it, from here they pass...
Pass by this bend!

Like a storm,
whooshes by a road!
Another descends;
rather shy and soft...
Among these roads,
there must be the one,
the one I sought...
The one that leads to you!
It passes by this bend...

From a distance
one of those does approach;

and then returns once close!
Another stands there, so still,
forlorn and morose...
I sit here thinking,
there must be one....
to you that goes!
It passes by this bend...

By this bend they all pass...
A few steps, steady
along the street!
And, a few along the highway,
faster than the heartbeat...

From the palaces of stone,
to fragile homes of glass...
to the nests made of twigs;
all of it, from here they pass...
From this bend!

 – Trans-created on 23rd January, 2017 by SharadKamal Bezboruah.

150. Dhan Dhan Dharti...

Lyrics: Gulzar. (Celebrating the spirit of a nation, as it sets feet into its 'diamond' year)

The skies aged,
look down upon the earth.
Hail this soil,
hail; hail this soil.

This soil has borne
so much bloodshed for ages.
The corpse, always,
on its back carries the Ganges.

So many shooting stars,
on it have fallen.
So many suns, on it did set.
Hail oh, this soil,
Hail oh soil! You are indeed great.

Hail this soil! Hail, hail this soil.

At a partition,
on it are the boundaries marked.
In drought, it is this soil that cracks;
this second it lives,
the next, it faces the sharks.

Hail oh, this soil;
for it takes upon itself these tasks.

Hail this soil! Hail, hail this soil.

May these stains on the soil be washed;
by someone, to say at the least.
May its gardens, that lay crushed,
again be replenished!
As the drops of dew descend,
every night, every day,
the same, they have wished.

Hail this soil! Hail, hail this soil.

The skies aged,
look down on the earth.
Hail this soil,
hail; hail this soil.

  – Trans-created on 18th August, 2017 by Sharad Kamal Bezboruah.

151. Jalte Hai Jiske Liye....

– MAJROOH SULTANPURI.

The song for which
the lamps in your eyes sparkle...
I have brought here,
for you; the same jingle.

The one which, remained,
in the heart...
Like a pain, failing to lessen...
The one which, like magic,
stuck to your eyes, stiffened...
The song for which your eyes glow...
today, I have brought for you...

It, in your heart,
you must keep...
From the hands,
never let it slip...
The song is delicate,
more fragile than glass...
Make sure it doesn't break!
I shall hum this very song;
I shall hum on, for you, thus...

Till it doesn't reach your lips,
it shall wander on,
under the shade of your tress...
I shall sing on, this very song,
I shall sing on, for you, yes...!!

The song for which your eyes glow...
I have brought the same,
for you...
The song for which your eyes glow...!

– Trans-created on 6th June, 2016 by Sharad Kamal Bezboruah.

152. *Kabhi Kisiko Muqqammal Jahaan Nahi Milta...*

— Nida Fazli.

When does one ever get the world entire?
For somewhere there isn't the earth;
and somewhere there aren't the skies.
When does one ever get the world entire?

When does one ever get the world entire?
Everyone here appears lost;
never of themselves are they ever tired!
We have all a tongue,
yet to speak to, but there is none...
When does one ever get the world entire?

When does one ever get the world entire?
Who has ever been able to extinguish,
of time, the flames!?
For this is the fire;
of which the smoke none sees...
When does one ever get the world entire?

When does one ever get the world entire?
For somewhere there isn't the earth;

and somewhere there aren't the skies.
It's only that you don't find it where you desire;
otherwise, there's enough love in your world to suffice!
When does one ever get the world entire?

– Translated on 23rd June, 2017 by Sharad Kamal Bezboruah.

153. Mujhse Pehli Si Mohabbat

– FAIZ AHMAD FAIZ.

From me,
love like times olden;
oh beloved, sought not.

I thought, with you around,
radiant is life;
with the agony of your separation,
battling the pain of the world;
where stands?
From your face,
learns endurance, the very essence of spring;
in this world, beyond your eyes,
what else does lie?

'Were you to be mine,
faith; at my feet would rest;
but it weren't so...
Only a desire that didn't manifest.

The world knows of more pain,
than of love alone;
to comfort other than that of union
they are known. '

Of the countless centuries,
the dreary dark spells;
in silk, satin and the like, spun.
In souks and corners, sold are the bodies
as it is; wrapped in ashes
drenched in blood...
(And), bodies popping out of the ovens of diseases;
and humours oozing out,
of tender wounds and scratches.

"The eyes, that way,
even today they turn; alas;
Even today, your beauty
compels to yearn, but, alas;

The world knows of more pain,
than of love alone;
to comfort other than that of union
they are known. "

– Trans-created on 12th July, 2018 by Sharad Kamal Bezboruah.
(At the 'Bhuyan's'; Itavata, Digboi)

154. Ae Gham-E-Dil

— Majaz Lucknawi.

The night of the city;
and I wander,
jobless and dismal;
on the streets awoke,
under the twinkle;
oh, how many strokes;
oh, how many more,
on how many doors?
Oh heart in agony,
what do I do?
Tell me you loony,
what do I do?

The Kumkum
that on foreheads twinkles;
along its way,
lay like shackles...
In the hands of the night,
like a portrait,
the enchantress
of the day; but, alas,
like a sword, straight
straight on my chest...

strikes!
Oh heart in agony,
what do I do?
Tell me you loony,
what do I do?

This silver shade;
in the skies,
of stars, the knots...
like the fancy of a Sufi poet;
or of a lover, the thoughts.
Oh! But, who would know,
why this heart wreaks and does wrought?
Oh heart in agony,
what do I do?
Tell me you loony,
what do I do?

Yet another shooting star,
yet again the sparklers fountain...
On whose lap did fall,
the string of pearls, who did gain?
The wound was on the heart,
and in the chest; arisen, the pain.
Oh heart in agony,
what do I do?
Tell me you loony,
what do I do?

It isn't much of me,
on way, to pause;
to breathe or wait...

Nor is it to return;
to turn my feet
or change my gait.
And, that I find someone
along the way,
when was ever such my fate!
Oh heart in agony,
what do I do?
Tell me you loony,
what do I do?

The night, giggling,
tells me
"come along,
to the tavern…if you would;
then, we shall head to the boudoir
of the lady so lovely and good…
If neither would suit you fine,
then very well, let's head to solitude."
Oh heart in agony,
what do I do?
Tell me you loony,
what do I do?

Scattered all over,
is the colour and the grace;
at every yard,
intimacies stretch,
and with arms to embrace,
the detractions, forth they pace.
Oh heart in agony,

what do I do?
Tell me you loony,
what do I do?

These stars and the moon, dead;
all of it, I wish to pluck,
to pluck at this end,
I wish, and at that end too
I wish to pluck.
Of one or two, what is to be said,
spoken of?
Let me just pluck
the entire hundred
zillion in a bulk.
Oh heart in agony,
what do I do?
Tell me you loony,
what do I do?

Oh heart in agony,
what do I do?
Tell me you loony,
what do I do?
As fate would put it,
I, a lotus in water, soiled.
The palaces of my aspirations
would all be shattered.
And leaving me in turmoil,
who knew my fate too would be altered...
Oh heart in agony,
what do I do?

Tell me you loony,
what do I do?

Oh, will you turn away, sulk,
at a helpless, and
more helpless make?
Will someone come,
and everything will take;
the same way I have been robbed by fate?
Oh broken heart, tell me,
if even more, you are yet to break.
Oh heart in agony,
what do I do?
Tell me you loony,
what do I do?

Awaits me yet another,
storm of trails;
Oh! How many doors for me,
even today, there do lie.
The only hindrance here;
is alone this loyalty of mine.
Oh heart in agony,
what do I do?
Tell me you loony,
what do I do?

To break the promises
of loyalty, oh how I wish.
All the hope of her being mine
too I must leave...
Also, cut free the shackles

that these winds did weave.
Oh heart in agony,
what do I do?
Tell me you loony,
what do I do?

A heart, ablaze,
what do I do?
In the goblet, a splash,
what do I do?
Fragrant, the scratch,
the wound in the heart;
what do I do?

From the corner of the castle,
gleams the yellow moonlight.
Like the humility of the Mullah,
like the ledger of the merchant;
like the youth of the penniless,
or the youthful widow left to lament.
Oh heart in agony,
what do I do?
Tell me you loony,
what do I do?

Penury and these reflections,
lie before me, behold.
Hundreds of experts too,
who come to console;
of Genghis Khan and Nadir Shah,
before me lies an army whole.
Oh heart in agony,

what do I do?
Tell me you loony,
what do I do?

From the hands to Genghis
I shall snatch the dagger
and break it...
Such is my anger,
that I shall even break the stone
glimmering on his crown.
Whether someone does it or not,
I shall do it on my own.
Oh heart in agony,
what do I do?
Tell me you loony,
what do I do?

I shall burn down
everything in this court...
Burn down this one's garden,
and this one's chambers.
Along with the throne of the mighty,
I shall reduce everything to embers.
Oh heart in agony,
what do I do?
Tell me you loony,
what do I do?

— Trans-created on 22nd November, 2017 by Sharad Kamal Bezboruah.

Extended and Adapted: 11th February, 2018.

155. Channa Mereya

Lyrics- Amitabh Bhattacharya.

Well then,
I take your leave...
Remember me in your prayers!
The taste of these words,
do keep, on of your lips, the layers...
In the treasury of your heart,
do keep my good deeds...
In the stars tiny too;
my greetings do read!
Taking away your darkness, gloom;
I leave for you, my star lit!
Of the light of my soul,
oh beloved, every bit...

From your doorstep
my way I turn and leave...
For, Sandal am I,
to leave my fragrance;
I burn and leave!
All the attachment I had,
underneath your pillow you'd spot;
I, a wanderer, leave now,
wrapping myself in a nomad's thin cloth...

So what if I am not in your gathering,
I know, I ought not sulk...
For, instances of our intimacy,
are how many; do you need to ask?
Oh! How many mornings;
sitting, in your yard,
I have watched turn to dusk...

Taking away your darkness, gloom;
I leave for you, my star lit!
Of the light of my soul;
oh beloved, every bit!!

True love is perhaps that
which your sanity does seize...
But, in the friendship of two hearts too,
there is so much peace!
Separating me from you thus,
perhaps the lord wanted to show me this!

Taking away your darkness, gloom;
I leave for you, my star lit!
Of the light of my soul;
oh beloved, every bit!!

– Trans-created on 2nd April 2017, by Sharad Kamal Bezboruah.

156. Agar Tum Saath Ho...

Lyrics: Irshaad Kamil.

For a second pause,
so that; for once,
the heart can settle...
Tell me how I can hold you back!
Every pain coming my way;
be it large or little-
shall slip away... before it can attack...
I shall pull and absorb you
into my eyes black...

Without uttering a word,
I shall speak, what I is to spake...
If it is with you,
that every step I shall take...

I flow on,
in your world...
Like a river in it...
My world,
in and into...your love; it does fit...
It's like; I fade away, mingle,
in your every habit...
If it is with you, that I take
step every single...

In your eyes, are dreams,
in your dreams, is annoyance…
I feel the talks from the heart,
are all tricks of the words, nothing else….
Whether you're around or not,
what does it make any difference…!
Ruthless has been life, lifelong,
and still remains ruthless…

If it is with you,
that every step I would take…

With the blink of the eye,
the day ends…
As I sit on,
my mind wanders off…
and I rush about there, wherever it takes!
Every pain coming my way;
bit it large or little-
shall slip away… before it can attack…
You, I shall pull into,
my eyes black…

Without uttering a word,
I shall speak, what I is to spake…
If it is with you,
that every step I shall take…

In your eyes, are dreams,
in your dreams, is annoyance…
I feel the talks from the heart,
are all tricks of the words, nothing else….

Whether you're around or not,
what does it make any difference…!
Ruthless has been life, lifelong,
and still remains ruthless…

If it is with you,
that every step I shall take…
the heart shall settle…
If it is with you,
that every step I shall take…
Every pain; large or little…
shall slide away…
If it is with you,
that every step I shall take…
The day shall pass with a blink…
If it is with you,
that every step I shall take…
Every pain shall….slip and sink…!!!!

– Trans-created on 11th February 2016, by Sharad Kamal Bezboruah.

157. Aye Mere Pyaare Watan…

Lyrics: Prem Dhawan.

Oh my country,

so close to my heart!

Oh my, long-lost orchard…!!

This heart, to you I surrender…

You are my desire,

my honour…

You, thus are my life, no wonder…

Oh my country,

so close to my heart!

Oh my, long-lost orchard…!!

This heart, to you I surrender…

From your lap;

the breeze that comes…. I salute…

I shall kiss the very lip,

onto which you lovely name comes…

Most beautiful, your morning,

most colourful is your dusk…

This shall be my answer,

let anyone ask…

You are my desire,

my honour…

You, thus are my life, no wonder…

Sometimes, like the heart of a mother,
me you come and hug…
And, sometimes, you being a little daughter,
me your memories bug…
As much you are remembered,
so much you make me anxious…
This heart, to you I surrender…
You are my desire,
my honour…
You, thus are my life, no wonder…

Leaving behind your place, your land…
So far, I have come…
So far away, today I sit…
Even then, in the heart does stand,
the same desire…
I swear in the name of your every bit…
That, my life, there itself it must end,
where I had been born,
where I had begun it…
This heart, to you I surrender…
You are my desire,
my honour…
You, thus are my life, no wonder…

Oh my country,
so close to my heart!
Oh my, long-lost orchard…!!
This heart, to you I surrender…

– Trans-created on 25th September, 2014 by Sharad Kamal Bezboruah.

158. Chal Wahaan Jaate Hain...

– Rashmi Virag.

Beyond the skies,
there must be a world.
Where, of the concept of truth and lies;
none has heard.

Where the light
has a divine glow;
where beyond the bodies,
rush the shadows;
let's move there,
into that world let's go.

Let's move there,
into that world let's go.
Our love, to share;
into that world let's go!

Come,
come close.
What do you fear?
Come, hold me close.
Let me listen to the music,
from these heartbeats;
that arose.

Let's move there,
into that world let's go.

Let's move there,
into that world let's go.
Our love, to share;
into that world let's go!

Where no dawn
meets the night bleak;
let you and I
such a world seek.
I've brought the wings,
come, put them on;
let's go!
Let's move there,
into that world let's go.

Let's move there,
into that world let's go.
Our love, to share;
into that world let's go!

– Translated on 26th June, 2017 by Sharad Kamal Bezboruah.

159. Aa Chal Ke Tujhe...Main Leke Chalun...

– KISHORE KUMAR.

Come... Let me, take you there, underneath
such skies, where...
There would be no sorrow, no tears,
where only sprout, of love the seeds...
Such, the skies, and we underneath!

With the first ray of sunlight,
where the dawn of hope awakes!
And, bathed in the moonlight,
where the darkness bleak breaks...
Once the sun, let shine,
once....the shade, let greet...
And, the long pathway does not,
tire yours and mine feet...
Where would be no sorrow, no tears,
where only sprout, of love the seeds...
Such, the skies, and we underneath!

Where the sight sprints...far...
And, the vast skies flutter!!
Where the colourful-winged birds,
messages of hope they deliver...
Where, in dreams blossom,
the blossoms filled with laughter...

Where the delightful dusk sets neat!!
Where would be no sorrow, no tears,
where only sprout, of love the seeds...
Such, the skies, and we underneath!

In such a world of dreams and aspirations,
where love has bloomed...
like the blossoms fragrant.
Let us lose ourselves there;
without an issue, without a complaint...
Be there no enemy;
none a stranger, no reason to lament...
Let us move hand in hand,
wherever takes the roads bent...
To there...
Where would be no sorrow, no tears,
where only sprout, of love the seeds...
Such, the skies, and we underneath!

– Trans-created on 5th August, 2016 by Sharad Kamal Bezboruah.

160. Chand Tanha......

AASMAAN TANHA
– MEENA KUMARI 'NAAZ'...

The moon, forlorn,
the skies, all forlorn;
the heart, though found,
but somewhere lies, all forlorn.

Hope extinguished;
the star, hid in disguise...
All along, the smoke
shivered on; did rise, all forlorn.
The moon, forlorn,
the skies, all forlorn!

Is this what is called life?
The body and soul lay apart,
both lay aside, all forlorn.
If I ever did get a companion;
he would stay beside
but we both would stride, all forlorn.
The moon, forlorn,
the skies, all forlorn!

Like a flickering light,
shrinking, cringing a house;

whose walls, in do slide; all forlorn.
The moon, forlorn,
the skies, all forlorn!

The world shall await me,
for centuries to come;
I shall leave...
At my demise; all forlorn.
The moon, forlorn,
the skies, all forlorn!

– Translated on 08th June, 2019 by Sharad Kamal Bezboruah.

161. Ik Tu Hi Tu Hi Tu Hi...

Lyrics: Irshaad Kamil.

Your town, now that it's being left behind,
something is shattering deep within.
From where does this waterfall slide?
Astonished are both my eyes…

Whenever you wanted to, you made be cry,
whenever you wanted to, you made me smile.
Whenever you wanted to, in yourself you made me dwell.
Now it's only you, all the while.

I live on still though,
my Lord, my Almighty King is lost.
I live on still though,
all of it, everything is lost.

Your love,
my shadow it has annexed.
Your love,
it has troubled so much and made me vexed.
I went empty-handed
and returning empty-handed is what I did next.

I live on still though,
my Lord, my Almighty King is lost.

I live on still though,
all of it, everything is lost.

Whenever you wanted to, you made be cry,
whenever you wanted to, you made me smile.
Whenever you wanted to, in yourself you made me dwell.
Now it's only you, all the while.

It's like, on broken glass
on a journey when you embark.
It's like, blazing on the flame,
arising from that painful spark.
All the pain, this life now can't bear.
Somehow drinking poison or getting crucified,
if I lose my life. Only then shall the pain no more be there.
This is how time passes, my life gets shorter
and all the dreams are crumbled into a disorder.

It's like, on broken glass
on a journey when you embark.
It's like, blazing in the flame,
arising from that painful spark.
All the pain, this life now can't take.
Against the distances, no other pain does seem to matter,
and all joy and bliss seems to be fake.
Every second, bit by bit, this heart does shatter.

I still live on though,
my Lord, my Almighty King is lost.

From the pot of the heart, reaching for the seven seas,
why do these tears spill?

These five streams too now are astonished.
The notes of body and mind,
once so melodious, now this pain did kill.
How do I kill this pain?
How do I forget you?
The lost one, how do I regain?
Someone tell me, how to,
if this bond I have to maintain…

From the pot of the heart, like for the seven seas,
why do these tears spill?
The streams too now are astonished.
Your love has given rights too, and its pain also did kill.
Without you, I've lived, all dead, a million times.

I still live on though,
my Lord, my Almighty King is lost.
I still live on though,
all of it, everything is lost.

Whenever you wanted to, you made be cry,
whenever you wanted to, you made me smile.
Whenever you wanted to, in yourself you made me dwell.
Now it's only you, all the while.

Whenever you wanted to, you made be cry,
whenever you wanted to, you made me smile.
Whenever you wanted to, in yourself you made me dwell.
Now it's only you, all the while.

– Trans-created 23rd November, 2013 by Sharad Kamal Bezboruah.

162. Poore Se Zaraa Sa Kam Hai...

Lyrics: Irshaad Kamil.

A little less than complete…
A little less than complete…

The fact you and I
are here, is there…
You and I being there;
You're the air that fleets,
I'm its weather…
I am,
A little less than complete…

You're the river,
I am its bank…
I am its current…
And without you,
thus I vent,
A little less than complete…
A little less than complete…
And hence, I go looking for you,
at every square, every street.

I am,
A little less than complete,
a little less than complete…

Without you, what is a gain,
what is loss!
You're my messiah,
the remover of my pain;
you're my beloved.
One who fills life with delight…
You are the eye,
I am the view seen by the sight.
I am your signal, the sign;
Without you,
A little less than complete…
Though not much
only a bit…
But, yet,
a little less than complete…

I am…
A little less than complete…
A little less than complete…

– Translated on 28th June, 2014 by Sharad Kamal Bezboruah.

163. Rabba Main Toh Marr Gaya Oi..

Lyrics: Irshaad Kamil.

Someone came and made this heart lose control,

for with love, this heart she has fed.

Oh! Not speaking a word,

with her eyes, so much she has said.

God knows what she came and did,

it made me feel like I'm dead.

Now this heart, feels like writing,

on the lips of silence, many words sweet.

For few moments, let her take my name,

and in her name, God, let us meet!

At the first glance, she made a mark on my life;

her eyes were imprinted on this heart of mine.

Where else shall I go?

This heart is stuck there.....

Where she had (took) a glance of me and had moved ahead.

God knows what she came and did,

it made me feel like I'm dead.

Do the blossoms of spring dance to her tune,

or are the free birds of the weather in her custody?

She's like the sunshine of the winter, she the evening of the summer,

she's like the first rains of monsoon!

(She's the season in which my love awakens, my perfect lady!)2

In her two eyes, God knows what not I had read!
(God knows what she came and did,
it's made me feel like I'm dead.)2.

Someone came and made this heart lose control,
for with love, this heart she has fed.
Oh! Not speaking a word,
with her eyes, so much she has said.
God knows what she came and did,
it made me feel like I'm dead.

–Translated on 19th April, 2013 by Sharad Kamal Bezboruah.

164. O Rangrez

Lyricist: Prasoon Joshi.
(Credits, team 'Drenched' and others)

Oh dyer,
oh beloved dyer;
in of your colours,
the stream...
I wish to drown away,
forget how to swim.
Never do I wish to stay another.

Nor even one breath,
I wish to breathe, away;
Pull the life out of me, instead...
If I had to be another,
I'd rather be dead.

In your colour, oh beloved;
so subtle...so fragrant;
dip me, paint me, colour;
so that I remain, no different.

Anklet, you are;
I the feet...jingle,
you the Peepal, I the shade;
and thus at peace, I settle.

Oh! In the eyes,
your picture alone does sparkle;
and then they brim,
and finally drizzle.

In your colour, oh beloved;
so subtle...so fragrant;
dip me, paint me, colour;
so that I remain, no different.

Into a garland, come
let me weave you, together
and wear, oh beloved...
Onto my lips, come, become a melody;
so, I can rote you; remember.

Oh beloved!
All the pain, lingering;
grind away, mince, crush...
and then, into me, blend;
blend away into me, melt;
melt and further blend into me.

In your colour, oh beloved;
so subtle...so fragrant;
dip me, paint me, colour;
so that I remain, no different.

Oh dyer,
oh beloved dyer;
in of your colours,
the stream...

I wish to drown away,
forgetting how to swim.
Never do I wish to stay another.

In your colour, oh beloved;
so subtle...so fragrant;
dip me, paint me, colour;
so that I remain, no different.

– Trans-created on 11th April 2020, by Sharad Kamal Bezboruah.

165. Kisi Ranjish ko Hawaa Do!

— Sudarshan Faakir.

Fan the flames of some pain,
for now I still live…
The fact that I still am alive,
make me feel and believe…
Fan the flames of some anguish...
So that; this life,
from death, I can distinguish...

If I pause,
so will my breath…
But, I still live,
so, of the journey ahead,
increase the length…
The fact that I still am alive,
make me feel and believe…
Fan the flames of some anguish...
So that; this life,
from death, I can distinguish...

To drinking poison…used to,
(habituated) I've always been…
I still live,
so, oh people, now,
some other medicine,
bring…

For I still live…
Fan some (yet another) anguish…
So that; this life,
from death, I can distinguish…

In the journey so long,
travelling…
the tired eyes have shut,
but only for a while…
I still go strong, Faakir,
so, ask the crowd to step aside….
I still live,
and will now take things on my stride…
Fan the flames of some anguish…
So that; this life,
from death, I can distinguish…

Fan the flames of some pain,
for now I still live…
The fact that I still am alive,
make me feel and believe…
Fan the flames of some anguish…
So that; this life,
from death, I can distinguish…

Fan the flames of some pain,
for now I still live…
The fact that I still am alive,
make me feel and believe…
Fan the flames of some anguish…
So that; this life,
from death, I can distinguish…

– Trans-created on 11th February 2016, by Sharad Kamal Bezboruah.

166. Ae Dil E Nadaan.

– Jan Nisar Akhtar.

Oh humble heart,
what do you seek?
Oh humble heart,
what do you wish for?

I wander,
Oh why I wander
in the forest,
and in the desert.
Like in the river
too; the currents feel
of water, the dearth.

What a dilemma,
why so much it puzzles?
Like a shadow
before the eyes,
what is it that settles?

Oh humble heart,
what do you seek?
Oh humble heart,
what do you wish for?

What doom, oh,
what trouble, oh lord;
none can say whose wishes.
Like, life be lost somewhere;
this life, all of this astonishes.

The skies and the earth,
silent they do sit.
Then, from where does
all around, arise this heartbeat?

Oh humble heart!

– Trans-created on 19th August, 2017 by Sharad Kamal Bezboruah.

167. Samandar Saare Sharaab Hote...

– UNKNOWN.

If all the seas were filled with wine...
Imagine what disorder!!
If for crimes,
there were rewards and not fine!
Imagine what disorder!!

What one hides within him,
only knows the Divine...
Imagine what disorder!!
If their faces; masks didn't define...

For years, I went on doing
what I had to, with a whine...
For my nature; it has always been of silence!
If there were answers on the lips of even mine,
imagine what disorder!!
I wasn't ever too bad,
but, in their eyes I remained a swine...
Imagine what disorder!!
If I was truly one;
if I too did cross the line...!

If all the seas were filled with wine...
Imagine what disorder!!

– Trans-created on 5th November, 2016 by Sharad Kamal Bezboruah.

168. Solah Baras Ki...

– Anand Bakshi.

(Celebrating the spirit of 'Sixteen', 2013; our time; yet upholding timelessness of this piece, nonetheless)

Salutations to the tender age of sixteen...
A salutation to you, the first sight of love's beginning.
Hats off to the one who lost his heart for first time ever,
salutations to the world's first lover.
Which begins from this heart, a million times I thank that street.
I offer salutations to that path, the other heart which goes and meets.
A salutation to you....the first sight of love's beginning.
A salutation!
Oh! To you, the first sight of love's beginning.

Where we grew young and were accused thus,
hats off to that town, at the gate of that house, the street which bends.
That which made as meet, that which separated us,
salutations to that time, that second, that very moment.
A salutation to you....the first sight of love's beginning.
A salutation!
Oh! To you, the first sight of love's beginning.

We have met many times here, here it is writ...
Hats off to the victory of these writings,
for over so many years, them none could defeat.

My heart once swayed on the sands of this beach.
Of this ocean, I offer a salutation to wave each.
The beautiful, deep lakes of the eyes;
salutations to the whirlpool; for in those lakes drowned
me; and that spread open and glided down from the head,
to salute the bravery of that worn, green veil I am bound...

The enemies of love, they did try a lot;
but yet never were lowered,
salutations to those eyes...

A salutation to you....the first sight of love's beginning.
A salutation!
Oh! To you, the first sight of love's beginning.

Salutations to the tender age of sixteen...
A salutation to you, the first sight of love's beginning.

    – Trans-created on 18th February, 2014 by SharadKamal Bezboruah.

169. *Jaane Woh Kaise Log The Jinke Pyaar Ko Pyaar Mila...*

Lyricist :-Sahir Ludhiyanvi.

God knows who were those;
whose love found love...at the end...
When I sought for blossoms,
instead, I was presented with, of thorns a garland...
God knows who were those;
whose love found love...at the end...

When I went in search of a place of joy,
I found, of sorrow the sand, the dirt...
Of affection, love when I sought melodies,
I was treated with sighs chilled or replies curt.
The burden on this heart was doubled,
by whoever, made the pain descend.
When I sought for blossoms,
instead, I was presented with; of thorns a garland...
God knows!! Who were those;
whose love found love... at the end...!

Drifted away...
Drifted away...
Drifted away every companion,
every journey mate...

stopping by for a moment or two...
Who had the leisure to wait,
to pause to hold, of an inane the hand...
To me, even my shadow,
showed cold shoulders, and went...
When I sought for blossoms,
instead, I was presented with; of thorns a garland...
God knows!! Who were those;
whose love found love... at the end...!

If this is called life,
I shall live on this way...
Not a word I shall utter,
my lips I'll stitch...
I shall drink every tear,
not one drop I shall let scatter...
Now, from pain, why fear,
a hundred times to me, many did send...
When I sought for blossoms,
instead, I was presented with; of thorns a garland...
God knows!! Who were those;
whose love found love... at the end...!

– Trans-created on 21ˢᵗ August, 2016 by Sharad Kamal Bezboruah.

170. Main Shaayar Badnaam...

– Anand Bakshi.

A poet defamed,
I leave now, farewell...
In the alliance of poets,
a title, incapable to claim...
Farewell!

In the house of this poet,
you shall find laid...
the following:
A cot, my bed;
and another thing that is,
a broken bottle, of ale red...
Farewell...

A poet defamed,
I leave now, farewell...

I was to walk on many an ember;
and sleep on many a thorn!
Many a time I was to cry,
questioning why I was born...
I wonder how many more,
jobs remain of kind the same!
Farewell!

A poet defamed,
I leave now, farewell...

The path is obstructed;
a bit of life remains...
In the heart, destructed,
wonder what wishes remain!
Let it be, oh heart,
taking the lord's name...
Farewell! Farewell to all...
A poet defamed,
I leave now, farewell...

A poet defamed,
I leave now, farewell...
In the alliance of poets,
a title, incapable to claim...
Farewell!

– Trans-created on 22nd August, 2016 by Sharad Kamal Bezboruah.

171. Aur Kya..Ehd-e- Wafaa Hote Hai...

– Anand Bakshi.

What else to uphold, than faith and loyalty?
People only meet and to soon depart...

"No doubt, the ones who love, are not less,
yet... without your company, I remain in a mess".

Who knows when we separate,
we're only journey mates.
Who knows when it might,
flip over, and alter; that one sight...
To which are etched, lost, both my soul and heart!
People only meet to soon depart...
What else to uphold, than faith and loyalty?

"I have lost for I said we're two,
the truth is...I am yours, and mine are you!"

A talk of this generation did arise,
the one that is in the habit of forgetting...
But, why is it that you get annoyed,
only to see me lamenting...?
When one doesn't show up, there isn't a point in waiting!
What else to uphold, than faith and loyalty?

When he has made me cry till his heart's content,
when he has troubled me till his heart's content…
he seems to be a bit happy only then!
What else to uphold, than faith and loyalty?

    – Translated on 31st July, 2013 by Sharad Kamal Bezboruah.

172. Maana KE Hum Yaar Nahin...

Lyrics: KAUSAR MUNIR.

Agreed, I am not your beloved...
Sure, there isn't love!
Even then, don't look into the eyes,
for, of the heart, nothing can be said...
Agreed, I am not your beloved...

If ever you cross;
to shake hands,
do pause...
If you are with someone then;
from a distance,
just smile across...
But the smile be such,
that no one knows,
if it has, of commitment
the slightest touch!
That which you can't deny,
never through the eyes,
speak of it, you must!

Agreed, I am not your beloved...

The old rose
between the pages,

crumple, crumble and
turn to dust!
If anyone asks of me ever;
call it a mistake,
if you must...
But, let the mistake be such,
that it brings no regrets...
And, when you sleep,
be it that, to have peace;
you too, something never lets!

Agreed I am not your beloved...

– Translated on 23rd June, 2017 by Sharad Kamal Bezboruah.

173. Sun Ri Baavli
(Lyrics: Manoj Yadav)

– Angaraag Papon Mahanta.

Listen, oh crazy gal…
Call out prayers for yourself
on your own…
You shall have none to call a pal,
no one of your own…
The one in front,
who seems to be a saviour…
shall not be one…

The apartment of the body frame,
of the heart, the room…
of the breaths the game!
In your hair, keep the sunlight safe,
of the night; you might have to face the gloom.

Listen, oh crazy gal…
Call out prayers for yourself
on your own…
You shall have none to call a pal,
no one of your own…

Pick the shooting stars,
out of them make the moon…

Holding the edge of your cloth,
with it, the skies you must weave…
For shade, the bride,
the palanquin, sunlight,
has been brought.
The habit of loving yourself, never leave.
In your hair, keep the sunlight safe,
a fight with the night may have to be fought…

Fly away whenever you wish to…
What's there to ask the elders?!
You are your own inspiration…!
Let the moment imprint the letters
it wishes to… Don't stop its fingers…
In your hair, keep the sunlight safe,
a fight with the night may have to be fought…

Listen, oh crazy gal…
Call out prayers for yourself
on your own…
You shall have none to call a pal,
no one of your own…
The one in front,
who seems to be a saviour…
shall not be one…

The apartment of the body frame,
of the heart the room…
of the breaths the game!
In your hair, keep the sunlight safe,
of the night; you might have to face the gloom.

Listen, oh crazy gal…
Call out prayers for yourself
on your own…
You shall have none to call a pal,
no one of your own…
Listen, oh crazy gal…!!
Listen, oh crazy gal…!!
Listen, oh crazy gal…!!

– Trans-created on 16th April, 2014 by Sharad Kamal Bezboruah.

174. Ik Sapne Mein Atkaa Hain Mann.....

Angaraag Mahanta.
Lyrics - Vaibhav Modi.

Why is there something like a miracle, a wonder…?
God knows where, why, how and when,
this heart has gone and got stuck.
God knows where, why, how and when,
this heart has gone and got stuck.

Its attitude; is now like that of the wild weather.
Earlier it never, anywhere, ever, did wander.
At a dream, a hope
the heart has gone and got stuck.
At a dream, a hope
the heart has gone and got stuck.
And with that said; I barely can cope.

It has in it, like an afternoon,
of a lukewarm smile, a sip.
In it a soft, cozy shawl takes wone;
in it; a sweet, tickling sunray it does keep.

In the dream is a hope too…
It's your own too and yet not your own….
It all goes by luck.
At a dream, a hope, the heart has gone,

gone and got stuck.
At a dream, a hope
the heart has gone and got stuck.

– Translated on 27th December, 2013 by Sharad Kamal Bezboruah.

175. Deewano Ki Hasti...

– Bhagawaticharan Verma.

What is our existence?

We have been wanderers,
we're the same today.
Today we're here, tomorrow there.
A sense of humor followed along,
wherever we've gone, blowing dust off the way.
What is our existence?
We have been wanderers,
we're the same today.

Now, we've come as happiness;
and now, we're gone... flowing away as tears.
All looked on and only called out,
"Oh! How did you come, where are you off to?"
What is our existence? We are and always have been wanderers!

Do not ask, in which direction we go,
for we only move for we're meant to move.
Taking something from the world and then,
giving it back a lot more, hoping it'll improve.

Two words I spoke, two words I heard,
laughed a bit and then cried out.

Though it sounds a bit absurd,
I drank in joy and pain together,
through the same mouth.
What is our existence?
We are, and always have been wanderers!

In the world of beggars,
I went squandering, the wealth called love.
I now go carrying at heart, this burden of failures,
like a token, a memory forever.
I was neither insulted nor honored.
I only gambled till my heart's content.
Now, here itself, laughing, giggling,
I have wagered my life too, in this last bet.

Now, who the loved ones, who foreigners,
happy shall remain the ones who live.
I had made them myself,
and now myself, break all ties,
wrongly must none perceive.

   – Translated on 2nd August, 2013 by Sharad Kamal Bezboruah.

176. Tu ISS Tarah Meri Zindagi Mein Shaamil Hai.

– Nida Fazli.

You are in my life thus,
that wherever I head to,
I find your gathering, your conclave.

The skies, the clouds, the roads,
the breeze… the wind…of the season,
everything is where it belongs…
For a long time, I haven't had,
any complaints with the age, the generations…
Life is a journey,
of which you are the destination…

Every blossom is fragrant,
like vivid memories…
In your thoughts, awakens the atmosphere…
Are these trees, or are they blessings of love?
Though you be or be not here,
yet your presence is felt.

Everything to be done,
is illuminated by of love, the light…
Life is incomplete in its absence!
In front, the roads of loyalty which run,

along those,

there must be a companion…

It shall be difficult, if

in case; the road is to be travelled alone.

In your absence,

there seems something missing….

Youth, it has been wandering in the dark…

Peace and stability, the heart has attained,

in your arms…

You're the shore, for me, an ark,

that has lost its way!

My universe is lightened up by your radiance;

my search, your sooth,

let them remain!

Oh lord! Be so, that,

this craze, this insane mood,

remain… Be the crazy around….

For, in your commitment,

every joy would be found…

You are in my life thus,

that wherever I head to,

I find your gathering, your conclave.

– Trans-created on 11th February 2016, by Sharad Kamal Bezboruah.

177. Jeevan Ke Safar Mein Raahi...

Lyricist:-Sahir Ludhiyanvi

In this journey of life,
people meet only to part...
And, in solitude, to make you anxious,
they leave memories in the heart!

The ones rich of beauty
....who stand tall...
when do they ever hear;
the heart's call...!!
God forbid, if ever;
in the traps of fate,
their lovers fall...

In this journey of life,
people meet only to part...
And, in solitude, to make you anxious,
they leave memories in the heart!

Whoever with their eyes,
does play...
They get pain in life,
and on them, trouble lay...
All of them, they wander;
to seize hearts and turn away...

In this journey of life,
people meet only to part...
And, in solitude, to make you anxious,
they leave memories in the heart!

In return of the heart,
they can only cheat...
On us, of illnesses,
they leave a fleet...
Laughing away, each time,
like the moth, their lovers they lit...

In this journey of life,
people met only to part...
And, in solitude, to make you anxious,
they leave memories in the heart!

– Trans-created on 1ˢᵗ July, 2016 by Sharad Kamal Bezboruah.

178. Jeena Isi Ka Naam Hai...

– Shailendra
(Shankardas Kesarilal)

When you lose yourself watching someone smile;
when someone's sorrow you borrow for a while...
When you fall in love with one in style...
That's what I would call life!
Now, that's what I would call life...

When you lose yourself watching someone smile;
when someone's sorrow you borrow for a while...
When you fall in love with one in style...
That's what I would call life!
Now, that's what I would call life...

I admit in the pocket, there isn't a penny...
Even then, in the heart, lives affluence...see!
Life is that, for love that does wane...
Life is that, for spring that burns in pain!
Whether or not anyone has faith in it,
I do believe very well...
That to be called life, only this is fit...

The bond between hearts, of trust;
it is for us that love hasn't yet caught rust...
Even after death, me,

I shall see someone remembers...
I shall dwell and smile,
within someone's tears...
The flower shall speak to the buds and say,
repeatedly, this line...
that, if asked what is to be called life,
it is described in these words of mine...

When you lose yourself watching someone smile;
when someone's sorrow you borrow for a while...
When you fall in love with one in style...
That's what I would call life!
Now, that's what I would call life...

   – Trans-created on 6th September, 2016 by Sharad Kamal Bezboruah.

179. Bahaut Pehle Se...

– Firaq Gorakhpuri.

I know the approach of those footsteps
at one instance!
Oh life, you I recognise,
I recognise you, oh life;
from quite a distance...

When I get the shivers, in the silent night,
I pull over me, the blanket of your memories!!
Oh life...I know it is you,
even when I hear, yours, a movement slight...

My eyes; even these,
are the life and faith of those...
When eyes meet,
one's life and faith, who seize!!

At one instance...

Often the wicked comes disguised,
says Firaq;
sometimes I know, and sometimes,
the distinctions I succeed to mark!

I know the approach of those footsteps
at one instance!

Oh life, you I recognise,
I recognise you, oh life...from quite a distance...

At one instance...

– Trans-created on 30th November, 2016 by Sharad Kamal Bezboruah.

180. Mera Kuch Saamaan...

Lyrics: Gulzar.

A few of my belongings
lay there with you...
A few wet days of monsoon!!
And, wrapped in a letter of mine,
a night under the moon....
Let that night pass by,
smoothen this crease...
send them all down,
return all of it, please...

There's of autumn too, a handful;
isn't there??

....The sound of leaves shedding in autumn,
on my ears, I once wear,
and away I come...
The branch still hangs there,
trembling...
Break it off...
And, return all of my belongings...

When we were two,
and umbrella, only one single...
As we walked down under it,

half dry each, and half wet in the drizzle...
I brought the bit,
which was not wet...
The drenched heart of mine,
you shall perhaps find by the bed!
When you do,
please, to me do send...

A hundred and sixteen nights,
under the moonlight...
And, one, your shoulder,
the essence of wet Hena...
The few false complaints....
And, all the false promises; let me remind!!
It would be generous of you;
if you sent...
all that I have left behind...
If once, the assent you ever gave...
I shall bury it all,
and I too shall sleep,
there itself shall be found my grave...

I shall bury it all,
and I too shall sleep,
there itself shall be found my grave.

    – Trans-created on 1ˢᵗ July, 2016 by Sharad Kamal Bezboruah.

181. Yun Hasraton KE Daag...

– RAJINDER KISHAN.

The stains of desires,
thus, in love, I have washed...
The words of the heart,
I spoke out to itself...and,
then wept, and fell apart...

I set out, from home,
in search of joy...
There stood pain on the way,
and along it chose to come...
The words of the heart,
I spoke out to itself...and,
then wept, and fell apart...

The stains of desires....

The heart is a flower,
although withered...
Now, it's your choice,
if instead, you wish to
count the thorns gathered...
The words of the heart,
I spoke out to itself...and,
then wept, and fell apart...

The stains of desires....

When my lips
I chose to zip,
then the world said...
If there's something, speak;
to yourself, why do you keep...!!?
The words of the heart,
I spoke out to itself...and,
oh! How I did weep!!!

The stains of desires.....

– Trans-created on 26th May, 2016 by SharadKamal Bezboruah.

182. Jo Humne Daastaan Apni Sunaayi...

Lyrics: Raja Mehdi Ali Khan.

When my tale
I happened to narrate...
why did "You" whine and wail!!?
The turmoil was in my fate...
why did "You" whine and wail!!?

This is my pain and sorrow,
why do you take it all in!!?
Why these tears, do you borrow,
for, they're mine...
From your eyes, why let them flow!!?
The fire of pain I have lit myself;
into it, why yourself do you come, throw...!!?

When my tale
I happened to narrate...
why did "You" whine and wail!!?

A lot I did cry, now, for you,
I shall assure no tear pours...
No!! I shall not lose my peace,
nor make you lose yours...
These are but your tears
that are wasted!

Why do you cry...
when my tale you hear!!?

Then, when my tale
I happened to narrate...
why did "You" whine and wail!!?

If these tears, of yours, do not stop,
look, even I now feel an urge...
to cry! I too shall cry and,
these stars,
the moon, shall in tears submerge...
The entire divinity, the heavens;
nowhere it shall stand...
Why did you cry...!!?

Then, when my tale
I happened to narrate...
why did "You" whine and wail!!?

– Trans-created on 24th September, 2016 by Sharad Kamal Bezboruah.

183. Na Kisi Ki Aankh Ka Noor Hoon...

– MUZTAR KHAIRABADI.

Nor I am of one's pupils, the star;
nor the solace of one's heart.
Of use to none which are,
I am those few specks of dirt.

Nor I am the ointment
on the hurt
of the bosom;
neither, of one, the glance kind;
nor I am hither; nor thither,
nor the relief;
nor the sufferer.

I am discoloured, deformed;
my fate too has been, against me altered.
I am the bloom of spring
of the garden that autumn shattered.

Who would come and read me hymns,
who would offer flowers four.
Who would come and a candle light,
for I am the grave, in which are laid, the poor.

Nor I am an attachment, nor love,
nor a relationship to pursue.
Nor I am the knot of the wedding,
nor a long-sustained virtue.
I am the sculpture defaced,
of your maquillage, the faded hue.

I am not the song of the atmosphere,
not really something
that you would want to hear,
not at all.
Of the ailing, I am the moan,
of the anxious, I am the call.

Nor, I Muztar; am their beloved,
Nor, I Muztar, their foe.
I am but the fate re-writ,
I am but the town that was lit.

Nor I am of one's pupils, the star;
nor the solace of one's heart.
Of use to none which are,
I am those few specks of dirt.

   – Trans-created on 12th August, 2017 by Sharad Kamal Bezboruah.

184. Raat Hamaari Toh

Lyrics: Swanand Kirkire.

This night,
So black, oh so deep.
This night,
So dark, oh! So bleak!

Our night, of course, to be,
a friend of the moon is known;
but, after ages, today,
it has arrived, all alone.

Silence, sings a song
Of separation, of lament;
And, alongside;
the music of the cricket.

Our night, of course, to be,
a friend of the moon is known;
but, after ages, today,
it has arrived, all alone.

Of the evening lamp,
someone please blow out the wick;
for, today; with darkness,
I have a lot to speak.

The night is insane,
so, so, bleak;
But yet, it's mine to call,
Though it bites, stings, oh it pricks.) 2

On its lap, I am, to lean
My head and sleep;
In its arms, I ought to
Silently weep.

From the eyes,
as kohl;
This darkness
Thus, does roll.

Our night, of course, to be,
a friend of the moon is known;
but, after ages, today,
it has arrived, all alone.

– Translated on 25th April, 2020 by Sharad Kamal Bezboruah.(3:30 am)

185. Aankhein Khuli Ho Yaa Ho Bandh...

Anand Bakshi.
(Celebrating the spirit of 'Mohabbatein'; Shweta Pandit and YRF)

There was a girl, a bit crazy;
she was crazy for a boy.
With eyes bent,
a little coy,
she passed through many a street.
Silently and secretly,
many letters she had writ.
Perhaps, there was something she had to say,
but god knows whom she did fear.
Whenever we would meet,
she would enquire....
"How people fall in love,
can you tell me friend?"
And every time, I remember,
this was all I had said....-

"Be the eyes close or open...
it is the loved one you always see.
Dear mate...How do I say when,
and how in love people can be!"

Be the eyes close or open...
it is the loved one you always see.

Dear mate...How do I say when,
and how in love people can be!

Male:
Today itself, we shall check out,
for someone, how it is to die.
Female:
What love is all about;
to understand today we shall try...

Male:
Lost in the memory of someone,
many dreams I have woven...
Female:
Asleep in someone's arms,
it's he now whom I have chosen...

Male:
Oh mate! In love,
none sleep, none stay awake.
How do people fall in love, oh my...
The answer to this when anyone did spake?!!
So, how can I??

Female:
Is it some kind of magic,
which is just casted.
Male:
When in love, even a thousand guards,
against the heart has never for long lasted.
Female:
All these decisions, are made,

somewhere up above in the heavens.

Male:

Who knows when a meeting with the journey-mate,

of life is written in one's fate!

Male:

Whosever name is written in the heart,

it is that person whom the heart chooses.

I wonder how I should start,

to explain how one's heart one loses.

Be the eyes close or open...

it is the loved one you always see.

Dear mate...How do I say when,

and how in love people can be!

    – Trans-created on 6th March, 2014 by Sharad Kamal Bezboruah.

186. Keh Do Na...

– Shweta Pandit

Come on…
Say, you've got something in the heart, it seems.
Listen…
Listen to what I carry in my dreams.
Listen to it…
Listen…
Listen…

It's magic, so wild.
For long, the heart is desperate.
It is dementing… Listen,
it's a mistake I have made.
It is really intoxication… and yes it does pain,
something has definitely begun to happen.

Please read what is in the eyes,
I want you to keep with you what I have within,
you see.
Keep it…
Keep it, please.
It's a conspiracy, a desire.
This waiting has been so long,
it has begun to tire.

It is dementing… Listen,
it's a mistake I have made.
It is really intoxication… and yes it does pain,
something has definitely begun to happen.

It's a desire, a conspiracy.
For so long, the heart has been
desperate to see this intimacy.

It is dementing… Listen,
it's a mistake I have made.
It is really intoxication… and yes it does pain,
something has definitely begun to happen.

Say it…. Listen please.
Say what you have in the heart.

– Translated on 26th December, 2013 by Sharad Kamal Bezboruah.

187. Main Zindagi Hoon...

– Shweta Pandit

I admit I only listen, to the very heart my own,
a bit mischievous I am, I agree.
In the abode of dreams, I have grown.
What can I say, what my name is...?
I am life!
I am life!

Open up the wings of desires;
choose your happiness by yourself.
Sway along with the wind often;
by the heart is all the happiness...
To the heart, always listen.

I admit I only listen, to the very heart my own,
a bit mischievous I am, I agree.
In the abode of dreams, I have grown.
What can I say, what my name is...?
I am life!
I am life!

Do spend few moments like this,
with the flowers, you too sing.
Listen to the tunes sung out by waterfalls,
with open eyes, many dreams together do string.

I admit I only listen, to the very heart my own,
a bit mischievous I am, I agree.
In the abode of dreams, I have grown.
What can I say, what my name is…?
I am life!
I am life!

Life!!

Yes, I am Life….!!

  – Translated on 26th December, 2013 by Sharad Kamal Bezboruah.

188. Rangon Bhara Tumhara Jahaaan....

Shweta Pandit
Lyrics: Ajay Jhingran.

Full of colours is your world…

Full of colours is your world…
Whenever I think of you,
I give out fragrant sighs.
Why are you looked for
everywhere by my eyes?
You are my earth,
you are the skies.

Full of colours is your world…
Full of colours is your world…

It's because of you,
that built is the world of dreams.
Being a sort of feeling,
you dwell in my thoughts all the while.
Wherever my eyes go,
they see only your smile.
Even the mirrors do show,
only you, I tell.

Only this much,
is what makes my tale.

Full of colours is your world…
Full of colours is your world…

– Translated on 26th December, 2013 by Sharad Kamal Bezboruah.

189. Yeh Inaayatein Gazab Ki...

– Nazeer Banarasi.

This concern too is rather strange;
A fatal benevolence, this is...
To hear about my well-being too;
from another, now they please!

Has made to you weep
already' oh beloved, my pain!
The clouds that overhead sweep;
they speak, 'long gone is the rain'...

Your beauty lay asleep;
It was awakened by my stir light...
Your youth is now adorned,
for such was my sight!

My voiceless eyes;
from them...a few droplets did patter!
If she sees them, they're tears,
if not, they be called water...

This concern too is rather strange;
it is the benevolence of this crisis...
To hear about my well-being too;
from another, now they please!

– Trans-created on 27th *January, 2017 by Sharad Kamal Bezboruah.*

190. Manjaa...

Lyrics: Swanand Kirkire. (Dedicated to the ones lost along the way, fondly remembering; Sushant Singh Rajput)

We shall console,
the dreams turned cold...
The strings of cut kites
we shall jump to grab and hold...!!
There's the determination within,
all of it, to handle...
The passion... the knots
of complex ties, to untangle...

The fate asleep...
by us, shall be awakened!
Tomorrow, the skies,
we shall make to bend...
We have it within,
the passion... The knots
of those ties; shall be untangled...

The ties, the bonds...
they shall give wind to wings!
The bonds shall heal,
the wounds, the stings...
Sometimes victory,
sometimes defeat...

Sorrow and pain, friends,
shall be our guests for
barely a week...

The ties, they shall step across doorsteps...
They shall even sought for blood!
Sometimes tears,
sometimes pearl beads...
Even life, let's let them have, studs!

Separated buddies,
we shall gather...
The hope asleep,
we shall waken together...
There's the determination within,
all of it, to handle...
The passion... the knots
of complex ties, to untangle...

From the heart of glittering aspirations,
we shall remove the guard of fear!
The colourful dreams, it like they weave
a headdress of hope...
Let us sing on...and let none conquer,
our tunes and melodies...
Let us dream on, for
what happens tomorrow...who cares...!!

We shall console,
the dreams turned cold...
The strings of cut kites
we shall jump to grab and hold...!!
There's the determination within,

all of it, to handle...
The passion... the knots
of complex ties, to untangle...

In the frozen eyes,
we shall see of tomorrow,
a melted picture...
In the bosom of rock,
we shall feel boiling, thick lava...
The spark of devotion within, a fire;
let not the fire die...
Devoted...always been,
we have...let not the fire die...
What happens tomorrow...who cares...!!

We shall console,
the dreams turned cold...
The strings of cut kites
we shall jump to grab and hold...!!
There's the determination within,
all of it, to handle...
The passion... the knots
of complex ties, to untangle...

We shall console,
the dreams turned cold...
The strings of cut kites
we shall jump to grab and hold...!!
There's the determination within,
all of it, to handle...
The passion... the knots
of complex ties, to untangle...

The fate asleep...
by us; shall be awakened!
Tomorrow, the skies,
we shall make to bend...
We have it within,
the passion... The knots
of those ties; shall be untangled...

The ties, the bonds...
they shall give wind to wings!
The bonds shall heal,
the wounds, the stings...
Sometimes victory,
sometimes defeat...
Sorrow and pain, friends,
shall be our guests for
barely a week...

Separated buddies,
we shall gather...
The hope asleep,
we shall waken together...
There's the determination within,
all of it, to handle...
The passion... the knots
of complex ties, to untangle...

– Trans-created on 7th August, 2016 by Sharad Kamal Bezboruah.

191. Satyamev Jayate...

Lyricist: Prasoon Joshi.
Courtesy: Aamir Khan.

Your colour has now polished me so well;

no other colour can ever again do so.

Your name's written in this heart, I tell...

anyone who wishes can come and see.

Yes...!!

There is this passion...

The passion of your affection...

Yes...!!

Your love flows in my veins...

This blood is raging with an incredible craze...

It is you who taught,

me the meaning of truth.

Only after I approach you I got,

to know...of my existence the reason.

Truth alone triumphs!!

Truth alone triumphs!!

True is my love...

Truth alone triumphs!!

In the customs of your divine light,

let there be no creases, no wrinkles.

I wish that shining bright,

your divinity forever twinkles.
My attempts are only for this,
let the fragrances remain... May the gardens too remain!
I've set out to untangle the strands of your hair.
I've set out to come even more close to you, since
I wanna show that I really do care.
In which not a note anybody could miss....
To sing songs to such music, I've now set out to dare.
Yes...!!
There is this passion...
The passion of your affection...
Yes...!!
Your love flows in my veins...
This blood is raging with an incredible craze...
It is you who taught,
me the meaning of truth.
Only after I approach you I got,
to know...of my existence the reason.

Truth alone triumphs!!
Truth alone triumphs!!
True is my love...
Truth alone triumphs!!

Your colour has now polished me so well;
the passion has increased even more.
It's because of your rain that I've bloom and blossomed...
And hence, you so much I adore.
However I am...Be it,
I shall not ask you to accept me thus, be sure.
So that somehow, for you I become enough fit,

I wish to open such a door.
The pace of this breathing,
and the carnival of heartbeats...
This world of mine that's bleeding,
and every victory...every defeat...
I shall transform it all... For you!!
Yes...!!
There is this passion...
The passion of your affection...
Yes...!!
Your love flows in my veins...
This blood is raging with an incredible craze...
It is you who taught,
me the meaning of truth.
Only after I approach you I got,
to know...of my existence the reason.

Truth alone triumphs!!
Truth alone triumphs!!
True is my love...
Truth alone triumphs!!
Even myself, I shall investigate at my will...
In case there's a fault, I shall say...
If there are stains, why conceal...
Like this, from the truth why turn away...!!
Myself, if I have to change,
I shall change... For you!!
Even to walk on ambers and flames, if I need the courage,
I shall gather the courage... For you!!
In my blood flows the pledge of your love....
Thus it must seem.

If they cut me, in streams may you flow out!
And, red be the colour of each such stream.
Yes...!!
There is this passion...
The passion of your affection...
Yes...!!
Your love flows in my veins...
This blood is raging with an incredible craze...

Truth alone triumphs!!
Truth alone triumphs!!
True is my love...
Truth alone triumphs!!

– Trans-created and Adapted on 2nd March, 2014
by Sharad Kamal Bezboruah.

192. *Main Jise Odhta Bichata Hoon...*

– Dushyant Kumar.

The ones I shroud, the ones I spread;
those couplets, by me, to you, be read.

I wander into the woods within your eyes,
but can barely find my way ahead.

The ones I shroud, the ones I spread.

And, I, along the way, like a culvert clattered;
each time, you, like a train, across sped.

The ones I shroud, the ones I spread.

Whenever I step into the luminescence,
everywhere, only protests are bred.

The ones I shroud, the ones I spread.

Ever since I have lost an arm,
things even heavier, I have begun to held!

The ones I shroud, the ones I spread.

I have found you grow closer by the day,
each time, your memories I have tried to evade.

The ones I shroud, the ones I spread.

Who, on earth, shall ever cover the distances;
I, an angel...only the truth, forever, I have said.

The ones I shroud, the ones I spread.

– Translated on 25th August, 2021 by Sharad Kamal Bezboruah.

193. Teri Mehfil Mein Kismat Aazma Kar Hum Bhi Dekhenge...

Lyrics: Shakeel Badayuni.
Credits: Voice Kids. (Battle round, Asmi, Ankita and Tiyasha)

I too would like to try my luck,
at your court...
To experience being close to you,
for a moment, I too sought...

I too would like to try my luck,
at your court...
To bow at your feet,
I too sought...

Spring, the message of love,
it has brought...
To watch the buds of hope smile,
after ages we have got!
The darts that pain has to throw to the heart;
to dodge; I too shall give a shot!

'If there be no pain,
what fun is life, do think...
If be not blood,
then tears, what fun is to drink!!?
In your love, tears,

I too shall shed, and blink...'
To try my luck at your court,
I too do seek...

The tale of lovers is just this bit...
that they suffer silently, sigh;
and then suffocate,
and then die...
And so, smiling, someday,
the same chaos, I too shall watch...

I too would like to try my luck,
at your court...

Yes, love of course does ruin,
one's life... I admit...
But, being remembered by the world,
at death or after... isn't any less now, is it??
In love for someone,
I too shall lose my every bit...
I too sought,
to bow at your feet...

To experience being close to you,
for a moment, I too sought...
I too would like to try my luck,
at your court...

– Trans-created on 14th September, 2016 by Sharad Kamal Bezboruah.

194. Ranjish Hi Sahi

– AHMAD FARAZ.
(and Talib Baghbanpuri)

Be it pain, displeasure;
come, come to hurt the heart.
For, it is just that, I shall treasure;
Come, even if it is;
to leave me again and go; come.

Might not possible, the ties like before;
come to accomplish, the rituals;
that this land, has for centuries bore.

To how many shall I convey;
the reason of our separation.
If it is only me you detest,
come, for the rest of the generation.

Till date, this heart full of complacency
has expectations from you, and does wish.
Come, even the remaining flames of hope,
come to extinguish.

It has been an age since I had
the luxury of 'even grieving';
oh! Healer of the heart, come for once;
come, to leave me weeping.

At least a little, honour, the efforts,
in your love, that I have made.
Even you,
at least someday, come to persuade.

I admit that love is about concealing it all,
but yet;
but yet, for once, stealthily;
someday, even you; come to vent.

As you have known....
As much as you have known, all this while;
of not showing up, a dozen excuses.
Come, someday; to stay; and say,
that to ever return, the heart refuses.

Be it pain, displeasure;
come, come to hurt the heart.
For, it is just that, I shall forever treasure!

         – Translated on 14th July, 2015 by Sharad Kamal Bezboruah.

195. Woh Subah Kabhi Toh Aayegi...

Lyricist :-Sahir Ludhiyanvi

There must be a day,
when that dawn shall arrive...

There must be a day,
when that dawn shall arrive...

From above these bleak centuries,
the day when shall shift...the shade of the night grim.
When the clouds of sorrow shall melt and fade;
and the waters of the sea of joy shall brim.
When the skies would sway in utter bliss;
and the earth would sing a ballad...
There must be a day,
when that dawn shall arrive...

The dawn for which since ages,
we all have lived a thousand deaths...
The dawn, to whose eternal sweet tune;
we swallow goblets of poison into our breaths...
To these hunger, thirsty souls,
at least someday, it shall shower mercy...
That very dawn arriving,
at least someday we hope to see...

There must be a day,
when that dawn shall arrive...

I know and admit that our dreams
are now of no value...
Even for soil a handful, there's a price,
but of us humans, there is no value...
When the price of human dignity,
is not measured in worthless coins...
There must be the day when we see,
us, the splendid sun rejoins...

There must be a day,
when that dawn shall arrive...

For wealth,
when is not sold...
of women, the fate...
When love shall not be crumpled,
and modesty not sold!
When, at their darkest deeds,
the world shall mourn...
There must be a day,
when shall arrive that very dawn...

Someday, this phase;
of unemployment and of hunger...
Shall pass...and shall,
stop...the monopoly of wealth; of power...
When the foundations shall be laid,
of an incredible world, better, stronger...
There must be a day,
when shall come such an hour...

There must be a day,
when shall arrive that dawn...

When helpless seniors of the nation
shall not sweep dust beneath their feet...
When innocent childhood,
no more plead for pennies on the street...
When we, who fight for rights and needs,
shall not be shown spears and
threatened with defeat...
There must be a day,
when such a dawn we shall meet...

There must be a day,
when shall arrive that dawn...

When in the pyres of differences
humans shall not be lit.
Nor in the hell within the heart,
flames of aspirations shall sit...
When this place, more dreadful than hell...
shall be transformed to heaven, its every bit!
There must be a day,
when us that dawn very shall visit...

There must be a day,
when shall arrive that dawn...

When the earth shall flip over,
when prisoners shall be set free...
The nests of sins, when shall sever,
when shackles of oppression

shall loosen and break...
When the world shall run without prisons...
For the arrival of such a dawn,
we shall be the reason...

Yes! We shall be the reason,
for the arrival of such a dawn.

In the set-up of this depraved society,
when oppression and tyranny is no longer bred...!
Where no longer; hands are cut;
neither the people, any longer, does anyone behead...
When the world will run without of dirt a speck...
Yes! We will bring the dawn,
when we shall all rise from this wreck...

When all workmen and peasants,
shall come out of the fields and mills...
When, in the hearts of the homeless,
every wound and slit heals...
When the world,
will even more wonderful,
delightful flowers fills.
When such flowers,
the world adorn...
Yes! We shall be the reason,
for the arrival of such a dawn.

Yes! We shall be the reason,
for the arrival of such a dawn.

– Trans-created on 15th August, 2016 by Sharad Kamal Bezboruah.

196. Yeh Duniya Agar Mil Bhi Jaaye Toh Kya Hai!?

Lyricist:-Sahir Ludhiyanvi.

This world of monuments,
of thrones, of crowns;
this world full of enemies of humanity,
of the society, and of the towns;
this world of customs and duties,
whose hunger never goes down;
what good is such a world,
even if your own!?

Every body lays crippled,
thirsty every soul;
Eyes all puzzled,
hearts all cold...
This world where on one's self
too, none has hold...
what good is such a world,
even if owned!?

Here, the existence of humans
is like a toy to keep.
This is a slum,
where the dead all worship.
Here, rather than life itself,

you'll find death is cheap.
What good is such a world,
even if your own!?

Here, the youth roam astray;
on young bodies,
a sale out is laid...
Here; even love is now
but a trade!
What good is such a world,
even if your own!?

The world where humans,
to nothing are reduced;
by loyalty, by friendship,
no feelings are induced;
where by love too remains no value;
by such a world,
how can one be amused?
What good is such a world,
even if your own!?

Burn it down,
reduce it to ashes.
Remove this world
from in front of my eyelashes.
It's yours; keep it to yourself;
this world of clashes.
What good is such a world,
even if your own!?

– Translated on 23rd June, 2017 by Sharad Kamal Bezboruah.

197. Usko Juda Hue Bhi, Zamaana Bahaut Hua.

– AHMAD FARAZ.

It's been ages since we separated.
What do I speak of it?
The story is now outdated.

The dusk of separation
hasn't yet passed,
even after all the efforts.
Oh untimely death,
how long will this game last?

Oh good lord!
We've left your Paradise...
But, from this,
yet another long fable did arise.

Now, I stand alone;
to be my enemy chose
the world whole;
only because we came,
just a little more close.

It's time that this love
on this life, I sacrificed;
for in love; as in this life;
this much of losses shall suffice.

To this date, the heart,
to this heart hasn't been introduced;
agreed that to come across it oft,
it is now very well used.

What not of myself
I have vitiated.
Yet, oh memories of my beloved,
in my heart,
for long you are seated.

I told my friends,
not to speak.
Well, that was the one excuse
that they always seek.

The name of that traitor,
yet again on your lip!
I told you, Ahmad Faraz,
enough already; for so long you did weep!!

It's been ages since we separated.
What do I speak of it?
The story is now outdated.

– Translated on 23rd June, 2017 by Sharad Kamal Bezboruah.

198. Umr Guzregi Imtehan Mein Kya?

– Jaun Elia.

Shall life pass by only through tests?
Bruises alone shall you send in bequest?

Each word I utter, leaves no effect,
does each of them have only defects?
Shall life pass by only through tests?

Is this what prevails in the clan, for,
for my deeds, no one does detest?
Shall life pass by only through tests?

We only strive to conceal our deficits,
of us, the destitute, what lies in respect?
Shall life pass by only through tests?

You find yourself to stand out in the crowd,
is that what my surmises attest?
Shall life pass by only through tests?

The shops are shut, wherever I see,
do they not incur even losses in net?
Shall life pass by only through tests?

"Do you still bathe in the river of love, 'Baan'";
is what I ask the heart's dawns and sunsets.

Shall life pass by only through tests?

Why do you not speak in my favour?
Has your tongue grown too many cysts?
Shall life pass by only through tests?

Is it something I only presume, or do silences
whisper in the ear with every breath?
Shall life pass by only through tests?

I wish to meet her, for once and ask,
"Is it 'me' your prayer 'still' protects?"
Shall life pass by only through tests?

The way you look on at the skies,
tell me, if up there, someone rests.
Shall life pass by only through tests?

The breeze of spring too, blows dusty,
is it that only dirt blows, in our nest.
Shall life pass by only through tests?

Why do I not find peace at all,
apart from that one, shall I find no next?
Shall life pass by only through tests?

– Translated on 1ˢᵗ December 2021 by Sharad Kamal Bezboruah.

199. Thoda Likha...

– Tehzeeb Hafi.

I wrote a little
and left the rest;
to give way to
the upcoming nexts.*.

Each day a leaf;
to me it does send.
Ever since, to the forest
I no longer head.

Only for a moment,
on my ears, my hands I kept.
And then, that voice,
no longer did follow; it left.

What do you know,
what the brook has underwent?
Ever since, water;
you no longer fetch.

These girls, they rush at one ring,
(of the phone); with the fire all set:
Imagine, how deeply by them,
love is felt.

I wrote a little
and left the rest;
to give way to
the upcoming nexts.*.

– Translated on 6th June, 2019 by Sharad Kamal Bezboruah.

---

*nexts: here, has been used to refer to the next, next to next and all subsequent nexts.

200. Teri Har Baat...

– Rahat Indori.

In love, to every word of yours,
giving an 'aye',
embracing the deficit;
in the heart's souk, desolate I lie.

I am the stream, a whirlpool
in whose every speck does hide.
You were wise to have stepped
away from me, gone aside.

My face does, both flush,
and turn pale.
They all amuse themselves,
speaking of our tale.

For the stars to blink an eye,
I await the entire night.
For, the moon, onto my roof,
I shall thus invite.

He watched the flame in the slums
that ablaze did stay;
and then, stepped aside;
to the storms, giving way.

– Translated on 24th October, 2021 by Sharad Kamal Bezboruah.

201. Sarfaroshi Ki Tamanna…

– Bismil Azimabadi.
Credits: http://en.wikipedia.org/wiki/Sarfaroshi_ki_Tamanna (Wikipedia).

In desire of revolution,

our hearts now rebel.

All we need to see is this,

in the arms of the executioner,

what strengths and powers dwell…

Oh Motherland, why nobody else…

talks about you, here today…?

I look on, at the one who sits silent,

about you, in the function, nothing who tells…

Oh martyrs of the nation and land,

in honour of you,

my head I bend…

Now, tales of your bravery,

in another's assembly

they are heard, they are said…

In desire of revolution,

our hearts now rebel.

When the time comes, oh skies,

was shall announce it to u…

What do say from now, about what we have planned!?

By the hope of being murdered we've being brought pulled

to the streets and lanes of the enemy...
for, this nation; we've risked our lives to defend…
in love for the nation….
In desire of revolution,
our hearts now rebel.

The enemy there stands in guard,
with the weapons in hand.
With the bear chests,
all prepared to die, here we stand…
We are all ready, even if
with our blood we would need to play…
For now our own nation and land,
in deep trouble it now does lay…
In desire of revolution,
our hearts now rebel.

The vicious swords cannot cut,
the arms filled with fire and rage…
The heads held high, shall not bow,
with merely an enemies' challenge…
By that, even more shall blaze;
the flame-like fires, that
in our hearts are placed…
In desire of revolution,
our heart now rebel.

As we set out of our homes,
we already had our lives at stake…
And our steps, as they go on,
our lives, on our palms we take…
All we know is that-

in the gathering of death,
life's only a guest…
And we move on now with this,
leaving aside all the rest…
In desire of revolution,
our heart now rebel.

That murderous fellow,
he asks if anyone wishes to bear the testimony…
Standing there in the gallows,
We carry in the heart; hurricanes,
and waves of revolutions in the veins…
The enemies shall lose their senses;
we shall drive them insane….
To stop us, let try not today any…
Where is there strength in destinations to stay away…!?
Today, we've set out to change even our destiny…

What is a body, if within it there isn't blood raging…!!?
After all, how can one fight the storms
when his boat's at the shore and doesn't sail!!?
In desire of revolution,
our hearts now rebel.

– Trans-created on 15th August, 2014 by Sharad Kamal Bezboruah.

202. *Tum Itna Jo Muskura Rahe Ho...*

– Kaifi Azmi...

What's the matter?
Tell me what makes you smile…
What pain are you hiding in there,
tell me what pain, within do you pile?

Moisture in the eyes,
smile on the lips…
What's your actual state,
what is the disguise?
What's the pain that,
you so anxious keeps…?

As you drink on,
these tears that you drink;
shall turn into poison…
What pain do you try to hide?
Of your smiling so much,
what is the reason?
Of your smiling so much,
what is the reason?

The wounds that have been filled up by time…
Why do you again, go tearing them apart?
Tell me what makes you smile so much…

What pain do you hide in the heart?
Tell me what makes you smile so much…

Of the lines that run,
along your palm…Fate is the game.
Yet, you are being undone,
by lines the same…!
What pain do you hide in the heart?
Tell me what makes you smile so much…

What's the matter?
Tell me what makes you smile…
What pain are you hiding in there,
tell me what pain, within do you pile?

– Translated on 22nd April, 2014 by Sharad Kamal Bezboruah.

203. Kadam Milakar Chalna Hoga (Extract)

– Late Atal Bihari Vajpayee.(Sung by Late Jagjit Singh)

'Come the hindrances as they may,
and cast their shadows
the dark clouds of doom;
Along the road,
Underneath be embers,
and overhead,
of flames the showers;
Our own hands, setting ablaze,
smiling, we ought to embrace fire.
We ought to pace forth together.

In laughter, in sorrow,
in the wild tempest;
the outnumbering sacrifices
made on duties' behest...
In parks and playgrounds,
in solitude;
in honour
or in disrepute;
to hold our heads high,
and our bosoms forth;
in deep turmoil too,
we must resort.
Together, we ought to pace forth.

In the light, and in the shade;
on the cruel banks or at mid-sea-
in deep despise or in love pure;
in victory transient
or in defeat, long endured.
A million dreams, each so tempting;
you ought to cast aside, decline;
we ought to pace forth; together in line.'

— Translated on 17th August, 2018 by Sharad Kamal Bezboruah.

204. Koi Yeh Kaise Bataaye.

– Kaifi Azmi…

How does one say,
why he remains a loner?
Whoever was once yours,
why, is now another's?
If this is what happens here; in this world,
why does this happen, I wonder!

I shall pull her back, by her dress,
if she extends, for once, her wrist;
into her heart, let immerse;
my each and every beat.
If so close,
then, why, in between, this fleet?
From the desolate heart,
no one ever did exit;
at the door of a home, robbed;
someone does repeatedly hit,
a hope, long snapped;
why strive to again hitch?

Whether of joy, or call it,
of sorrow;
if love, is meant to be lifelong,
why does it change tomorrow?

How does one say
why he remains a loner?
Whoever was once yours,
why, is now another?
If this is what happens here; in this world,
why does this happen, I wonder!

– Translated on 24th December, 2021 by Sharad Kamal Bezboruah.

205. Mohabbat Karne Wale.

– Hafeez Hoshiarpuri.

(*Celebrating the spirit of 'rekhta', the Hindustani language, on making it all the way to Barrack Obama's personal playlist and finally merging into the winner's list at the 64th Grammy Awards 2022; and Arooj Aftab's contribution in the same.)

(For;) Among the ones who love,
none shall ever refrain.
But alas, in your gatherings,
someday, I shall no longer remain.
Among the ones who love,
none shall ever refrain.

Oh! All the worldly sorrows, cluttered;
if against your strain, I scale.
Before the pain, the sorrows of losing you;
Oh, so many more, shall not even prevail.
But alas, in your gatherings,
someday, I shall no longer remain.

By some chancy fortune,
your proximity, even if I do regain...
The turmoil of your separation;
not even a bit, shall wane.
But alas, in your gatherings,
someday, I shall no longer remain.

The hearts would continue to
grow increasingly perplexed;
if words of wisdom,
to cope, none gen.
But alas, in your gatherings,
someday, I shall no longer remain.

Upon this concern,
I often, in depth, dwell.
For how much longer, shall the flowers not,
heed to the dewdrops that bewail?
But alas, in your gatherings,
someday, I shall no longer remain.

Hafeez, as much as those wiles,
I do not rely on, yet go insane.
Never by me, shall she be vexed,
in ways, the same!
But alas, in your gatherings,
someday, I shall no longer remain.

Among the ones who love,
none shall ever refrain.
But alas, in your gatherings,
Someday, I shall no longer remain.
Among the ones who love,
None shall ever refrain.

– Translated on 27th December 2021
by Sharad Kamal Bezboruah. (3:30 am)

Having covered a wide range of songs, Ghazals, Nazms, along 'The
Unsung'; it would only be fair and just to dedicate a sub-section to an

industry that we as a generation can barely stop learning from. And so, as we now move towards the end of this marathon, or so to call it a rollercoaster ride; even though I have covered Bollywood to a great extent, in the sections above, here; in the words of Prasoon Joshi, is a tribute to the 'Satrangi Jaadugar'.

Never did I ever imagine when I started off with this project; that, what began with the event of the nation losing one crown jewel, would only end after loss of yet another Bharat Ratna, Late Lata Mangeshkar ji. However shattered and devastated we are as a nation; here is celebrating the life and times of the 'Nightingale', with translations of several of her iconic numbers; those that precede; and those that follow hereafter.

"Satrangi Jaadugar…
Lyricist: Prasoon Joshi.
Courtesy: Wiz-craft.; and Celebrating 110 years of Indian Cinema.

You disperse from the golden sun,
through thick and thin, with me you did run.
Every eye of the nation,
offers you a salutation….
Thank you, oh multifaceted wizard!
Thank you for all that you've done.

Yes… We have learnt from you,
how to push aside every difficulty.
No matter how much the trouble,
to move on with dignity.
If you have been in love, why fear…
that's something that you've told.
Life itself is a riddle, you say,
a truth that we shall forever hold.
If it's the entire world that we've got,
even then it's you we'd sought.

Every eye of the nation,
offers you a salutation....
Thank you, oh multifaceted wizard!
Thank you for all that you've done.

With your eyes representing lips,
you have been a smile full of beauty.
Of my motherland, my country,
you have been a glorious identity.
Whenever has faded the fragrance in life,
you've given off fragrances,
burning bit by bit.
The thread of hope;
you are a pathway of light...

Every eye of the nation,
offers you a salutation....
Thank you, oh multifaceted wizard!
Thank you for all that you've done.
Thank you, oh multifaceted wizard!
Oh magician!
Oh magician, full of miracles!
Oh magician!

When tired, all dreams were turning to dust,
and the bare feet stood on the burning ground, compelled...
Then, you were the one who said new dreams must
awaken. It was by you that our hands were held.
Hope then again stood tall, the clouds giggled out loud.
We pride you.
Yes... of you, we are all proud!
Yes... of you, we are all proud!!

Every eye of the nation,
offers you a salutation....
Thank you, oh multifaceted wizard!

Thank you, oh magician full of miracles!

Thank you, oh multifaceted wizard!
Thank you for all that you've done...

Oh magician....!!
Oh magician full of miracles!

Thank you, oh multifaceted wizard!
Thank you for all that you've done...

    – Translated on 8th July, 2013 by Sharad Kamal Bezboruah."

206. Ajeeb Dastaan Hai Yeh.....

– Shailendra
(Shankardas Kesarilal)

This indeed is a strange tale,

neither the beginning is known, nor end....

Neither of us, neither he nor I can tell,

where we are heading....where the roads bend.....

With the light,

why did smoke rise from the lamp!!?

A dream I do sight,

that by dreams I am awakened...

This indeed is a strange tale,

neither the beginning is known, nor end....

Neither of us, neither he nor I can tell,

where we are heading....where the roads bend.....

Felicitations to you,

for you've become the light for someone...

To someone, you are so close now,

that from everyone else, far you've run...

This indeed is a strange tale,

neither the beginning is known, nor end....

Neither of us, neither he nor I can tell,

where we are heading....where the roads bend.....

Now, it's time you build a new home,
with affection unhampered….
Whenever such an evenings come,
by me, you shall be remembered….

This indeed is a strange tale,
neither the beginning is known, nor end….
Neither of us, neither he nor I can tell,
where we are heading….where the roads bend…..

– Trans-created on 22nd July, 2014 by Sharad Kamal Bezboruah.

207. Chalte-Chalte Yun Hi Ruk Jataa Hoon Main...

Anand Bakshi.

Male:
As I walk on...I often pause...
As I sit, in many a thought
without a cause
get lost oft....
As I speak on,
I often become silent.
Is this itself love?
Is this itself love?

Female:
Yes...This is it, what you call love...!!
Yes...This is it, what you call love...!!

Male:
For you, why does the heart die,
I know not...!
Why I do so, why do I,
I know not...!
Through blocked streets,
secretly now I've begun to tread.
As I lived away from the world,

I've now begun to be scared...
Oh my,
what have I begun to do!!

Is this itself love?
Is this itself love?

Female:
Yes...This is it, what you call love...!
Yes...This is it, what you call love...!!

Male:
As I walk on...I often pause...
As I sit, in many a thought
without a cause
get lost oft....
As I speak on,
I often become silent.
Is this itself love?
Is this itself love?
Female:
Yes...This is it, what you call love...!!
Yes...This is it, what you call love...!!

Male:
Your words,
on making mischief they are bent.
On my lips,
there is many a complaint.
Your eyes with my eyes I seem,
to have begun to kiss.
Taking you in my arms in my dreams,

I seem to have begun to dance about in bliss.
Is this itself love?
Is this itself love?

Female:
Yes...This is it, what you call love...!
Yes...This is it, what you call love...!!

Male:
As I walk on...I often pause...
As I sit, in many a thought
without a cause
get lost oft....
As I speak on,
I often become silent.
Is this itself love?
Is this itself love?

Yes...This is it, what you call love...!!
Yes...This is it, what you call love...!!

– Trans-created on 6th March, 2014 by Sharad Kamal Bezboruah.

208. Diye Jalte Hai...

– Anand Bakshi.

The lamps, they give out light,
the blossoms, their fragrance extend.
But with great difficulty,
in this world you shall find a friend.

The moment a friend departs,
never to be back.
Do not ask, oh,
it leaves the heart sacked.
Like, with the arrows of memories,
it has been attacked.

The lamps, they give out light,
the blossoms, their fragrance extend.
But with great difficulty,
in this world you shall find a friend.

On this glamour, do not pride.
Sacrifice your life,
but never a friend's trust degrade.
For, this glamour shall fade;
the sunlight too,
shall turn to shade.

The lamps, they give out light,
the blossoms, their fragrance extend.
But with great difficulty,
in this world you shall find a friend.

Your youth shall one day fade;
your wealth; shall run out of stock.
The world shall turn against you,
but your friend shall always, by you walk.

The lamps, they give out light,
the blossoms, their fragrance extend.
But with great difficulty,
in this world you shall find a friend.

– Trans-created on 4th August, 2017 by Sharad Kamal Bezboruah.

209. Hai Apna Dil Toh Awaara... (Sad).

– MAJROOH SULTANPURI.

This heart of mine,

a vagrant...

No clue, as to whom,

to fall for, it is meant...

It has never paused, nor will...

No clue, of, what tune,

has got into it...

He takes this route at noon,

and, by dusk he's at another street...

It rolls on, door to door...

anxious and vexed...

No clue, as to whom,

to fall for, it is meant...

This heart of mine,

a vagrant...

No clue, as to whom,

to fall for, it is meant...

It had come across someone,

somebody please tell me what it was...

Was in my senses,

or just a dream...! Tell me,

for curiosity it does cause!!?
It has lost to its own sorrow, pained...
No clue, as to whom,
to fall for, it is meant...

This heart of mine,
a vagrant...
No clue, as to whom,
to fall for, it is meant...

– Trans-created on 9th June, 2016 by Sharad Kamal Bezboruah.

210. Hai Apna Dil Toh Awaara...

– MAJROOH SULTANPURI.
Credits: Sanam Puri's rendition.

This heart of mine,
a vagrant...
No clue, to fall for whom;
it is meant...

The ladies, they called,
and embraced it...
It was explained, times a dozen,
yet, it never faced it...

It is too innocent,
oh, poor thing...!
No clue, on coming across whom,
the bell within would ring...

This heart of mine,
a vagrant...
No clue, to fall for whom;
it is meant...

Incredibly insane,
no home, nor an abode...
No ties, neither to the soil,

nor to the skies, it has ever showed...
(Like) a shooting star, fallen,
yet showing no repent...
No clue, as to,
to fall for whom, it is meant...

This heart of mine,
a vagrant...
No clue, to fall for whom;
it is meant...

I looked around everywhere,
everyone has someone
as their strength and support...
This heart of mine, alone
to keep none could afford...
In a journey, like a nomad,
along a road bent...
No clue, as to whom;
to fall for, it is meant...

This heart of mine,
a vagrant...
No clue, to fall for whom;
it is meant...

If ever it had agreed,
there wasn't, to find, a priest...
Every bet, in every game,
to lose, it never could resist...
In the entire world,
the most incompetent...

476 | *Maj-rooh*

No clue, as to whom,
to fall for, it is meant...

This heart of mine,
a vagrant...
No clue, to fall for whom;
it is meant...

– Trans-created on 9th June, 2016 by Sharad Kamal Bezboruah.

211. IshaaronIshaaronMein Dil Lene Waale.....

Lyrics by: Shamshul Huda Bihari.

Female: Oh, the one who takes the heart away through signals!
Where have you learnt this art, be kind enough to tell…
Male: Listen, oh beloved of mine! I've learnt it from the same place,
from where you've learnt to use your eyes to cast spells.

My heart just fell for you… Tell me what was my mistake?
God!! This was that merciless grace…
This was what made the heart's peace break.
This was it!
The tales of Romeos and Juliets down the lane of memory,
I believe they're no different than my own story.

Female: Oh, the one who takes the heart away through signals!
Where have you learnt this art, be kind enough to tell…

The ones who love never do speak of it, old or young.
The beat of their heart, they don't ever make others hear.
What fun would there remain, when one has already sung,
the tale and has said all about love, with one's own tongue.

Male: Listen, oh beloved of mine! Tell me from where;
from where did you ever learn to use your eyes to cast spells.

I admit dear one, that you're one in a million,
but at least to the prowess of my eyes, pay a bit of heed.
For, the flower of which even spring was proud of,
I've chosen that very blossom, the best indeed.

Female: Oh, the one who takes the heart away through signals!
Where have you learnt this art, be kind enough to tell…
Male: Listen, oh beloved of mine! I've learnt it from the same place,
from where you've learnt to use your eyes to cast spells.

Female: Where have you learnt this art, be kind enough to tell…
Male: From the same place from where you've learnt to use your eyes to
cast spells.

– Translated on 17th November, 2013 by Sharad Kamal Bezboruah.

212. *Jeena Yahaan ..... Marna Yahaan...*

– Shailendra (Shankardas Kesarilal)/Shaili Shailendra.
(Celebrating the spirit of the showman,
Raj Kapoor and RK Films)

Here I am to live, and here itself to die,

whenever you want, just call out my name.

Apart from this… where do I go?

For my dwellings shall forever be the same!

It all lays here, both worlds of mine,

everything earthly and everything divine.

This song of mine, the song of my life,

tomorrow too shall be sung by another with a mask.

Another clown shall come, to make the world laugh,

and he would then carry forth my task.

Here lies my heaven, here my hell,

apart from this place, where else do I dwell?

Whenever you want, call out my name.

Apart from this… where do I go?

For my dwellings shall forever be the same!

It all lays here, both worlds of mine,

everything earthly and everything divine.

Tomorrow, whether I am in this world or not,

the skies shall forever be filled with stars.

You shall forget, they too would say they forgot,

but I shall be forever, forever yours!
Here itself shall lay, my footprints, my marks,
Where else shall go, in this world so dark?
Whenever you want, call out my name.
Apart from this… where do I go?
For my dwellings shall forever be the same!
It all lays here, both worlds of mine,
everything earthly and everything divine.

Here I am to live and here I am to die,
whenever you want, just call out my name.
Apart from this… where do I go?
For my dwellings shall forever be the same!

– Translated on 5th August, 2013 by Sharad Kamal Bezboruah.

213. Kahin Door Jab Din Dhal Jaaye...

– Yogesh

Somewhere far away,
when the day ends,
the sun sets...
The bride of dusk, shy
slowly, in, she sneaks...
The lamps of dreams and fantasies,
she lights in the courtyard bleak
of my thoughts...
Somewhere far away,
when the day ends,
the sun sets...
The bride of dusk, shy
slowly, in she sneaks...

Some moment,
when turned heavy the breath...
Sitting on...when,
the eyes turned wet...
Sometimes,
Tripping...and coming close,
someone... Someone's touch is felt...
But, not one sight,
of her, I can get...

Somewhere far away,
when the day ends,
the sun sets...
The bride of dusk, shy
slowly, in she sneaks...

Somewhere, the hearts;
they do not even meet...
While elsewhere,
prevailing through births;
arise the bonds sweet...
Such are the dilemmas;
the heart's a foe,
rather queer...
My own, though,
it goes through
the pains of another, near...

Somewhere far away,
when the day ends,
the sun sets...
The bride of dusk, shy
slowly, in she sneaks...

The heart knows how,
these differences deep...
Turned into dreams golden!
Only these dreams,
these are mine to keep...
To nowhere else,
away from me....
their shadows shall ever sweep...

Somewhere far away,
when the day sets...
The bride of dusk, shy
slowly, in she sneaks...
The lamps of dreams and fantasies,
she lights in the courtyard bleak
of my thoughts...
Somewhere far away,
when the day sets...
The bride of dusk, shy
slowly, in she sneaks...

– Trans-created on 14th February 2016, by Sharad Kamal Bezboruah.

214. Kasme, Waade, Pyaar, Wafaa....

– *Indeevar.*

Promises and vows,
love and loyalty...
are all merely words,
not one of them is an entity!
No one is a relative to anyone here;
these false bonds do not exist in reality!
Promises and vows,
love and loyalty...
are all merely words,
not one of them is an entity!

The saviour shall stand right in front of you,
and yet he shall not be all save
you even if he desires....
Your own siblings or descendents shall have
to light your funeral pyres.
Oh! The one who flies high,
you shall come crashing into the land...
Promises and vows,
love and loyalty...
are all merely words!

In happiness, all shall be together,
in pain their backs they shall turn.

The people of the earth, they pretend
to be yours...And, once your trust they earn...
Your heart they shall break and they; roads, shall bend.
To trick the Almighty too they yearn,
how would they let go of humans?!!
Promises and vows,
love and loyalty...
are all merely words!

If it is the work of a Hindu
then who has looted the temple?
All its wealth who did take?
All this, if a Muslim did do,
then why did the Lord's abode break?
The beliefs, the religion that allows all of this,
that religion can only be called fake!!
Promises and vows,
love and loyalty...
are all merely words!

– Trans-created on 17th March, 2014 by Sharad Kamal Bezboruah.

215. Kaun Aaya…

– RAJINDER KISHAN (Celebrating the grandeur and life of Prabodh Chandra Dey)

Who….!!!??
Who has arrived???
Who has arrived???

Who has arrived,
at of my heart the gates;
and has brought along,
the jingle of anklets!??
Who has arrived???

The eye doesn't recognize,
but to the heart it is familiar…
Such a face, has today,
to me, come near…
The crazy heart, it drowns deep into thoughts,
taking along with it,
the world of dreams entire…
Who has arrived,
at of my heart the gates;
and has brought along,
the jingle of anklets!??
Who has arrived???

For a second, I feel,

my hope has come in whole new attire.

The next moment, a possibility revealed,

is that it could be a shadow; which

has come to the home of a stranger…

with a heart, which with an extraordinary affection is filled.

Who has arrived,

at of my heart the gates;

and has brought along,

the jingle of anklets!??

Who has arrived???

– Trans-created on 22nd October, 2014 by SharadKamal Bezboruah.

216. Khoon Chala....

Lyricist: Prasoon Joshi.

To do something before I die,
my blood now rages.
To descend onto the mirrors of the eye,
my blood now rages.
From the body, the drops descend,
and then it embraces the land…
From the roads and streets…
it arises and emerges…
To fill in brand new colours,
my blood now rages.

With the wounds open,
with an increasing pain…
Slowly!
Steadily!
Moving with, of accusations the fingers
and a fist full of answers…
My revolutionary instinct I wish to trigger…
To do something before I die
my blood now rages.

To do something before I die,
my blood now rages.
To descend onto the mirrors of the eye,

my blood now rages.
From the body, the drops descend,
and then it embraces the land…
From the roads and streets…
it arises and emerges…
To fill in brand new colours,
my blood now rages.

My blood now rages!!
My blood now rages!!

    – Tran-created on 30th March, 2014 by Sharad Kamal Bezboruah.

217. Lukka Chuppi

Lyricist: Prasoon Joshi. (Among Lata ji's last few gems)

Enough you have played hide and seek...
Come on, now show up....!
All over the place, so much I have searched,
I am tired now...Come on, grow up!!
Come back, for evening has set in,
I am worried about you....
my sight...so blur it is getting...
Come on, show up now....!

What do I say, mother...
about where I am...!!
Here, to fly,
I am given
the sky...
the skies open...
Like your tales,
so innocent...
To dwell,
I have a wondrous world, full of dreams....
My kite....It flies here,
fearless...not afraid even a little.
None shall snatch the thread;
none shall cut it through the middle.

How shall I show to you,

what I have here...

I have drunk water,

from the waterfalls....

Bunches of dreams on trees,

I have leaped to touch...

With shade, the sunlight is here,

this place of mine is such...

Everything seems to be of new form...

There's everything here, but yet,

I feel alone, without you, away from home...

– Tran-created on 25th March, 2014 by Sharad Kamal Bezboruah.

218. Khud Se…

– Angaraag Mahanta..
Lyricists: Manoj Tapadia

The heart of itself is afraid,
somewhere within it seems to be dead.
Now, the heart fears itself,
from itself, it's far away being spread.
Yea… from itself!
Yea… from itself!

The lost moonlight,
too now isn't a delight.
Now this life too seems like a curse,
imagine my plight.

Of those poisoned wounds, these scratches,
these spots and these dark, red patches.
Someone come and see, for I have examined them only on my own,
their sight no eye apart from mine ever catches.
Yea… only mine…!
Yea… only mine…!

The heart of itself is afraid,
somewhere within it seems to be dead.

Now, the heart fears itself,

from itself, it's far away being spread.

Yea… from itself!

Yea… from itself!

    – Translated on 14th August, 2013 by Sharad Kamal Bezboruah.

219. *Jaane Kahaan Chupke Baitha Hai Khuda…/Kyun Main Jaagoon*

– Anvita Dutt Guptan.

This way, separating me from my aspirations,
god knows where God gone and hidden…
I know not when I went missing, away from myself…
How shall I live on, for with my soul too now;
my meeting is forbidden!!

Why!? Why do my own streets and lanes,
ask the address of my home…
Why!? Why do the knocks enquire,
where they'd find the door…
Now… In those streets I roam,
you may come and look for
me… For now, I dwell,
in those streets which do not lead to any destination.
The heart's somewhere; and the beats,
somewhere else they fell…
My pair of lungs though; somewhat it breathes…
Yet, I do not seem to be alive…

It turned into sand…
and from between the fingers
of my hand…

It has flowed… and my fate is now scattered…
all across that land…
all around…
How do I write another new tale!?
After all…Where is the ink of pain found??
I've chosen sighs… I've chosen them, very well….!!
Then why do I live so lost from myself like this!?
What was my mistake as such, oh Lord…
that you've given me the punishment of living on in this hell…!!??

Oh fella, across your forehead,
the lines that are pulled…
Only as much as that bit is the world…
My tears… They will definitely wipe me out...
One cannot forgo the orders of the one who rules….

Now…In those streets I roam,
you may come and look for
me… For now, I dwell,
in those streets which do not lead to any destination.
The heart's somewhere; and the beats,
somewhere else they fell…
My pair of lungs though; somewhat it breathes…
Yet, I do not seem to be alive…

Why do I stay awake,
while the Lord… his dreams he now weaves…?
Why my Lord…In this way,
with his eyes open, he sleeps….
Why do I stay awake……..!!?

– Trans-created on 24th August, 2014 by Sharad Kamal Bezboruah.

220. Lag Jaa Gale…
(As timeless as ever)

Lyrics: Raja Mehdi Ali Khan.

Open your arms,
for who knows if again…
There'll be this night,
full of charm…
And, in this life;
if ever our roads shall ever cross…
Open your arms…

These moments,
they've come to us by fate…
Look at me from close,
to your heart's content…
For, in your fate a night like this,
be or be not who knows…
Who knows if again…
in this life…
if our roads shall ever cross…

Come close, for
I shall come often not…
Let me put these arms,
upon the shoulders your…

and cry my heart out!
For, who knows if ever again, of love, the rains;
shall be, from of eyes, the cloud...
Who knows if again...
in this life...
if our roads shall ever cross...

Open your arms,
for who knows if again...
There'll be this night,
full of charm...
And, in this life;
if ever our roads shall ever cross...
Open your arms...

   – Trans-created on 14th February 2016, by Sharad Kamal Bezboruah.

221. Lambi Judaai...

Anand Bakshi.

We just have separated only yesterday or the day before.
I just wonder how I shall live on like this for ages more....

Death hasn't come yet...
But, the image of your memory has...
Oh... For so long remain the distances...!!
Love is only of four days, Oh Lord!!
Oh... For so long remain the distances...!!
For so long remain the distances...!!
Oh! My heart has now risen up to my lips, alas!!
For so long remain the distances...!!
Love is only of four days, Oh Lord!!
Oh... For so long remain the distances...!!

My beloved is not near in the first place.
Secondly...We aren't meeting soon in any case.
On top of it all, came monsoon...
In the heart, it raised a blaze!!
Oh... For so long remain the distances...!!
Love is only of four days, Oh Lord!!
Oh... For so long remain the distances...!!

Oh this Generation!! Let your merciless hands break...
thus is my curse...

For with these very hands,

the glasslike hearts you did crush...

And, you built...

the high wall of separation,

and felt not even wee bit of guilt.

Oh... For so long remain the distances...!!

Love is only of four days, Oh Lord!!

Oh... For so long remain the distances...!!

The flower beds were devastated,

before the buds could blossom.

The birds got separated,

before their good times could come.

The call of the cuckoo

made me feel within the heart an acute pain.

Love is only of four days, Oh Lord!!

Oh... For so long the distances remain...!!

Oh... For so long the distances remain...!!

Oh... For so long the distances remain...!!

– Trans-created on 1st February, 2014 by SharadKamal Bezboruah.

222. Main Har Ek Pal Ka Shaayar Hoon...

Lyricist :-Sahir Ludhiyanvi

I am a poet of every moment;

every moment is my story...

In every moment is my existence;

in every moment is my youth, my glory.

Of relations, only the forms change,

the foundations are never finished.

Of dreams and emotion, the value,

never does it get diminished.

In a flower lies my youth,

and in a flower dwells your beauty.

Only a face is the identity you have,

and only a face is my identity.

I am a poet of every moment;

every moment is my story...

In every moment is my existence;

in every moment is my youth, my glory.

The divine syrup of life, to drink,

to you and me, these hands shall give.

In their heartbeats, we shall have to dwell,

in their breaths we shall have to live.

Hand over your grace to them,

I hand over my loyalty.
For myself, all that I had once dreamt,
I give all those well-wishes to them.

I am a poet of every moment;
every moment is my story...
In every moment is my existence;
in every moment is my youth, my glory.

– Translated on 11th November, 2013 by Sharad Kamal Bezboruah.

223. *Main Pal Do Pal Ka Shaayar Hoon...*

Lyricist :-Sahir Ludhiyanvi

"Tomorrow,
new buds shall bloom...new flowers smile.
And, on the new floor of new grass...
new feet shall
They did not come between me,
why should I come in between them...
Of the mornings and their evenings...
their dusks and dawns...
why should I receive even a second..."

I am a poet of a moment of two,
of a moment or two is my story...
For a two or two is my existence,
for a moment or two is my youth, my glory.

Before me so many poets, oh my!
Came and left a while after coming.
Few returned only calling out a sigh;
few went off their way humming.
They were all tales of a moment,
after a while, I too shall depart...
I shall be separated from you, do not resent,
though today, in your life I play a part.

I am a poet of a moment of two,
of a moment or two is my story...
For a two or two is my existence,
for a moment or two is my youth, my glory.

Tomorrow more of them shall come,
the flowers of melodies who gather.
Those who speak better than me
and than you those who are, in listening much better.
Tomorrow if anyone would remember me,
why by anyone would I be remembered?
Why should the busy generation, this busy world,
waste time thinking of me, of whom they've never heard.

I am a poet of a moment of two,
of a moment or two is my story...
For a two or two is my existence,
for a moment or two is my youth, my glory.

    – Translated on 7th September, 2013 by Sharad Kamal Bezboruah.

224. Main Zindagi Ka Saath Nibhata Chala Gaya....

Lyricist:-Sahir Ludhiyanvi.

I went on always,

accompanying life…

Every thought, every worry,

into smoke I turned with a swipe.

I went on always,

accompanying life…

Mourning my downfall

was a waste…

And hence, celebrating my downfall,

on I went…

And hence, celebrating my downfall,

on I went…

Every thought, every worry,

into dust I turned with a swipe.

Whatever I've found,

I now regard it as fate…

Whatever I've found;

now I regard it as fate…

Whatever I've lost,

I've chosen to rather forget…

Every thought, every worry,
into dust I turned with a swipe.

Where between happiness and sorrow,
the boundaries can't be demarked…
To bring the heart unto that point,
on a quest I've always embarked…

I went on always,
accompanying life…
Every thought, every worry,
into dust I turned with a swipe.

– Trans-created on 19th April, 2014 by Sharad Kamal Bezboruah.

225. Mera Saaya...

Lyrics: Raja Mehdi Ali Khan.

Whichever way you go,
along shall move my shadow...
My shadow!
My shadow!

If ever you tears flow,
remembering....me...
Then, there itself, do know;
my tears shall go obstruct
their way, for sure...
Whichever way you turn,
to head... along shall move
My shadow!
My shadow!

Whichever way you go,
along shall move my shadow...
My shadow!
My shadow!

If ever you are sad,
I too shall fill with sorrow...
I shall be there, somewhere around,
whether or not myself I show!

Wherever you shall,
along shall move my shadow...

Whichever way you go,
along shall move my shadow...
My shadow!
My shadow!

If ever I happen to,
separate from you...
Never lament over it!
Nor, remembering my love,
ever cry a bit...
For, if you turn and look,
following you, you shall find it,
my shadow!
My shadow!

Whichever way you go,
along shall move my shadow...
My shadow!
My shadow!

My pain has been a part of
your sorrow, your hurt!
My love has been with you,
in your every birth...
Whatever birth you take,
along shall move my shadow...
My shadow!
My shadow!

Whichever way you go,
along shall move my shadow...
My shadow!
My shadow!

– Trans-created on 17th October, 2016 by Sharad Kamal Bezboruah.

226. *Mora Gora Ang Leile…(Gulzar Saab's very first; in the voice of our very own Lata ji)*

Lyrics: Gulzar.

Take away my fair complexion;
and make me ebony...
I'll fade away in this night,
if you give me,
of my beloved the company...

On one hand, I'm held back by reticence;
on the other...I'm pulled,
by endearment...
Someone please guide me,
I do not know
which way is to be went...

Sliding aside the clouds,
the moon silently peeps...
Curse you foe,
you smile, while making me weep...

Take away my fair complexion;
and make me ebony...
I'll fade away in this night,
if you give me,
of my beloved the company...

Something I lost, after finding...
Something I found, losing...
Wonder where the heart takes me...
along the path winding,
taking away my senses!

Take away my fair complexion;
and make me ebony...
I'll fade away in this night,
if you give me,
of my beloved the company...

– Trans-created on 18th September, 2016 by Sharad Kamal Bezboruah.

227. Naam Gum Jaayega...(and, the voice, shall remain in the memory)

Lyrics: Gulzar.

The name shall be lost,
and shall change, this face, pretty...
If at all, it remains in your memory;
my voice is my identity...

The name shall be lost,
and shall change, this face, pretty...
If at all, it remains in your memory;
my voice is my identity...

The woes of time
aren't any less amusing...
Today we're here,
tomorrow, nowhere to be seen...
Somewhere, beyond time,
if our roads happen to be crossing...
In the same tone,
I shall sing...

"If at all, it remains in your memory;
my voice is my identity..."...

The name shall be lost,
and shall change, this face, pretty...

If at all, it remains in your memory;
my voice is my identity...

That which has passed,
is from yesterday...
It wasn't a lifetime,
just one night...
If traces of it, somewhere,
find, I might...
If at all, it remains in your memory;
my voice is my identity...

The name shall be lost,
and shall change, this face, pretty...
If at all, it remains in your memory;
my voice is my identity...

Where the day sets,
where the night is close...
The torch of flame,
high you must hold...
If I'm remembered,
and you ever feel morose...
If, remembering me,
you ever feel morose...
If at all, it remains in the memory;
my voice is my identity...

The name shall be lost,
and shall change, this face, pretty...
If at all, it remains in your memory;
my voice is my identity...

– Trans-created on 26th May, 2016 by SharadKamal Bezboruah.

228. Naina Barse...Rimjhim Rimjhim...

Lyrics: Raja Mehdi Ali Khan.

The eyes overflow with tears,
awaiting your arrival...
The eyes overflow with tears!!

Those days in my eyes,
those memories...
in my breath still linger!
In the lanes of your love,
this heart still does go wander...
The roads; forlorn...
Through my arms run chills!!
The eyes,
an age old thirst kills...
The eyes overflow with tears!!

Without you, the eyes,
they are rather disturbed...
And, its palms,
love has oft rubbed...
Of loyalty, commitment,
still burns the flame...
It awaits you, the moth,
it's time you came...
Listen oh, companion,

I roam in fear, anxiety...
Come now, wherever you are,
at least show some pity...
The eyes overflow with tears!!

I am a tale, incomplete...
Do come, if ever you recall
me! Come and see,
without you, how I crawl...
The eyelids wet,
tears spill like...
beads from an anklet...
The eyes, lost...and in pain!
The eyes overflow with tears!!

These million sorrows,
this loneliness in the air...
This way how love does defame
me... Thus passed, a lot many nights,
neither had you come, nor death; it came!!
This star I wear on the forehead,
now burns like an ember from a flame!
The Hena of my hands; disheartened...
The eyes overflow with tears!!

The eyes overflow with tears, awaiting your arrival......

– Trans-created on 25th September, 2016 by Sharad Kamal Bezboruah.

229. O' Paalanhaare...

– Javed Akhtar.

Oh keeper of our nourishment…
Oh absolute and distinctive divine…!!
Save us for we have no one…
Listen to this prayer of mine…
Solve our dilemmas and puzzles…
Oh Almighty, Bhagwaan….
Save us for
apart from you, we have no one…

You are the one,
our situations, who does settle…
You are our guardian,
without you, nothing we can handle…
Oh Almighty, Bhagwaan….
Save us for
apart from you, we have no one…

Oh! In the moon…
the moonlight, you are the one who does fill…
The sun-rays of sun too are from you…
The skies too, delighted they feel…
you are the one who has given it the stars old and new…
Oh Almighty!! This life of ours…
if you don't adorn and enhance…. Who will!!?

Oh Almighty, Bhagwaan….
Save us for
apart from you, we have no one…

If you listen, I shall speak….
Oh Almighty!
A boon that we seek…
is that, to the ones in pain you must give patience…
so that they never have to bow before pain…
Oh Lord! Give shelter the weak…
So that they can live in peace….
Give strength to devotion…
Give strength to devotion…

You are the keeper of the universe…
Listen to this plea of ours…
Along the way there is only darkness,
give light as a boon and free us from this curse….

Oh keeper of our nourishment…
Oh absolute and distinctive divine…!!
Save us for we have no one…
Listen to this prayer of mine…
Solve our dilemmas and puzzles…
Oh Almighty, Bhagwaan….
Save us for
apart from you, we have no one…

 – Trans-created on 9th August, 2014 by Sharad Kamal Bezboruah.

230. Pairo Mein Bandhan Hai…

Anand Bakshi.

Female:
There are chains around our feet;
noises are made by our anklets.
Shut the doors properly dear mate,
there come the thieves again, I bet.

Male:
Break all the chains today,
let noise be made by your anklets…
Open all the doors of your heart, give us the way…
The thieves of your hearts, in you must let.

Female:
What shall I say? What shall I do?
I die of shame.
Male:
Don't torment this way, dear!
Slowly it moves out, my life I fail to tame.

Female:
You are my true lover;
I still am not convinced yet.
Male:
If you still have doubts,

if I love you or not...
Then about me just forget.

Female:
So soon, I shall not remove,
of shame, the veil...
I'll think first, and then I shall,
some other day come to you and tell.
Male:
Even today, you did not agree;
watch out gal, your palanquin...
maybe be taken away by of wind a gust!
Don't say later, warned you had not been.

Female:
There are chains around our feet;
noises are made by our anklets.
Shut the doors properly dear mate,
there come the thieves again, I bet.

Male:
Break all the chains today,
let noise be made by your anklets...
Open all the doors of your heart, give us the way...
The thieves of your hearts, in you must let.

Female:
Those would have in their fate,
their meetings definitely do come.
Male:
Not much they have to wait,
for of the hearts the blossom...

their ability to bloom is so great,
that they are found even in autumn.

Female:
The world, dear friends,
it says the heart doesn't have sense.
Male:
The crazy heart, it says
that the world too, has no brains.

Female:
Look, oh beloved
I've come now....
Leaving the entire world behind.
Breaking all the chains and shackles,
that had for so long kept me tied.
Now, I've tied myself to your chains.
Male:
To each other, let us get tied...
Come oh beloved!
Let us together take flight...
Like the string it is tied to,
and the free, flying kite.

Female:
There are chains around our feet;
noises are made by our anklets.
Shut the doors properly dear mate,
there come the thieves again, I bet.

Male:
Break all chains today,
let noise be made by your anklets...

Open all the doors of your heart, give us the way...
The thieves of your hearts, in you must let.

Female:
There are chains around our feet;
noises are made by our anklets.
Shut the doors properly dear mate,
there come the thieves again, I bet.

Male:
Break all chains today,
let noise be made by your anklets...
Open all the doors of your heart, give us the way...
The thieves of your hearts, in you must let.

Male:
In this world there is so much hatred...
But yet, in the hearts of many,
there is this feeling of love spread.
Even if lovers are no more,
even if the ones who love are dead.
By many others to come,
forever immortal, their love is made.
Forever immortal....their love is made!!

Female:
Even if lovers are no more,
even if the ones who love are dead.
By many others to come,
forever immortal, their love is made.
Forever immortal....their love is made!!

– Trans-created on 5th March, 2014 by Sharad Kamal Bezboruah.

231. Piya Milenge...

Lyrics: Irshaad Kamil.

Whom you go about looking for
all around...
He sits there inside,
of your heart the door!!
The sea within you
can quench your thirst...
Looking for water why
wander you must??

The curtains of the mind,
you must push behind...
And, the veil
over your head; slide...
And then, shall appear
your beloved,
within you who does hide!!

This has happened
times a lot...
What is got is lost,
and what is lost is got!
This shadow of mine
is who has been by me the most...
None you did cheat,

so live with all your heart!!
And "He" shall sow for you to reap...
You shall meet...

Whom you go about looking for
all around...
He there, isn't inside,
of your heart the door!!
The sea within you
can quench your thirst...
Looking for water why
wander you must??

"IT IS 'HE' ALONE WHO IS 'HE',
BEYOND 'HIM', THERE LIES NO OTHER 'HE'!"...

What have you seen
if you have seen that which all have!
See that which seen
has yet not been...!!!
With open eyes, never are seen
things such...
Close your eyes, and...
Everything appears thus!!
And thus, you will blend...

It is he you wish to touch;
it is he who is always sought...
Yet, somewhere he isn't there,
somewhere you are not!!

It is he you wish to touch;
it is he who is always sought...
Yet, somewhere he isn't there,
somewhere you are not!!
Where he is not...it is lonely, forlorn...
Yet, you shall find him,
because you ought....

– Trans-created on 9th December, 2016 by Sharad Kamal Bezboruah.

232. Poocho Na Kaise....
(Manna Dey)

— Shailendra
(Shankardas Kesarilal)

Ask not how I've passed the night,
a second passed as if it were an age.
Ages passed, yet I couldn't sleep.

On one hand burns the lamp through the night,
on the other my heart burns.
Yet of light there is no sight.
I passed the entire life anxious and nervous.
Do not ask how I've passed the night.

Neither anywhere is there the moon,
nor anywhere a star.
The helpless eyes look for light,
near and far.
Even now, light isn't brought on,
by the soon approaching dawn.
Ask not how I've passed the night.

— Translated on 19th November, 2013 by Sharad Kamal Bezboruah.

233. Rula Ke Gaya Sapna Mera...

– Shailendra(Shankardas Kesarilal)

The nightmare zoomed passed,
leaving me to mourn.
Thus, I sit awake,
awaiting the dawn.
The nightmare zoomed passed,
leaving me to mourn.

Of the bosom, same is the pain;
the same is the moon;
the same stars twinkle.
And, the same old me;
helpless and feeble;
the same old midnight,
and the same, are all the things little...

Even then,
that wretched thief,
up, yet hasn't shown.
The nightmare zoomed passed,
leaving me to mourn.
Thus, I sit awake,
awaiting the dawn.
The nightmare zoomed passed,
leaving me to mourn.

Oh! This life...
My breath too
me does irk.
This heart and I,
together we sunk.
This damsel;
helpless, ill-fated...
In the hands of life;
well defeated;
and on top of it all,
this grief that overshadows.

The nightmare zoomed passed,
leaving me to mourn.
Thus, I sit awake,
awaiting the dawn.
The nightmare zoomed passed,
leaving me to mourn.

– Trans-created on 27th October, 2017 by Sharad Kamal Bezboruah.

234. Sandese Aate Hai...

– Javed Akhtar.

Letters from home,
raise a turmoil in the heart...
They go on questioning,
"Coming home....when thou art!!?...
Write (of) when you are coming....!!
For without you, this home is like a desert...!"...

The good hearted,
the inebriated...
girl writes to me...
and questions, as for so long she has waited...

Someone's breath,
The beats that someone's heart has bet...
Someone's bangles,
and...also questions, someone's bracelet...

The kohl with which her eyes are done,
the flowers hung about her bun...
The fragrant mornings which arrive,
and the anxious evenings of the setting sun...

The lonely nights,
the incomplete conversations...

The arms that await a hug tight,
and question…the eager, awaiting sight…

"Coming home….when thou art!!?…
Write (of) when you are coming….!!
For without you, this heart is like a desert…!"…

Letters from home,
raise a turmoil in the heart…
They go on questioning,
"Coming home….when thou art!!?…
Write (of) when you are coming….!!
For without you, this home is like a desert…!"…

My friends, my pals…!!
Back home, my beloved people…
They write, asking… "Would you care to tell;
return home, when you shall?"

People of my hamlet,
of the mango tree, the shade…
The old tree of Peepal;
and the clouds of monsoon, wet…

The farms, the barns…
The lush green fields along which I once did run….
The swaying sunflowers,
the spring carnivals that were so much fun…

The swings elastic,
the flowers which give out fragrances…
the tender buds, fragile and weak,
and, the lanes of my village… an answer they seek!!

"Coming home….when thou art!!?…
Write (of) when you are coming….!!
For without you, this village is like a desert…!"…

Letters from home,
raise a turmoil in the heart…
They go on questioning,
"Coming home….when thou art!!?…
Write (of) when you are coming….!!
For without you, this home is like a desert…!"…

Often of a mother's care,
of the river of love…comes a letter…
It brings along…childhood days,
games played in yard, running hither and thither…
The black spot put on me, saying, "far be the evil!";
and the shade of her shawl, nothing could be any better…

Of the nights, the lullabies,
the tender hands…
The love in her eyes,
the worry, in her words that lies…
Showing annoyance on the outside,
her love within, she couldn't hide…
and so….questioning me, in her letters,
these lines she does write…!!!

"Coming home….when thou art!!?…
Write (of) when you are coming….!!
For without you, this courtyard is like a desert…!"…

Letters from home,
raise a turmoil in the heart…
They go on questioning,
"Coming home….when thou art!!?…
Write (of) when you are coming….!!
For without you, this home is like a desert…!"…

Oh Winds!! As you pass,
I would like to ask;
if you could do me a favour,
do this one task… -
Go to my village,
and to my friends, give my hello…
And, then, the lane of my village,
where my beloved lives; to that lane, go!
Go and give her the wine of my love…
A few steps away, is my house, you know!!
There, lives my old mother…
GO, and touch her toes;
and my name, don't forget to utter…

Oh Winds…
Listen…
To my friends,
my beloved, my mother…
this message I need to send…
Please do me the favour!!
Please do me the favour!!

Let them know,
I shall return…
To my village,

Someone's shade…to embrace…
To the place,
where lays that old Peepal…
The shade of my mother's shawl…
99and, the kohl of someone's eyes…
The promise I had made to them all…
I shall keep!!
For, to break promises,
I never did learn…
And, so…
One day, I shall return!

Someday, I shall return!
Someday, I shall return!
Someday, I shall return!

– Trans-literated and Trans-created on 11th November, 2015
by Sharad Kamal Bezboruah.

235. Zindagi Ke Safar Mein....

Anand Bakshi.

In the journey of life,

the landmarks you might have crossed.

They never show up again,

they're forever lost.

Flowers bloom,

people meet…

But, the flowers that fall off in autumn,

never do they bloom again in spring.

One fine day, when few people move away,

those people, not even a thousand meetings bring.

Life long, to meet them even if one yearns,

their names are called out, but they never return.

They just don't return…

The eye is a trick,

about it, nothing one can tell.

Friends, suspicion is an enemy of friendship;

in your heart, do not let it settle.

Tomorrow, in whose memory you might be anxious,

stop them, don't let them get annoyed,

don't let them go.

For later, all greetings of love you send them would be void.

They never return.

They just don't return…

The morning comes, and then the night passes.
The morning comes, the night passes this way.
Time moves on, for no one it does wait,
in a second, it moves ahead we've seen.
One can't even see properly and yet,
the picture changes on the screen.
Once days and nights; dawns and dusks go past.
Never do they return.
They just don't return…

In the journey of life,
the landmarks you might have crossed.
They never show up again,
they're forever lost.

    – Translated on 20th November, 2013 by Sharad Kamal Bezboruah.

236. Suno Mere Bandhu Re...suno Mere Mitwa...

– MAJROOH SULTANPURI.

Listen, oh....friend...
Oh beloved!
Listen dear companion, oh!

If you were the Peepal,
I would be your roots,
eternal...
Around your neck,
smiling, I would...
lay like a garland!

Listen dear companion, oh!

Listen, oh....friend...
Oh beloved!
Listen dear companion, oh!

The heart, says;
if you would be the sea...
I would be your river!
Flowing in waves,
I would go join my lover...

Listen dear companion, oh!

Listen, oh....friend...
Oh beloved!
Listen dear companion, oh!

– Trans-created on 17th September, 2016 by Sharad Kamal Bezboruah.

237. Tu Jo Mila...

– K.K.
Lyrics: KAUSAR MUNIR.

A safe, secure refuge for you;
is here, with me… A shelter!
In search of your lane,
a home I found…
…For you, food and water;
are in these hands….
And, the knowledge I did gain,
of the abode of my God…
as I looked for Your Lord, in alien lands…

When you, I found…
Look, I turned competent….
When you, I found…
I found everything, to the heart's content…
When you, I found…
aside the hurdles bent!
For you are the beat, that,
to beat, in this heart is meant…

You getting annoyed; after
that, my saying, listen, cheer up…
In search of your laughter,
I found joy…

I'm your path destined,
you are the soul…
that is within
me.…
Looking for your traces,
I found identity, I found consciousness;
found my senses…

When you, I found…
Look, I turned competent.…
When you, I found…
I found everything, to the heart's content…
The journey, though tough, turned smoother,
easier seemed the destination.…
to which we head.…
For you are the beat, that,
to beat, in this heart is meant…

When you, I found…
Look, I turned competent.…
When you, I found…
I found everything, to the heart's content…
When you, I found…
aside the hurdles bent!
For you are the beat, that,
to beat, in this heart is meant…

– Trans-created on 11th February 2016, by Sharad Kamal Bezboruah.

238. Yeh Hawaa, Yeh Raat, Yeh Chaandni...

– RAJINDER KISHAN.

This breeze cool,
this night...
and, of the moon full,
this light...
All of it, I shall place at your feet...
On just on gesture of yours!
Why should you be not;
my longing, my fantasy...
Even the spring,
is in search of you, see...

What do you know,
oh! You are not aware...
What magic lay, what influence,
in just one sight of you...
Everyone turns tense,
when you get into a temper...
When you show little benevolence,
there spread relief and composure...

Why should you be not,
my longing, my fantasy...
Even the spring,
is in search of you, see...

This breeze cool,
this night...
and, of the moon full,
this light...

Every word of yours,
never fails to mesmerize...
There is none as wondrous as you,
little do you realize...
Each blossom, so merry;
each reflecting the
intoxication in your eyes...

Why should you be not,
my longing, my fancy...
Even the spring,
is in search of you, see...

This breeze cool,
this night...
and, of the moon full,
this light...
All of it, I shall place at your feet...
On just on gesture of yours!

– Trans-created on 7th June, 2016 by SharadKamal Bezboruah.

239. Taareefon SE...

Lyrics: KAUSAR MUNIR.

Hey you!
Yes, you!!

Yes, you are the most beautiful,
everyone you have baffled.
Yes, in everyone's heart,
you have gone and settled.
Yes, you're intoxicating,
and also, your tantrum,
everyone it amazes.
But, well, you are
definitely not settling for praises.

Hey you!
Yes, you!!

Hush, oh heart,
go slow;
to her your anxiety,
don't show.
On my helplessness,
she'll be smiling away...
But, well, you are
definitely not settling for praises.

Hey you!
Yes, you!!

Should I hum by your ears,
or scream from those peaks...
"It's you, only you!"
Or, should I just act silly,
like those movie freaks!?
Speak rubbish, give you gazes!
But, well, you are
definitely not settling for praises.

Yes, you are the most beautiful,
everyone you have baffled.
Yes, in everyone's heart,
you have gone and settled.
Yes, you're intoxicating,
and also, your tantrum,
everyone it amazes.
But, well, you are
definitely not settling for praises.

– Translated on 26th June, 2017 by Sharad Kamal Bezboruah.

240. Aisa Kyun Hota Hai Baar-Baar…??

Sameer.

What has this happened to my heart;
don't know where it has got lost in vain.
Why does it seem to be night in daylight,
like in sunlight it seems to rain?
Why does this happen again and again…
Is this what they call love?

New dreams began to build up…
The world too began to feel anew.
Never did anything of the sort happen before,
what kind of thirst has aroused, undue.
There seems of be spread, an intoxication, a senselessness.
The skies too seem to begin bending on its knee.
The silences have turned into speech;
they seem to narrate some story.
Even the heartbeat, something did intoxicate.
Why again and again does arise, this feeling so great?

When I looked at myself in the mirror,
my eyes lowered in shame.
With a thud, beat the heart;
for a second, static these breaths became.
Now thefts have begun to trouble,
to make me stay awake in the nights they have begun.

In vain, I've begun to remain anxious,
into someone else I've now begun to turn.
Is this it, what is called love?
God knows why I always yearn….
Why does this happen again and again…
Is this what they call love?

– Trans-created on 19th January, 2014 (1:30 am)
by Sharad Kamal Bezboruah.

241. Ishq Vishk Pyaar Vyaar.

– Sameer.

A boy meets a girl for the first time suppose,
what happens, tell me friend.
What else would happen, love of course!
On a straight road, one arrives at a bend.

A girl meets a boy for the first time suppose,
what happens, tell me friend.
What else would happen, love of course!
On a straight road, one arrives at a bend.

This heart is crazy,
of the heart, the tale…
The heart listened,
the heart itself did tell.
The heart thinks, the heart desires;
the heart, as beloved, you it chose.
Doing it again and again, me it tires,
nothing but love, is what this did cause.

Nor goes the pain,
nor comes the sleep…
nor does for a second come peace.
Neither in my senses I am, nor are you sane!
What kind of intoxication is this that fails to cease?

Why has everything made us anxious in vain??
Love is what's in the air… Love is what's in the breeze….
Love is what's in the air… Love is what's in the breeze….

A boy meets a girl for the first time suppose…
A girl meets a boy for the first time suppose,
what happens, tell me friend.
What else would happen, love of course!
On a straight road, one arrives at a bend.

– Trans-created on 19th January, 2014 by Sharad Kamal Bezboruah.

242. Tujhe Yaad Na Meri Aayi...

– Sameer.

Female:
Oh Lord… My Lord…
Never let love keep,
anyone so anxious…or helpless…
That the heart's word, in the heart it remains,
and never comes onto the lip…

My memory did not come to you,
now what is to be said…!?
The heart cried, tears filled the eye too,
now what is to be said…!?

I send your way now, every joy…
On your lips, be always a smile…
Male:
The clouds of strands from your head,
proclamations of faith they make to deploy…
Female:
Oh! You've fulfilled all your duties well,
now what is to be said…!?
Oh! About it, what do I tell…!!

Oh Beloved… Oh Beloved…

My memory did not come to you,
now what is to be said…!?

Male:
The heart cried, tears filled the eye too,
now what is to be said…!?

Both:
My memory did not come to you,
now what is to be said…!?
The heart cried, tears filled the eye too,
now what is to be said…!?

– Trans-created on 28th September, 2014 by Sharad Kamal Bezboruah.

243. Masha Allah... (Saawariya!)

– Sameer.

You are the moonlight gentle....
a fairy…
or are you an angel!?
You are wondrous…
You are the apple of my eyes…
or are you a ray,
of the divine light of paradise.
Grace to the Almighty lord!!
Grace to the Almighty lord!!
Oh, the lord!
Oh, the lord!

You are the gentle breeze
or in the clouds of the rains you dwell…
You are the galaxy, the universe…
My darling mademoiselle!
Like of morning, the first sunray…
Like the fearless breeze…
You give out fragrances,
engrossed in mischievous activities…
Grace to the Almighty lord!!
Grace to the Almighty lord!!

You are modesty…

You are content…
You are loyalty….
You are intoxication spelt…
Your solemn vision,
is like echoes…
Your words
are like well-wishes at the Lord's shrine…
You seem so far away
even though you dwell in every breath of mine!!

Grace to the Almighty lord!!
Grace to the Almighty lord!!

You are the moonlight gentle….
a fairy…
or are you an angel!?
You are wondrous…
You are the apple of my eyes…
or are you a ray,
of the divine light of paradise.
Grace to the Almighty lord!!
Grace to the Almighty lord!!
Oh, the lord!
Oh, the lord!

  – Trans-created on 19th April, 2014 by Sharad Kamal Bezboruah.

244. Piya O Re Piya....

– Priya Panchal.

Female: I'm yours now,
Oh dear, what an error!
I'm yours now,
this heart it is now compelled forever.

Male: Oh you've touched the eyes with your lips;
all wishes I made are at you now complete.
You're found by me where,
my entire world lay there.
At you itself, all the euphoria comes and greet.
Dear one… oh, dear one…
Dear one… oh, dear one… oh, dear one…

These distances, with intimacy….
They've made some kind of a deal.
Bowing down, the eyes have made
a promise of love to the heart, I feel.

Female: I'm yours now,
Oh dear, what an error!
Filling my arms with many a star,
take me somewhere, very far…

Both: Dear one… oh, dear one…
Dear one… oh, dear one… oh, dear one…

Male: In this life, something had always been absent
when did we ever know about?
And, now we meet like this with the Lord's consent,
like he's liberal to us.

Female: I'm yours now,
Oh dear, what an error!
The Lord's will that we're meeting,
today on us his light does shower.

Both: Dear one… oh, dear one…
Dear one… oh, dear one… oh, dear one…

– Translated on 2nd December, 2013 by Sharad Kamal Bezboruah.

245. Rang Jo Lagyo...

– Priya Panchal.

The paused breaths now have begun to live,
as it has now met with you.
This is the effect of your love, hard to believe,
and now….every cell of mine is lost within you.
The benevolent lord has showered over me,
ever since you have been found.
After finding you it seems, I have been missing,
only now am I to myself bound.

For this colour has colored me…..
For this colour has colored me…
for it's your colour…!!

This colour so deep
has begun to dissolve in the soul.
It doesn't fade,
doesn't fade at all.
What to care of the world,
when the heart has crossed all limits.
My world now illuminated,
and new and complete seem now, all my bits.

For this colour has colored me…..
For this colour has colored me…
for it's your colour…!!

Look at the melting sky,
to the droplets up there, it says…
About my love for you…
My love….limitless!
You've become a promise that can't be forgotten,
even if I try to forget.
That cannot be broken even if it's tried to be broken,
such a bond you've become.

For this colour has colored me…..
For this colour has colored me…for it's your colour…!!

– Translated on 23rd August, 2013 by Sharad Kamal Bezboruah.

246. Phir Le Aaya Yeh Dil....

– Sayeed Quadri

This helpless heart has pulled me along,
what is to be done?
It didn't fit really to live away,
what is to be done?
Listen to what this heart has to say.
It says, go on,
complete your words today....
Go on and complete your fragmented memories.
Go on and complete your fragmented memories.

Yes, I have confession to make,
what could be done?
I admit, I had done the mistake,
what is to be done?
Listen to what this heart has to say.
It says, go on,
and free it today....
The desire that you've kept suppressed for so long.
The spark that you've kept suppressed for so long.
The spark that you've kept suppressed for so long.

Fate too has no objections today,
what is to be done?
Let us then in this way always meet,

what else is to be done?
Listen, the heart says, go on,
Go move the stagnant street....
Go attend to the desire waiting for so long.
Go attend to the desire waiting for so long.

– Translated on 9th April, 2013, by Sharad Kamal Bezboruah.

247. Thamm Sa Gaya Hai...

– Priya Panchal.
– (Angaraag Papon Mahanta)

Time seems to have sort of paused...
since you have come in front of me!
Just with one sight,
you've made me all yours...
Your essence, it touches my heart thus...
Is it a dream, or am I falling for you?

Never knew what love is, nor now do;
but, at your sight,
it felt like this life's now synonymous to you...
In your presence, being, it felt like,
a new dawn, is found by my nights...

It's your influence,
that is...making this happen...
That has raised in this heart,
this impatience...
It somehow remains drenched,
in memories, all the time...
Forgetting myself, fading away,
I've begun to lose myself in you....
And, now, in it's like my dwellings,
are...your thoughts...

Time seems to have sort of paused…
since you have come in front of me!
Just with one sight,
you've made me all yours…
Your essence, it touches my heart thus…
Is it a dream, or am I falling for you?

– Trans-created on 11th February 2016, by Sharad Kamal Bezboruah.

And, now moving on to the final stage of this compilation, in the name of those poets of the 'rekhta' (the Hindustani) language, who can either only be fathomed so much, yet who have been beguiling, all the more. And, several others of our time, who have but carved along newer jewels onto the necklace of the language, and continue in their endeavors the same.

Constraints, as have been so many, but yes, I have always been tempted to go ahead and work on several more of the gems, (that is, select couplets or pairs of couplets, if not more), of yesteryears as well as of recent times, who, though are popular among 'rekhta' enthusiasts; but are yet to see as much light of the day, as they ought to. These, are those handpicked 'extracts', if I may say, that I have dearly treasured till this very point, each one worthy of a leisurely savour, though; as brief, crisp and incisive as they are.

248. 'Madhushala...'

– Shri. Harivansh Rai Bachchan

From his home, to the tavern,
heads the one who drinks…
Which route to take,
which not to… he thinks…
He, the innocent,
asks the road to me….
And so, to him I thus vent…
"Everyone gives you different directions,
I give you this one…
That the road where motion and movement are frequent,
that is the road to the tavern, dear mate"….

This is red wine, in a goblet.
Don't mistake it for fire…
just because it's red.
This too is wine,
from the soap nut tree here.
Don't call it a mark on the heart,
that makes u shed a tear...
Pain is as sweet as intoxication,
and the past memory of wine is the server.
Listen, in pain the one who finds bliss.
Must come to my tavern...
This goblet of wine he must kiss.

The religious books and testaments,
whose heart's rage has burnt;
they crazy one, who has broken all temples, mosques and churches
and to cut through, of priests and saints the traps,
the one who has learnt…
It is only he who can be welcomed by my tavern…

Priest be the server,
And water of the sacred Ganges be this ale…
In the hands be they counting on… the goblets,
like the beads of a rosary, and the same spell-
"Keep taking more, keep drinking more" must echo on…
In the tavern, near and far…
Let this tavern turn into a temple,
in which I be placed at the altar…

In a year, only once burns
the flame of the festival of colours…
Only once, are together lit,
a chain of lamps, showing splendor…
in the festival of lights…
But, oh people, someday come to meet
and see us at the tavern…
For, dear mates,
a fact you must learn….
is that… Here, everyday, the tavern celebrates
the festival of colours in the day; and that of light in the night…

Two are the Hindus and Muslims,
but one is their goblet…
One is the ale that fills that up to the rim,
one is their tavern…

They aren't together till
they go to mosque and temple…
Listen dear friends,
their unity these temples and mosques kill…
And, it's all quite simple,
that their bond is strengthen by the tavern…

Whatever be the liquid on the lip;
on the tongue, it only seems to be the ale…
In my hand whatever vessel I keep,
it seems to be only the goblet…
Every face turns into the face of the server…
In front of the eyes… be whatever, let;
in the eyes is the tavern, forever…

In this short life of mine,
how much do I go spreading love…
Let me instead just drink this wine.…
For at only my arrival,
I've already been named the" leaver"…
With my welcoming ceremony, I again tell,
of my farewell, I could see arrangements and patterns…
As soon as it was opened, within only a second,
was again closed…of my life, the tavern.…

Let not be on my lip the water of the Holy Basil!
The Holy water of the Ganges
on my tongue let not anyone spill.…
Listen, oh those who shall walk behind my corpse once I'm dead;
the need to call out "In God We Trust", I do not feel,
call out "True is the Tavern!" instead…

At my corpse, cry must he, who has ale in his tears….
He who is intoxicated by the fragrant ale,
to hear him sigh, I yearn….
Let I be carried on the shoulders of those,
whose feet go left and right, in utter delight.
And let my funeral pyre burn…
At that very point,
where once had stood a tavern….

And Into my pyre, be not
put ghee, nor oil,
but ale from the pot…
From the grape-vine they offer should hail,
ale, not water…
And if you wish to hold my funeral,
call all those who drink, and open the tavern…
To call the priest and make him chant hymns don't bother…

Do not hold up any other offering in hand,
but the goblet as libation on my death, son…
In place of the holy waters of the Ganges,
let this divine ale flow and run…
And, once this ale wets some alien land;
that would be all that peace to my soul would concern…
And, on my funeral, not hymns, dear son…
Read out lines from this poem of mine, "The Tavern"!!!

And, hence, pouring out the Ale, and unlocking the 'Tavern'… Here are,
'the Extracts'.

1.
"Come soon;
rush, whoever may wish to embrace;
for then I need put this frame to work
in an elsewhere place"

– Vipul Kumar.

2.
"The love which seeks union alone,
that love be defamed...
That pain be condemned,
which into couplets could be framed."

– Vipul Kumar.

3.
"Letters move to words, words to meanings;
all characters head back to the story;

Let her know; the smoke shall be noteworthy;
the day I head into the waters shrouding a coat fiery.

The heart is a river in the hollow bosom;
of which I no longer note the fury."

– Abhishek Shukla.

4.
"A day does come such,
when it all turns fine; and shone.

To me, now comes to be known;
whatever is meant to; happens on its own.

Love is a doing verb, meant to be done;
what!! You thought it happens on its own!?

Sharad Kamal Bezboruah | 563

Each one, as they pass by me;
leaves with so much thirst overhead borne. "

– Abhishek Dixit.

5.
"There's this ritual to raise the toast;
in bliss, in pain; and on occasions most.
At our end, love; to be upheld, ought;
at hers, the ritual to leave it foregone; lost."

– Surajmani Tripathi.

6.
"Such is the pain; that I cannot hide;
endurance such, that I cannot even cite.

Things would be different, if you were never to leave;
now even if you return, I can take no pride."

– Ismail Raaz.

7.
"Your lanes never left, even though you detest;
loosening it all, yet clinging on to the rest.

Your lover did not, from his town, move west;
that is, to tackle the spilt, didn't head to the forest."

– Ismail Raaz.

8.
"Nowhere, a confidant, and an entire night to pass;
in the tavern lies not, even half a glass.

Where do I head, carrying along the tattered heart;
it's not that she lives anywhere close by, alas!

These days, those beloveds, also long for a house, fanciful;
I do not even have clothes of proper class. .”

– Ismail Raaz.

9.
“Around the boundaries of the souls
to unfold a marvel,
it takes in fact bodies two
to entangle.

When I’m wiped out those eyes
may turn a little moist;
a lot of soil would go into,
making; drop, even a single. “

– Vipul Kumar.

10.
“Whoever on his heart, burns of love sustains
bears more candles than the candelabrum.
This time, I have come across a lover so learned;
that as big as my heart, is his brains.”

– Farhat Ehsas.

11.
“If you bow to it, the stone too, shall turn into a Lord;
don’t love her so; for she would turn faithless, go overboard!”

– Bashir Badr.

12.
“If you sit idle,
do me this favour if you could,
inflict upon me,
another fine little wound.

How religiously,
you serve the birds, water and food;
why don't you set them free,
if you are at heart, so good."

– Zubair Ali Tabish.

13.
"The heart isn't hapless,
it has only failed.
Only an evening, this sorrow;
though an evening sustained."

– 'FAIZ AHMAD FAIZ'

14.
"You no doubt a vice of mine,
but I have another ninety-nine.

Your city may be less of love,
but is never less of wine."

– Brrijbhan Singh Rajawat.

15.
"The doc shall no doubt provide a cure,
but I hope my pain isn't defamed.
What is this? A remedy!? Sure!
But I just hope my illnesses would not be tamed".

– 'JAUN ELIA'

16.
"Look into my eyes, give me an answer,
something, speak out.
How many times have I been robbed,
at least give me a count".

– Lt. Dr. Rahat Indori.

17.
"The pain of the world,
the face of my beloved, or the
enemies' arms tough.
Whatever I came across,
I embraced with love".

– 'FAIZ AHMAD FAIZ'

18.
"I was busy keeping count
of all the sorrows in the world,
but today, your countless memories
have unfurled."

– 'FAIZ AHMAD FAIZ'

19.
"Fear not in love,
on whatever; place the bet.
If you win, you win; cheers!
But even defeat, herein, isn't to resent".

– 'FAIZ AHMAD FAIZ'

20.
"The careless deceptions of expectations, never fleet,
a thud in the heart, and I started hoping, your feet."

– 'FAIZ AHMAD FAIZ'

21.
"Yes, oh, the wise, evidences of the lips and heart, bring along;
yes, dear singers; raise the echoes of another song!"

– 'FAIZ AHMAD FAIZ'

22.

"The rock first turns itself into a rock,

only then, does the sculptor's chisel knock"

– Madan Mohan Mishra 'Danish'

23.

"With one, he hands over the letter

and looks at me, with expression another.

Something more, he is to utter,

perhaps something more was said by the sender"

– Mirza Asadullah Khan 'Ghalib'

24.

"They ask me at the square,

on purpose, how life has been!

What can you say there,

about the soup you are in?"

– Mirza Asadullah Khan 'Ghalib'

25.

"If not, are in the souk,

the words on my paper.

At least the vendor

lends me a favour".

– Mirza Asadullah Khan 'Ghalib'

26.

"Lifelong, I have been committing the error,

the dirt was on my face, and I kept wiping the mirror."

– Mirza Asadullah Khan 'Ghalib'

27.
"At every word, you say, "what are you",
is this how things are to be said.
By its flow in the veins, I am amused;
what is blood, if as tears cannot be shed".

– Mirza Asadullah Khan 'Ghalib'

28.
"Faith holds me back, while,
I am pulled ahead by evil such.
Behind me, lies the Mecca,
while in front lies the church".

– Mirza Asadullah Khan 'Ghalib'

29.
"What work, without 'Ghalib',
shall cease to continue;
why weep your hearts out then,
why the cry and hue?"

– Mirza Asadullah Khan 'Ghalib'

30.
"Be there no movement in the arms,
at least the eyes still have enough strength.
So, let them remain, just leave them there,
the wine and the goblet".

– Mirza Asadullah Khan 'Ghalib'

31.
"The one yet not formed,
of that orchard very.
Of the branch of its tree,
I call myself the canary"

– Mirza Asadullah Khan 'Ghalib'

32.

"Something such has occurred that,
to speak of anything, my words refuse.
I live now, somewhere, where
from myself too, I hear no news".

– Mirza Asadullah Khan 'Ghalib'

33.

"What loyalty? What? Love??
Oh please; for God's sake!
If the head might as well be cracked open, then,
oh heart of stone, why on your mosaic?

– Mirza Asadullah Khan 'Ghalib'

34.

"Why would it not fill with pain,
it's a heart, after all, not stone.
Why shall someone come and bother me?
A thousand times, I shall mourn".

– Mirza Asadullah Khan 'Ghalib'

35.

"Oh humble heart, what do you seek for;
tell me, of this pain, what could be the cure.

The ones who know not of faith, constancy;
in hope of persistence; I stand at their door."

– Mirza Asadullah Khan 'Ghalib'

36.

"Fitted, within me,
so many sketches and cartoons;

they all might have gotten lost within,
in the woods.
I wished that the wounds fill soon,
but in fact ended up filled with wounds."

- Ammar Iqbal.

37.
"If you are ever tired,
you may leave behind your fatigue.
You may forsake me, in reality.

When have we, the trees
known the art of departure so closely;
you, a bird, may leave for overseas.

You may come, like comes
the fragrant breeze.
You may leave, leaving me
all claustrophobic.

I lose myself thus, into your words;
that you may leave, as all of it, I barely twig."

- Ammar Iqbal

38.
"The tears, they sought to be freed
so weep...
The eyes too, ought to be thus eased;
so weep....

If you are in glee,
you aren't travelling along the worldly street!
Weep; for, all along this forest,
only blisters are meant underneath.

Bound by endurance,
the leisure to cry, when in my fate?
You have all the liberty, weep,
weep on, I congratulate!"

- Abbas Qamar

--3

39.
"I did tell you, did I not,
that spring would visit me too, I trust.
The deal, of course, was just this,
that you must visit first."

- KAIFI AZMI

40.
"A few do call me insane,
the others think of me as a loon.
But the earth's anxiety, the pain,
is known to, only the clouds of monsoon.

From each other, separated,
however the two of us survived.
The journey, the stories of the hearts,
only in our hearts, imbibed."

- Dr. Kumar Vishwas.

41.
"There was a time when
a solace to you, I had been.
Look, I now stand all alone,
to the walls instead, I now lean.

Your beauty, like the river, spoken of;
in one phrase of the couplet;
at the other phrase; we shall meet;
along the same rivulet.

The ones ever-victorious often
are defeated by the ones, to them close.
Like, before you, my love;
all my love, I have but yet again, lost.

Each day,
you did drift me away, inch by inch.
And now, I twinkle, by the star, up here,
when the skies, hence I did reach.

In a way, we've won,
even though we had to split.
For, better than victorious apart,
is, together, we embraced defeat.

– Himanshu Pandey (Kota)

42.
"All the anxiety, turbulence,
from across the world, gathered;
when nothing could emerge out of it,
he made but the heart tattered".

– Najmi Naginvi

43.
"The eyes may still be filled with drops of dew,
there's still hope, if the blazing town, you wish to rescue.

Love, just one; that too failed,
but the same shall suffice to serve as a make-do!"

– Abbas Tabish.

44.

"People do often, each other meet;
But the hearts, only seldom together befit.

I often forget the woes inflicted by her;
with such simplicity, when she does greet.

The one, who disappears, is lost; after found,
the heart, to see her, always, into fragments does split"

– Jigar Moradabadi.

45.

"It is hence that so late by you, I arrive;
behind me, every footprint of mine, out I had to swipe.

I had to showcase to everyone, my prowess to swim,
yet, I had to come out of the ocean, but alive.

My desires of fame are but such, that,
in oblivion alone, to be acclaimed, I strive. ".

– Tauseef Tabish.

46.

"Oh February, oh! so darned, damned;
so many hearts, turned to dust, finished.
Not in vain, has someone wise,
its count of days, reduced; diminished".

– 'Unknown'.

47.

"Apart from life itself, there is no sentence; so stern;
and what the crime, the sin was, not that one could discern.

Into so many fragments, I have been split,
yet, in my name, remains fragment none.

Oh life, death alone is your end goal, whatsoever;
the same, to evade; there is no bend or turn.

Tell me, life, which way I should head now, for, toiling all day too,
along the souk entire; a vile of poison, I could not earn.

The truth, if added, or diminished; no longer remains true,
of the limits, bounds of the lie, no one can ever learn.

Even if you cast it in frame of gold, or even show a gun;
to sway away from the truth, the mirror shall ever wern.

And, in his writings shall shine, his light, the 'Sun';
'Noor' has never left, even after the 'Burn'.
                    – *KRISHNA BIHARI 'NOOR'.* (Zindagi se Badi...)

48.

"In this entire lifetime, times trying, for me, were but just two;
one that left just before 'you' came, the other that stayed on; seeing
off, 'you'.".
                                        – Muztar Khairabadi.

49.

"The breeze calm, by the stream, and us the two;
A moment spent in solitude's regime, and us, the two.

Three things alone do disperse, with such urgency, yes;
of any dawn, the earliest gleam; and us, the two".

– Vipul Kumar

50.
"The one whom, I have loved, as life;
she too, now, but as a stranger does arrive.

Who knew the darkness would only thus grow
like the moon, she too, into the clouds would dive.

Even more, made me yearn, and then away did turn;
her benevolence too was so, like in love, for love, a bribe.

Unrequited, even she, through the heart only strikes,
whose sorrow too, as if joys, to endure I did strive.

Never did it cross my mind, for her, Qateel so;
that, like every other, she too would someday, thus knife.

The one whom, I have loved, as life;
she too, now, but as a stranger does arrive."

– QATEEL SHIFAI (Kiya hai Pyaar Jise)

51.
"Neither have you arrived, nor is the night of fortitude, bygone;
in quest, every day, hence passes by the dawn.

Fruitful have been, only the ones passed in fervour;
albeit inflicted upon the heart, a thousand devastations, severe.

Whatever was not even mentioned, in of the tale, any page,
it is the same, which them, seem to exasperate, enrage.

Nor have flowers bloomed, nor have I met her, nor, a drop of ale,
even 'this' spring; has passed by thus, this pale.

Oh, god knows what woe, upon the blossoms, autumn does impose,
passes by the garden, yes; the breeze thus, perplexed blows... "
– 'FAIZ AHMAD FAIZ' (Tum aaye ho, na....)

52.
"My beloved, ever to meet; when was such my fate!
If I lived longer too, hence, on I would ought to wait.

I lived on; for, your promise was false, I did trust;
if ever I were to believe, I would right there, be long 'late'.

Oh, how, over what; would your half-stretched arrow mourn;
ask the heart tattered, if it were to pass through (it) straight?

What kind, is this friendship, why do they all come; and only counsel?
be someone at least a confidant; at the least, someone ameliorate.

What do I speak, of what misadventures the night of grief brings;
Only if death was to befall but just once; oh, it would have been how great!

My beloved, ever to meet; when was such my fate!
If I lived longer too, hence, on I would ought to wait. "
– Mirza Asadullah Khan 'Ghalib'
(Yeh Na Thi Humaari Qismat)

"Yet again the 21st, the last day of the third week;
Do 'they' continue to haunt you, in times bleak?

For how much longer shall you run away from the truth,
'Sharad'; is this all a child's play, or a game of hide and seek??"

– Sharad Kamal Bezboruah.

In Essence and in Spirit – 'THE MAGICAL SOULS'

Bhaiti 'Bordeuta', Shri. Dhirendranath Bezboruah (Padma Shri, 2016; Translator of the Jnanpith winning, 'Mrityunjay' by Lt. Shri. Birendranath Bhattacharyya, 1979, and more); reminiscing the 'Magical Times' he would spend with Bharat Ratna Lt. Dr. Bhupen Hazarika.

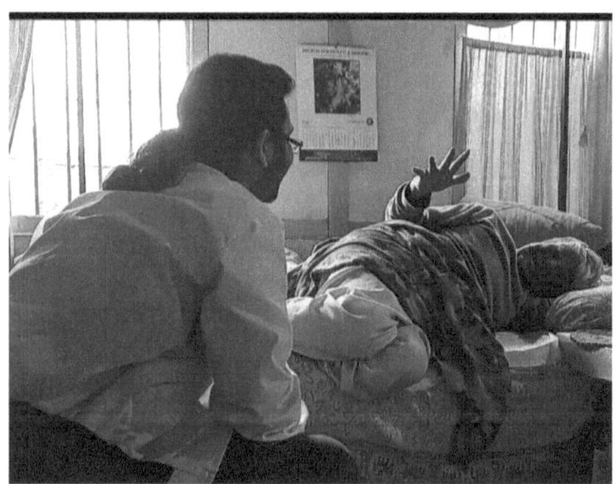

Eminent Academician, singer and litterateur; Padma Shri Dr. Birendranath Dutta 'Bordeuta'; discussing the nuances of his single take 'Mor Kontho Rudhile Kone', by 'Bokulbonor Kobi', Padma Shri. Lt. Shri. Ananda Chandra Barua (Sahitya Akademi, 1970); (Translation no. 72).

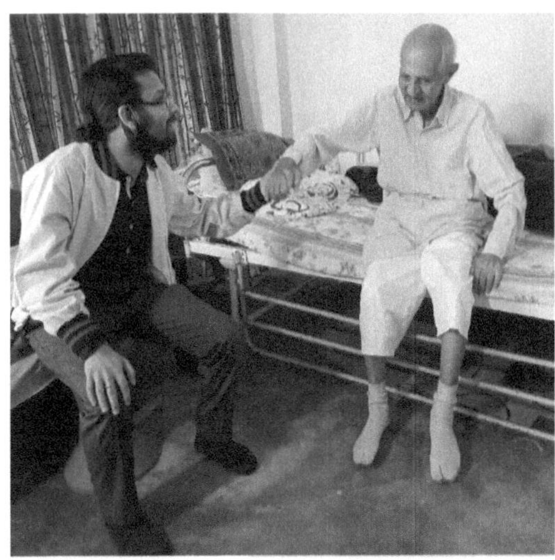

Under the magnificent, yet humbling shade of the state's 'Literary Banyan', Padma Shri. Nilomani Phookan Sir; Sahitya Akademi, 1981, (Kobita);the 56th Jnanpith, 2020.

The man who reigned over hearts for somewhat three-fourth of our lifetime; and continues to from above; the longest serving Chief Minister of the state of 'Oxom', former Union Minister and avid statesman; Lt. Shri. Tarun Gogoi Sir. (Padma Bhushan, 2021; also the very merited nephew of the noted Assamese poet 'Papori Kobi' Lt. Shri. Ganesh Gogoi); with Ananya 'ba'(Faculty, Hindu College, DU) and Abhinanda 'bou' (Jorhat, Assam).

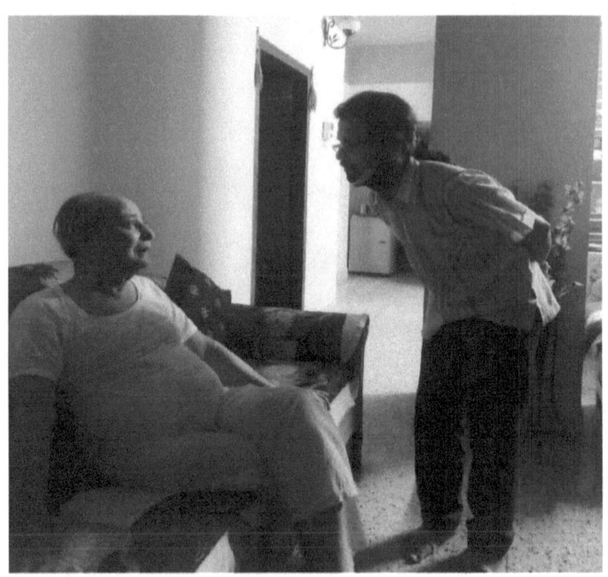

In Candid Conversation with Moina 'Mama', Shri. Bhaben Baruah; Sahitya Akademi, 1979, Xonali Jahaj; (the year, concurrent with the very first Jnanpith to the state, Lt. Shri. Birendranath Bhattacharyya, for 'Mrityunjay'.)

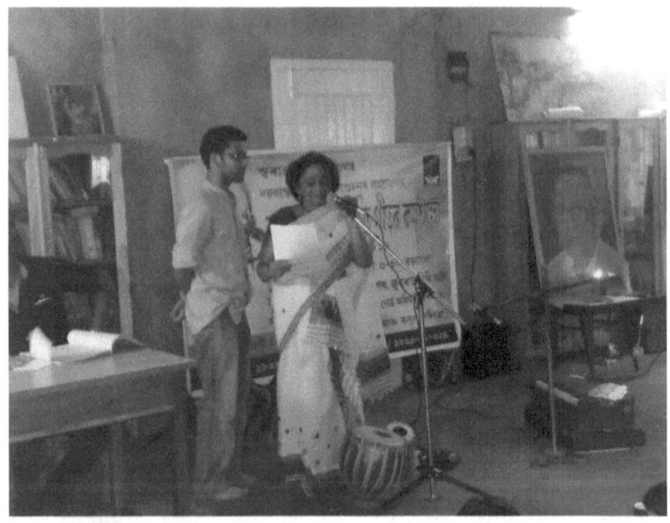

The honour of my translations of Padma Shri Lt. Navakanta Barua's (Sahitya Akademi, 1975, Kokadeutar Har) lyrics; being recited by his very own daughter Upala Barua 'Jethai' on his 15th death anniversary. (14.07.2017),(Translations- 12, 13, 35, 47, 51, and more).

With Eminent Translator of Assam, Mrs. Deepika Phukan 'Jethai', (Translator of Makam, Felani and many more; Grandma's Tales by Lakshminath Bezbaroa) and my niece Amrita.

With beloved 'Aita', Lt. Sharada Bezboruah, (left); (former maiden professor, English, Presidency College, erstwhile Madras; longest serving Principal, Jorhat College-Amalgamated- 1971 to 1985); and the ever-loving Gayatri Borgohain 'Jethai'; (lead actress, 'Mon Prajapati', directed by Bharat Ratna Dr. Bhupen Hazarika, 1979).

A Tribute – At the Nexus of the Generations

THE DEBEN-MOHEN CLAN, including Lt. Shri. Rajen Barua 'Mama' (Translator and Senior FASS Member, Houston, Texas); Smt. Anjana Chaliha 'Jethai', Shri. Niren Barua 'Mama', Smt. Arpana Khound 'Jethai', Mrs. Kalpana Sarma 'Jethai', Mrs. Archana Barua 'Jethai' and Mom, Mrs. Smita Bezbaruah. (Missing- Lt. J.P. Baruah and Lt. Dhrubajyoti Baruah).

Maternal Grandaunt Lt. Sewali Baruah.

Uncle Lt. Jyoti Prakash Baruah (son of 'AsomPran', Lt. Shri. Harendranath Baruah), with the family.

Beloved Maternal 'Aita' Lt. Kiron Barua, Ma & cousins.

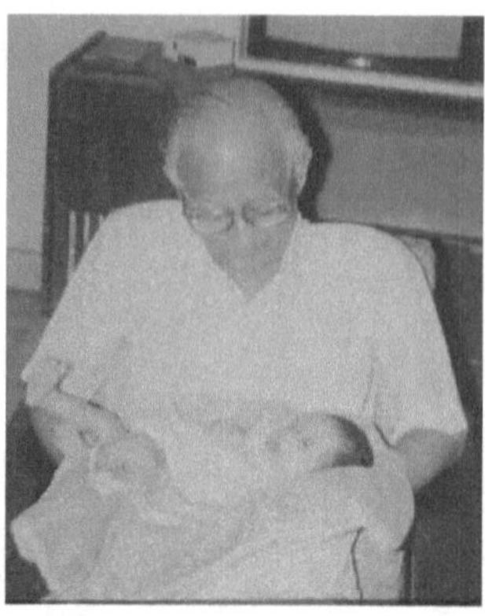

In 'Koka', Lt. Dr. N.K. Bezboruah's Lap.

Maternal Grandaunt, Lt. Renu Dowerah 'Aita'; (wife of Kalaguru Awardee, Lt. M.P. Dowerah).

'Borma Aita' Lt. Sushila Bezboruah with 'Aita-Koka' and the family.

Beloved 'Aita-Koka', Uncle Prabhat Kamal Bezboruah & Dad Kishore Kamal Bezboruah.

With 'Bordeuta', Shri. Prabhat Kamal Bezboruah (Chairman, Tea Board, India) and the family.

My brother, Rajat and I with Lt. Aaji, A'ti, Rupan Bai and Khetra Kokai (who have served three generations tirelessly).

Ma, Deuta and I with beloved 'Aita'. Lt. Sharada Bezboruah.

Eldest Paternal Grandaunt, Lt. Parvathi 'Aita'; with beloved 'Aita', Ma and myself. (Also remembering fondly, Lt. Malthi 'Aita', .Lt. Jimmy 'Koka', and dedicated to the greater.Nair family; Savitri 'Aita', R.K. 'Koka' & others).

The Future of Films, Theatre, Art and Music in Assam.

From Top: Actor- Director Kenny Basumatary da, (Local Kungfu- India's first kungfu film, Bornodi Bhotiai, Yaara, Raagdesh and more); Underground Artists Rocky Glock, A.VOID & Barcy Das with Abhi Saikia & Shankuraj Konwar; Arghadeep Barua, Lead Actor, critically acclaimed film 'AAMIS'; Actress Sukanya

Boruah (Nima Denzongpa, Bornodi Bhotiai etc); Singer Bornalee Deuri; Artist Annie Hazarika, Cinematographer Prayash Sharma Tamuly (Bornodi Bhotiai, Goru and more), Guitarist Mr. Zamatia & others.

The entire 'AAMIS' family at the screening; Director Bhaskar Hazarika ('Rajat Kamal' National Award, Kothanodi, 2015); Lead Actor Arghadeep Barua; Lead Actress Lima Das; Neetali Das, Sunayana Dutta and others.

The gems of Assam, Baharul Islam Sir (Manohar Singh Award 2005), Boloram Das Sir (best known for 'A Thursday', 'Badlapur Boys' and 'Gabbar is Back'); (Both Alumni, National School of Drama), Baharul sir's daughter, theatre artist and actor Barkha Bahar; Urmila Mahanta Ma'am (Alumni, Film and Television Institute of India; best known 'Padman', 'Bokul', 'Manjhi' 'Akira' and, of course, 'Kothanodi') and others.

With the much celebrated duo of Project Baartalaap, Maitrayee Patar (also an amazing poetess and lyricist, besides being the lead female vocalist) and Shankuraj Konwar (Lead Vocalist, Music producer and more); and childhood friend Rituraj Hazarika, at Shankuraj and Rituraj's AlmaMater, Jorhat Engineering College, Jorhat.

My mother and I with Mrs. Mrinmoyee Goswami Sarma, (very talented vocalist, musician, creator from Assam); the very merited daughter of Lt. Smt. Mamoni Raisom Goswami 'Jethai' (Indira Goswami, Sahitya Akademi, 1982, Mamore Dhora Tarowal; the 36th Jnanpith, 2000); soonafter Jethai's demise.

Poetry, Storytelling and Beyond.

Core Team for 'Irshaad- Jorhat Chapter', the first Open Mic in Jorhat, Assam; December 2018.

Renowned Anchor Reeky Sharma da, Prayash S Tamuli, Prabal Bora, Actress Maitri Das,Plabita (Founder, ART-ALAAP).

'Karwaan': Open Mic inspired by the Irshaad concept, first of its kind at Assam Agricultural University, Jorhat.

At the 'magical' altar, from where sprouts the 'Diwan -i- Ghalib'; 2018.

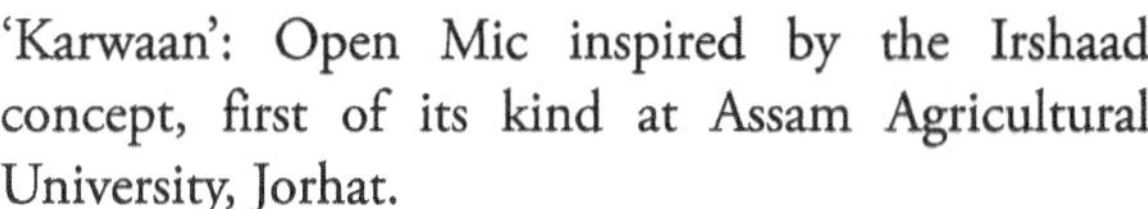

Attending the National Summit for Mediation, as a lead volunteer at the Indian Mediation Week,; aimed at resolving conflicts amicably and spreading the message of love; with the tagline of 'Suljhao Magar Pyaar Se'; 15th December 2018.

With Poetess Namrata Pathak 'ba' at her book release, and artist Reetuparna.

With noted Poet from Assam, Shri. Janardan Goswami 'da'.

With Internationally acclaimed poet Madhu Raghavendra 'da', who has been an inspiration, strength and guidance throughout the last 6 years.

With Nation-wide performers, Angshuman Sarma, (National Youth Poetry Slam finalist); and Bhawana Sarma (Performer at Dastak Nayi Pidhi Ki, Rashtriya Kavi Sammelan, New Delhi).

The thrill of opening for one of India's Best Spoken-Word Storytellers; Amandeep Singh (Assam,2019).

"Shitol Patir Niche Thaake,

Bheeje Maatir Moh;

Phirte Gele Pechu Daake,

Kon Shei Aapun Jon...

Nodir Baake

Jege Thaake

....Jhor.....

'Haariye Thikana Khonje Ghor'..."

– 'HAARIYE THIKANA KHONJE GHOR'
(Srijato, 2014; 'Buno Haansh'; Translation no- 111)

"Woh Agar Baat na Pooche,
Toh Kya Kare Hum Bhi;
Aap hi roothe, aap hi mann jaate hai...
Bulbulo nava-shauk hai un aankhon ki,
Jinse hum seekhne andaaz-e- sukhan jaate hai!
Rok sakta hai humein zindaan- e- balaa kya 'Majrooh';
Hum toh awaaz hai, deewaar se, Channn jaate hai!"

– MAJROOH SULTANPURI 'SAHAB'

"Rudaad- e- ghum- e- ulfat unse,
hum kya kehte, kyun kar kehte;
ik harf na nikla hothon se
aur aankh mein aansu aa bhi gaye.
Yeh Rang- e- Bahar ka aalam hai,
kya fikr hai tujhko, aye saaki';
Mehfil toh teri sooni na hui,
kuch uth bhi gaye, kuch aa bhi gaye.
Is Mehfil- e- kaif- o- masti mein,
is anjuman- e- irfaani mein;
sab jaam- ba- qaf baithe hi rahe,
hum pee bhi gaye, chalkaa bhi gaye. "

– ASRAR-UL-HAQ 'MAJAZ'.